5 CAPPETIZER

D1488465

Not War, Not Peace?

Not War, Not Peace?

Motivating Pakistan to Prevent Cross-Border Terrorism

GEORGE PERKOVICH AND TOBY DALTON

OXFORD
UNIVERSITY PRESS

OXFORD
UNIVERSITY PRESS

Oxford University Press is a department of the University of Oxford.
It furthers the University's objective of excellence in research, scholarship,
and education by publishing worldwide. Oxford is a registered trademark of
Oxford University Press in the UK and in certain other countries

Published in India by
Oxford University Press
YMCA Library Building, 1 Jai Singh Road, New Delhi 110 001, India

© Oxford University Press 2016

The moral rights of the authors have been asserted

First Edition published in 2016

All rights reserved. No part of this publication may be reproduced, stored in
a retrieval system, or transmitted, in any form or by any means, without the
prior permission in writing of Oxford University Press, or as expressly permitted
by law, by licence, or under terms agreed with the appropriate reprographics
rights organization. Enquiries concerning reproduction outside the scope of the
above should be sent to the Rights Department, Oxford University Press, at the
address above

You must not circulate this work in any other form
and you must impose this same condition on any acquirer

ISBN-13: 978-0-19-946749-5
ISBN-10: 0-19-946749-8

Typeset in Trump Mediaeval LT Std 9.5/13.5
by Tranistics Data Technologies, New Delhi 110 044
Printed in India by Replika Press Pvt. Ltd

CONTENTS

PREFACE

In a spacious and ornate office reflecting his rank and position, a senior Pakistani military officer discussed the implications of Pakistan's lengthy struggle to pacify militant groups that target the Pakistani state. The problem, he stipulated in this 2012 interview, is not merely one for the military or law enforcement. Counter-terrorism campaigns have wide-ranging effects on Pakistani civilians as well. The direct blowback can be severe, as was evidenced in December 2014 when the Pakistani Taliban attacked a primary school in Peshawar, murdering over 140 people including 132 children. More pernicious, he suggested, is the long-term psychological impact of living in a perpetual state of danger that comes from within. Generations of Pakistanis would feel the effects of this state of 'not war, not peace', he argued.

Indian officials and society, too, express the angst and policy dilemmas that stem from living in a condition of 'not war, not peace' with their neighbour, Pakistan. For India, the cause is less complicated: it is the Pakistani state's unwillingness or inability to prevent cross-border terrorism against India. This leads to a search for options to motivate Pakistani authorities to more decisively pacify groups and individuals that project violence against India.

In researching and writing this book we have thought about various ways in which 'not war, not peace' characterizes the India–Pakistan relationship. Our analysis suggests that the two states' possession of survivable nuclear arsenals makes conventional war mutually suicidal as a means to resolve the disputes that bedevil their relations. Some Indian and Pakistani strategists and officials do not share this conclusion. They seek to preserve space for limitable conventional military operations that they believe would not escalate to nuclear war. The uncertain outcome of their quest invites the question mark regarding 'not war' in our title.

The question mark also applies to 'not peace'. This book focuses primarily on Indian policymaking, so the range of options tends to reflect the parameters of Indian debate. Few Indian leaders argue that making peace with Pakistan—which unavoidably means give-and-take bargaining—should be India's leading policy. Many believe—with some justification—that even if India offered concessionary terms on Kashmir and other issues, the Pakistani security establishment would continue hostilities against India. Discussion focuses much more on how to compel Pakistan to meet Indian demands, short of major warfare.

'Not peace' invites at least two questions, then. First, assuming India will not seek peace by conceding to some of Pakistan's demands, are there other non-violent policies that could motivate Pakistan to do more to prevent cross-border terrorism? And second, will coercive policies alone be sufficient to motivate Pakistan to prevent cross-border terrorism and reduce risks of escalation if conflict does arise? Non-violent compellence, as discussed in Chapter 6, provides one possible answer to the first question, but it does not answer the second. Compellence is a form of coercion, and our analysis suggests that coercion alone is an insufficient motivator. More positive inducements are also necessary to modify behaviour. If the realistic prospect of negotiated peace is not on offer, then what other positive motivation is? We leave it to Indian and Pakistani officials and experts to answer whether and how their countries could negotiate lasting peace. We can only say that the condition of 'not war' is unsustainable if 'not peace' is the core of either state's policy.

ACKNOWLEDGEMENTS

Book writing requires big efforts by many people whose names do not appear on the cover. The authors therefore wish to acknowledge and express their gratitude to a number of people who played integral roles in the completion of this book.

First and foremost, we thank our colleagues in the Nuclear Policy Program at the Carnegie Endowment for International Peace, who provided feedback on our analysis at various points. We thank in particular Will Ossoff, Liz Whitfield, Lauryn Williams, Wyatt Hoffman, and Shane Mason (while he was a Scoville Fellow at the Carnegie Endowment) for very able research, editing and general support for the endeavor. Will Ossoff in particular critiqued multiple drafts and was an excellent editor. We also thank Jocelyn Soly, who designed the cover, as well as Becky White, Nick Parrott, and colleagues in the Carnegie Communications Department. Research for the book was aided significantly by Carnegie's excellent library staff, including Kathleen Higgs, Keigh Hammond, and Chris Lao-Scott.

Over the course of conducting interviews and writing drafts of the manuscript, we relied extensively on counsel, ideas, and critiques from a number of experts and officials in India, Pakistan, and the United States. We would like to thank Adm. (retired) Vijay Shankar and Zia Mian for going above and beyond in providing very valuable feedback. We benefited greatly from conversations and email exchanges, some of which are quoted in the text, with the late P.R. Chari, Arun Singh, K.C. Verma, and Vijay Shankar. We are also grateful to many other officials and experts who gave freely of their time and thoughts on background or in an anonymous capacity.

The authors wish to acknowledge Taylor and Francis Group for granting permission to re-use in Chapter 3 material that previously appeared in George Perkovich and Toby Dalton, 'Modi's Strategic Choice: How to Respond to Terrorism from Pakistan,' *The Washington Quarterly* 38, no. 1 (2015): 23–45, available at http://www.tandfonline.com.

We are indebted to the editorial team at Oxford University Press for agreeing to work with us and for very ably shepherding the book through the publication process. They are an asset to the press.

This book was made possible by financial support specifically from the Smith-Richardson Foundation and the Carnegie Corporation of New York.

Finally, the authors wish to thank their respective families— Sarah Vogel and Jake and Kate Perkovich; and Christie Sunwoo and Audrey Dalton—for support and toleration of the disrupted evenings, weekends, and vacations that went into producing the book.

ABBREVIATIONS

AESA	Active Electronically-Scanned Array
BCCI	Board of Control for Cricket in India
BJP	Bharatiya Janata Party
BMD	ballistic missile defence
C4ISR	command, control, communications, computers, intelligence, surveillance, and reconnaissance
CIA	Central Intelligence Agency
CSR	corporate social responsibility
DGMO	Director General of Military Operations
DRDO	Defence Research and Development Organisation
FDI	foreign direct investment
FRA	Flight Refuelling Aircraft
HAL	Hindustan Aeronautics Limited
IAF	Indian Air Force
IBGs	integrated battle groups
IED	improvised explosive device
IMF	International Monetary Fund
INSAS	Indian Small Arms System
ISI	Inter-Services Intelligence
ISIL	Islamic State of Iraq and the Levant
ISR	intelligence, surveillance, and reconnaissance
JuD	Jamaat-ud-Dawa
LCA	Light Combat Aircraft
LeT	Lashkar-e-Taiba
LoC	Line of Control
MIRV	multiple independently targetable re-entry vehicles

MoD	Ministry of Defence
MQM	Muttahida Quami Movement
NATO	North Atlantic Treaty Organization
NCA	Nuclear Command Authority
NFU	no first use
NPT	Treaty on the Non-Proliferation of Nuclear Weapons
NSAB	National Security Advisory Board
PGM	precision guided munition
PML-N	Pakistan Muslim League Nawaz
RAW	Research and Analysis Wing
RISTA	reconnaissance, intelligence, surveillance, and targeting acquisition
SAARC	South Asian Association for Regional Cooperation
SFC	Strategic Forces Command
SSBN	Nuclear Powered Ballistic Missile Submarine
TSD	Technical Support Division
TTP	Tehrik-i-Taliban Pakistan
UAV	unmanned aerial vehicle
UPA	United Progressive Alliance

INTRODUCTION

When ten young men entered Mumbai on 26 November 2008 and attacked the iconic Taj and Oberoi hotels, the Central Railway station, and a Jewish centre, it was not the first time that militants from Pakistan had inflicted dramatic terror on India. In 2001, five men believed to be affiliated with organizations in Pakistan attacked the Parliament in New Delhi, launching a direct assault on the seat of Indian democratic governance. Eight years prior, in March 1993, an Indian criminal don, Dawood Ibrahim, facilitated by Pakistan's Inter-Services Intelligence (ISI), orchestrated a series of bomb explosions in Mumbai that left 257 people dead.

Yet, when top Indian national security officials met in the prime minister's residence on 29 November 2008 to consider how they might respond to the latest Mumbai attack, they quickly found that they had no good and ready options for retaliation.[1] Communications intercepts and other intelligence had by then traced the attackers to Pakistan. A massive Army mobilization, like the one that occurred in 2001–2 following the Parliament attack, was immediately ruled out. That earlier response—known as Operation Parakram—had been hugely expensive and cumbersome and was widely seen as ineffective. The Navy Chief of Staff attending the meeting remained silent. The Army Vice Chief of Staff demurred from offering suggestions, wishing to wait for his chief to return to New Delhi. The Air Chief Marshal did speak up, suggesting air strikes on terrorist training camps in Pakistan-administered Kashmir, with the provision that intelligence agencies would have to provide the targeting coordinates. This meeting ended without a decision.

In subsequent days, additional meetings were held. The Army eventually suggested that a limited ground operation could be conducted against Pakistan with sufficient notice, but that this would carry high risk of escalation. Pakistan could respond across the Line of Control in Kashmir and also along the international border, requiring the government and military services to be prepared for a wider war. The prime minister reportedly asked whether Pakistan could misperceive an Indian conventional strike as a nuclear one and respond by launching its own nuclear forces. No one could answer with any certainty.

When Army and Air Force options were discarded as too risky, officials prepared lists of other possible responses. Covert operations could be conceived against targets in Pakistan-administered Kashmir or the Pakistani heartland, some with visible effects that could cause a sensation in Pakistan and some measure of popular satisfaction in India, even if Indian officials denied responsibility. But then it was learned that the Research and Analysis Wing (RAW), India's external intelligence agency, had no assets in Pakistan who could conduct such operations. The Army could be asked to conduct commando operations against targets in Pakistan-administered Kashmir, but the government would have to be prepared to deal with the possibility that Indian personnel could be captured, which would in turn cause a public relations nightmare.

In the end, the prime minister chose not to authorize military action or an immediate, dramatic covert operation. Instead, India pursued a course of non-violent pressure, urging others in the international community to join it in condemning Pakistan, while emphasizing that India would not allow terrorists to distract the nation from its economic advancement. It is impossible to say whether other options would have been more effective. The United Nations (UN) Security Council, held back by China, did not issue a Chapter VII resolution as it had after the 9/11 attacks on the US and the 2005 London subway bombings. Economic sanctions were not imposed on Pakistan. But Pakistan was further isolated and did find itself under intense international pressure to prevent similar attacks. Within Pakistan itself, the constant broadcast of the horrific carnage of innocent people in Mumbai registered with much of the population, to the point that in subsequent years many otherwise sophisticated people thought that India's RAW had been behind the attacks because the reputational effect had been so harmful to Pakistan.[2]

Nearly six years after the 26/11 Mumbai attacks, a former Indian national security advisor hosted a small group of eminent retired generals and diplomats for a freewheeling discussion with a visiting American. It was late April 2014 and the topic was the subject of this book: How can India effectively motivate Pakistani leaders to prevent future high-profile terrorist attacks against India, and, if that fails, to minimize the risk that the ensuing conflict could escalate to nuclear war? In essence, this is the question that Indian leaders wrestled with in the days immediately following the 2008 attack.

One passage in the discussion highlighted the tensions that remain inherent in the challenge:

'The Pakistanis need to know there is a feeling and a capability which we can bring to bear—"you will get hit!" exclaimed a former director general of military operations (DGMO). 'Who stops us from going after terrorist camps?'

'Yes, you can hit back,' a diplomat volunteered, 'but so what?'

'Did we get anything from the restraint we displayed after Mumbai?' another general complained.

'Is terror an act of war?' the former national security advisor asked wryly.

Another general—a former commander of the eastern forces—scoffed. 'Even some action if it had been taken would have demonstrated we are a serious state. The Pakistanis couldn't have done anything.'

'Did anyone change their policy toward Pakistan after Indian restraint?' asked the former DGMO. 'Did the US stop helping Pakistan? Of course not.'

'But you have to prove who did it,' the former national security advisor countered. 'There has to be solid attribution.'

'Operation Parakam,' a general said, referring to the ten-month stand-off with Pakistan after the December 2001 attack on the Lok Sabha, 'why did we mobilize? Why go through all of that? We should have done something.'

'We don't have a lot of capacity,' a diplomat noted. 'Covert military options can be the only one.'

'India must follow sober realism,' the retired national security advisor cautioned. 'In the CCS [Cabinet Committee on Security] I was asked, "Can we hit Pakistan?" I said, "Yes, but for what result?"'

'But how do you prove deterrence if you don't use force at any time?' the former DGMO replied. 'You get hit and you don't hit back. They conclude your deterrence is not real. It fails.'

'We have demonstrated neither the will not the capability to fight and to deter,' the former commander of India's eastern forces bemoaned.

'Well, both sides fire across the LoC [the Line of Control dividing Jammu and Kashmir],' the former national security advisor reminded.

'If your Parliament is attacked is that the time to assure the world?' asked the former DGMO. 'Does it help investment in India? No hard state does this.'

Despite the passing of years since 2008, Indian national security elites still struggle with how to effectively respond to the threats posed by terrorism emanating from Pakistan. This is an exceptionally difficult and pressing challenge. Groups like the ones that conducted these attacks continue to operate in Pakistan. Real risk remains that they will strike again. Such groups could attack India with or without the authorization or complicity of state authorities in Pakistan. Moreover, even if the leaderships of India and Pakistan achieved a diplomatic breakthrough to pacify relations, militant elements within Pakistan could attack India in order to break the peace and perpetuate conflict. Indeed, militants and some in the Pakistani security establishment believe that without ongoing threats of violence India and the international community will ignore the grievances of Kashmiri Muslims and Pakistan.

India's first priority, of course, is to enhance homeland security against terrorists. This entails improving intelligence on threats emanating within India and abroad, enhancing border monitoring including along India's coasts, strengthening police at the state and central levels, coordinating information flows amongst all of these actors, and upgrading police and security forces' preparedness to respond to threatening events.

Whatever confidence India can build in its homeland defences, the country will still need strategies, policies, and capabilities to deal with the threats of violence that emanate from Pakistan. Here, India's strategic aim is to motivate Pakistani leaders to act decisively and durably to prevent future attacks on it, and if an attack occurs, to desist from escalating in reaction to India's response.[3] Motivation can take multiple forms—which is why we use the term in the title of this book. It can entail positive inducements such as trade and diplomatic resolution of differences, as well as coercion. In this book we focus primarily on the latter. For, the predominant discourse among Indian security policymakers and experts in recent years has centred on coercion and downplays the utility of diplomatic conflict resolution with Pakistan. Whether or not this emphasis on coercion is sagacious and long-lasting, the options India faces in this regard merit careful analysis.

The American strategist Thomas Schelling coined the term 'compellence' to connote threats 'intended to make an adversary do something', as distinct from deterrence, which involves 'a threat to keep him from starting something'.[4] More than fifty years after Schelling coined the term, standard dictionaries still do not include it. Yet, the distinction Schelling identifies between deterrence and compellence is important and often missed. 'Coercion' is suitable to connote when force is involved in the threat intended to motivate an opponent. However, as Schelling noted, coercion could involve actions and policies meant to deter as well as compel. Thus, when we mean to distinguish between deterrence and the threat to use force in order to make an opponent change behaviour, we use 'compellence'. When we refer to non-violent exertions to motivate the opponent to change behaviour, we use 'non-violent compellence'.

Scholars and policy practitioners in South Asia and other countries, including the US, understand that deterrence is hard to achieve with confidence and that compellence is even harder.[5] There are no certain ways to achieve either deterrence or compellence, let alone both. The logics of deterrence and compellence suggest that Pakistani leaders—civilian and military—will not act decisively to prevent militant groups and individuals from trying to attack India again if India, perhaps joined by other states, is not able to inflict costs on Pakistan that are greater than any potential gains Pakistan might expect from allowing such attacks to occur. A RAND Corporation study following the Mumbai attack described the problem in terms applicable to both India and the US: 'The challenge for the U.S., India and the international community is how to selectively put pressure on the [Pakistani] military and intelligence agencies in the near term without destabilizing Pakistan's fragile civilian government.'[6]

The challenges of deterrence and compellence are even greater when the state—India in this case—is trying to affect multiple actors in the opposing state. That is, India is seeking to deter and/ or compel not only the government in Pakistan, which could be expected to possess the attributes of a unitary rational actor, but also violent non-state actors that may or may not be under the control of the Pakistani government. Indeed, the involvement of non-state actors, or proxies, in the confrontation between states blurs the distinction between deterrence and compellence. Leaders of the Pakistani security establishment, for example, could be deterred from ordering significant-scale attacks on India. This deterrence could be an effect of India's threats to respond to such attacks militarily. It also could be a consequence of international ostracism. Even more tellingly, Pakistani elites could feel self-deterred by the recognition that terrorism breeds terrorism and undermines Pakistan itself.

If and when deterrence is internalized, then Pakistani authorities would do their best to prevent militant groups from attacking India too. The authorities would extend this deterrence/ restraint to non-state actors in order to avoid the consequences of terrorism for which the Pakistani state would be blamed (fairly or not). Whereas at some earlier point Pakistani state leaders may have relied upon ambiguity of agency and attribution to get away with facilitating or tolerating attacks on India, now, if state leaders have concluded that any terrorist attacks are self-defeating, they would be less interested in 'getting away with it' and more interested in preventing such violence. But an internalization and extension of deterrence in this fashion could look like compellence. Applying the concept and phenomenon of compellence therefore may overstate the importance of externally exerted pressure here, and may understate the effects of deterrence, which are easier to obtain.

Whether India's objective is deterrence and/or compellence, the question arises, what strategy (or strategies) and capabilities would be *feasible and effective* to enable India to achieve this purpose? Feasibility and effectiveness are not easy to determine. A range of coercive policies and instruments could be useful (or not) in affecting Pakistani actions. In terms of military capabilities there are questions regarding the availability and operability of suitable reconnaissance and strike technologies. These technologies have variable costs, schedules, and implications for the structure and training of the forces that would deploy them. Effectiveness depends on the particular targeting and military objectives that need to be met, and the interactions between the attacking forces and the defences they will encounter. Then there is the issue of escalation and how to maximize gains and minimize losses as the scale and intensity of conflict potentially grows. Finally is the matter of whether the use of particular coercive instruments will be more or less likely to appear disproportionately destructive, perhaps by causing collateral damage, which can then affect the political, legal, or moral implications of using them, as well as the risks of stimulating escalation.

The conversation hosted by the former Indian national security advisor recounted earlier in the chapter referred directly and obliquely to these challenges. Indian leaders understandably are frustrated by the tension between the urge to retaliate forcefully to the attacks and the difficulties in finding ways to do so that will not trigger consequences worse than the initial injury. On the eve of the Narendra Modi-led Bharatiya Janata Party (BJP) government's arrival in office, this tension was apparent in further discussions in New Delhi with highly placed Indians with diplomatic and military backgrounds.

'The challenge is, how can you change the thinking of the other side—raise the cost, but not then have to face a dilemma that is existential?,' volunteered a former foreign secretary.[7]

A recently retired high-ranking Air Force officer, like many military leaders, evinced impatience. 'Political leaders in India always weigh many things before taking a stance. They are very hesitant to move toward war. The proactive approach is too escalatory they feel. Second, the connotation of potential use of nuclear weapons—they don't want to run that risk.... But escalation fears are quite misunderstood. You should plan for escalation control.'[8]

Outside powers, including the US and China, complicate the calculation of costs and benefits of Indian action. How and when might the US intercede diplomatically or otherwise in a burgeoning military crisis between these two states? Will China stand by passively if India inflicts military damage on its close partner Pakistan? What if an escalating conflict between India and Pakistan threatened the lives of Chinese citizens in Pakistan and Americans in India? Meanwhile, gaps between India's professed and actual military capabilities constrain options in ways that Indian leaders may be reluctant to admit for domestic political reasons. As an experienced foreign policy advisor in the BJP puts it, 'the notion that international pressure from the United States impelled India to hold fire in 2001-2002 and defuse the crisis was a political excuse. The real problem was a lack of viable military options.'[9]

The May 2014 electoral ascension of Narendra Modi, and subsequent gains by his party in state elections, created a sense of dynamism within Indian governance that has not been felt in decades. Known as a tough, decisive leader with muscular aspirations for securing India and building its economic and military strength, Modi inspired many observers to believe India will hit back hard if it is struck again by agents perceived to be affiliated with Pakistan. Days before the prime minister was sworn in, a close advisor said, 'Modi will have to respond to attack or he will lose all his credibility'.[10] Indeed, in October and November 2014, the Indian Army unleashed unprecedented disproportionate artillery barrages in response to shelling from Pakistan, leading Prime Minister Modi to exclaim: 'The enemy has realized that times have changed and their old habits will not be tolerated. People know my intentions, and I need not express them in words. Where jawans have to speak, they speak with their finger on the trigger and they will continue to speak that way.'[11]

On the other hand, domestic economic imperatives and the desire to limit escalation could temper the new government's behaviour. In the words of a long-time participant and observer in the Indian defence apparatus, 'the realities of the situation will force the new team to conclude that dialogue is the only way to proceed. Modi will have to transform into Vajpayee. They are very different personalities, but the situation will force adaptation'.[12] Indeed, in the past, after crises and wars the two states have managed to reach diplomatic agreements that tempered their competition, at least for a while. The Tashkent declaration in 1966 followed the 1965 war. The Simla agreement of 1972 followed the 1971 war. The Lahore declaration was negotiated shortly after the nuclear tests of 1998. And, following the December 2001 attack on the Indian Parliament and the ensuing mass mobilization of forces, Indian and Pakistani leaders negotiated a ceasefire along the LoC. Each of these agreements to pursue non-violent resolution of the two countries' disputes was soon overtaken by events, of course. India blames elements in the Pakistani security establishment for the return to violence.

Time and events will tell whether India's leadership will conclude that diplomatic solutions with Pakistan are impossible and therefore more emphasis must be placed on coercion. India traditionally has changed international policies slowly and cautiously. Yet, there is reason to think that if it experiences another shattering terrorist attack attributed to Pakistan the response will be more forceful than in the previous fifteen years. It is apt here to quote a statement by Tzipi Livni, then the foreign minister of Israel. During Operation Cast Lead, the December 2009 to January 2010 military campaign against Hamas in Gaza, she said, 'Israel is not a country upon which you fire missiles and it does not respond. It is a country that when you fire on its citizens it responds by going wild'.[13] This statement captures well the spirit of many Indians today, especially in the armed forces.

Indeed, one increasingly hears Indian national security professionals cite Israel as an example of resolute, forceful behaviour that India should emulate.[14] But Livni's statement also begs many questions which Indian decision makers would be wise to address. How well has 'going wild' actually worked for Israel? Israeli intelligence and military operations have killed many targets, but in the process, since the 1970s and the invasion of Lebanon in 1982, more extreme and effective perpetrators of terrorism such as Hizbollah and Hamas were created as a direct result. Israel has felt the need to repeat major military operations against Hamas in Gaza twice since 2009 when Livni espoused the imperative to 'go wild'. The most recent war, in the summer of 2014, yielded little sense of victory in Israel, notwithstanding the deaths of 67 Israeli soldiers and nearly 2,200 Palestinians, including more than 500 children.[15] Evaluating these episodes, Amos Yadlin, the former head of Israeli Military Intelligence, concluded: 'Three military campaigns between Israel and Hamas have ended in an asymmetric strategic tie.'[16]

Statecraft requires policies and capabilities that can shape adversaries' behaviours in desired ways and at the same time build domestic public confidence and feelings of security. Hitting back sometimes can achieve both objectives, but often it serves domestic political interests better than it changes the behaviour of the adversary. To achieve the latter objective, India needs a theory of how possible actions will or will not motivate Pakistani leaders to act decisively to demobilize anti-Indian terrorist groups and to eschew escalation of conflict in response to possible Indian military retaliation. Indian officials (and others elsewhere) need to realistically assess the circumstances in which their Pakistani counterparts operate, and what would be the satisfactory steps to meet Indian interests. The most effective anti-India organizations, especially the Lashkar-e-Taiba (LeT), do not attack the Pakistani state, unlike the Pakistani Taliban. Lashkar-e-Taiba's parent organization, Jamaat-ud-Dawa (JuD), is popular for serving social functions. As the Pakistani security establishment fights the extreme Deobandi groups who are killing Pakistanis and attacking the state, it is yet unwilling and probably unable to physically challenge the LeT and JuD too. Thus, a more feasible demand is that the Pakistani security establishment demobilize—that is, pacify—the LeT and other anti-India groups. In making such a demand, India (and other interested parties including the US) would merely be holding Pakistani authorities responsible for establishing monopoly control on the projection of violence from Pakistani territory, which is a basic attribute of state sovereignty.

The fundamental strategic imperative of defining a feasible objective and devising means to achieve it is often under-considered in Indian debates (as in similar debates in Israel and the US, to name two 'hard' states). 'We don't have empirical evidence that force will motivate them to change,' the recently retired high-ranking Air Force officer acknowledged, 'but the theory is to keep raising the costs, and over time they will change. Hit the practitioners, hit their leadership, hit what you can of the ISI, so they know that every time they do it, they will get hit back.'[17] This is a wishful assumption more than a studied assessment. As the former national security advisor notes from long experience of contesting Pakistan, 'The real problem for India toward Pakistan is that there is supreme indifference here. There is no real scholar of Pakistan here. There are very few real experts.'[18]

Indeed, India would not be acting in a vacuum. Pakistani military and civilian leaders and an array of terrorist and militant organizations in Pakistan and in India will respond to Indian action. As we discuss more in the next chapter, assessing how the various actors in Pakistan will respond, and what the interactions among them will produce, is extremely difficult. The resulting analysis and predictions inevitably will be uncertain. Yet, this difficulty does not spare Indian leaders from the responsibility to at least estimate the reactions that various options to motivate Pakistani authorities would most likely engender.

Assessing the Strategic Context

The following hypothetical scenario poses the main challenge we examine in this book. In 2017, a group of young men hailing from Pakistan conduct a terrorist attack in a major Indian city killing hundreds of people and severely damaging an iconic Indian landmark. While Pakistani authorities initially deny any direct or indirect involvement in the attack, and insist that in recent years they have exerted themselves to tame militant groups, Indian officials declare that they have intelligence tying the attackers to a group with infrastructure in Pakistan that is, or should be, known to Pakistani security officials. Within days, Indian military forces move to destroy targets in Pakistan. (The following chapters explore various modes of attack India could undertake.) Pakistan, expecting Indian military action, mobilizes its Army and other military and para-military forces for defence and possible counter-attack. To heighten preparedness and survivability, Pakistani personnel begin to disperse nuclear weapons. Pakistani military leaders repeat prior general warnings that if Indian forces intrude into Pakistan and threaten Pakistan's vital interests, Pakistan will use nuclear weapons to stop and repel them. Indian commentators associated with the ruling BJP seek to reassure the Indian public and warn Pakistan that if it uses nuclear weapons against Indian personnel anywhere, India will retaliate massively.

This general scenario points to key questions that Indian decision makers and, therefore, their Pakistani counterparts, must think through if they are to develop strategies, policies, and capabilities that would have acceptable chances of achieving their respective objectives. Indeed, these questions would apply to potential conflict emerging from any number of scenarios, whether the initial provocation came from the Pakistani or the Indian side. In particular, Indian decision makers must calculate sequentially how, with highest probability and most acceptable costs, to:

- satisfy the domestic political–psychological need for punishment, and thereby prevent loss of support for the government;
- motivate Pakistani authorities to act decisively against terrorists and thereby build Indian confidence, to the extent possible, that such terrorist acts will not be repeated;
- deter Pakistani authorities from escalating the conflict in reaction to India's punitive moves; and
- bring the conflict to a close in ways that do not leave India worse off in terms of casualties, costs, and overall power than it would have been if it had not responded militarily, or had responded with less destructive means than it chose.

Clearly, some actions that could most probably satisfy one of these objectives would lessen the chances of achieving others. For example, satisfying the desire to punish Pakistan could be achieved by a relatively wide range of military actions and international economic sanctions. But the more destructive of possible military actions could raise the overall scale and costs of the conflict to levels disproportionate to the harm done by the initial attack on India, and invite unwelcome international responses. Conversely, minimally destructive actions could achieve little more than short-term retribution. The most difficult questions to answer pertain to the type and level of action that would most effectively motivate Pakistani authorities to act decisively against anti-India terrorist groups and to eschew escalation in response to India's action.

The complexity and difficulty of meeting these objectives is unprecedented in the nuclear age. Unlike any other nuclear-armed antagonists, India and Pakistan directly border each other, have unresolved territorial disputes, and have engaged in armed conflict four times. Furthermore, terrorism poses an instigating threat of future conflict, creating a spectrum of potential escalation that runs from sub-conventional operations to conventional war to nuclear exchanges.[19]

The ambiguities that could surround the authorship of a conflict-instigating attack complicate the two states' capacities to conduct the signalling that is essential to manage deterrence and escalation. If Pakistan denied responsibility for a major terrorist attack on India—truthfully or not—this would severely complicate India's calculations of how Pakistani leaders would interpret India's responses. Compared to aggressors, defenders in armed conflict are generally assumed to have greater resolve and license to use whatever force is necessary to defend themselves.[20] In the words of the distinguished British military expert, General (ret.) Rupert Smith, 'defence enables the forming and sustaining of political will in a way attack or offence never does....[D]efence enables a moral advantage, which is appreciated and sometimes necessary for the people, considered a bonus by the state—or at least its political leadership—and preferred by the military'.[21]

Following another major terrorist attack on India, Indians naturally would feel aggressed upon and therefore act like defenders. Yet, in a scenario where the Pakistani state's authorship of an initial attack was disputed by Pakistan, India's military response could be seen as aggression. In such a situation, the psychology of deterrence signalling and escalation management would be more complicated than what classic models based on economic rationality and game theory suggest. Indian leaders will be hard-pressed to calculate what level and type of defeat of the Pakistani Army would be more likely to lead to the achievement of the four major Indian objectives listed above. Total defeat of the Pakistani Army appears to be impossible without inviting Pakistan's use of nuclear weapons, which in turn could lead to mutually destructive escalation. Thus, short of total victory, what sort of Indian military action would, in theory, leave Pakistan's civilian and military leaders and institutions with the *motivation and sufficient capabilities* necessary to control anti-Indian terror organizations?

No theories in the existing international literature or in other states' practices offer guidance as to how India could most effectively proceed here. Studies of strategies and tactics to deter and defeat terrorism have not addressed situations in which the major antagonists possess nuclear weapons. Theories and case studies of nuclear deterrence and escalation management in a nuclearized environment have not involved cases where terrorists with ambiguous relationships to one of the state antagonists are the instigators of aggression and the 'unitary rational actor' model may not apply. The Indo-Pak competition features both sets of challenges with the added complication that third states— primarily the US and China—also figure heavily in the calculations of decision makers.

To be sure, the international security literature does address two of the more challenging concepts or imperatives at play in this scenario: escalation dominance and war termination. Yet, in a nuclearized environment there are profound tensions between the two concepts that have never been reconciled convincingly in theory or practice.

Escalation dominance can be defined as a situation wherein 'a combatant has the ability to escalate a conflict in ways that will be disadvantageous or costly to the adversary, while the adversary cannot do the same in return, either because it has no escalation option or because the available options would not improve the adversary's position'.[22] Escalation dominance could 'require' a state to achieve an advantage at each level of potential conflict, at each rung of an escalation ladder. A gap in capabilities could surrender the advantage believed to be necessary to win the escalation process. Thus, the technical and military challenges and costs of dominating each rung of potential escalation could be enormous. In any actual conflict, of course, the competition would be defined by the relative capabilities and resolve of the antagonists. Even if one state could not acquire *all* the capabilities necessary to dominate all imaginable escalatory steps, it could 'win' if it had *enough* capabilities to prevail at the stages that the adversary could contest. Yet, the potentially unbounded nature of the challenge makes achieving escalation dominance much more difficult than conceptualizing it.

There is little historical evidence to draw on to assess practical implications of the pursuit of escalation dominance in a nuclearized environment. There are only two instances when nuclear-armed states engaged in direct warfare against each other: the Sino-Soviet border conflict in 1969 and the Indo-Pak Kargil conflict of 1999. Both, fortunately, ended without major escalation. Yet, both of these cases were less challenging than the scenario that India and Pakistan now must plan to manage. The Sino-Soviet conflict erupted over a riverine border dispute that was not central to either state's identity or interest, and neither state sought to escalate it, making termination relatively easy. Kargil occurred over disputed territory along the LoC in Kashmir, not in response to an attack on the Indian heartland. Moreover, Kargil was the first conflict to occur after India and Pakistan overtly demonstrated their nuclear status. While India mobilized a sizable portion of its ground and air forces, at the same time Indian leaders signalled that they would not allow air forces to cross the LoC. Importantly, Pakistan was unprepared to counter-escalate with ground or air forces in the conflict zone, due largely to faulty assumptions about how India would respond to the original incursion. In contrast, the subsequent experience of the 2001 and 2008 terrorist attacks on the Lok Sabha and Mumbai, respectively, changed the political, psychological, and strategic context in which a subsequent attack would be perceived in India, while also changing Pakistan's calculations of what it must be able and willing to do to deter Indian escalation.

It is easier to terminate a war that begins with a small-scale aggression focused on a marginally important piece of territory (or water resource) than it is to end a war that begins with major aggression against vital territory or interests. Yet, if conflicts that begin over small stakes are not ended quickly they can escalate to the point where the scale and importance of perceived interests become enormous. Then war termination is exceedingly difficult to achieve. If both antagonists believe they will prevail by raising the level of force they apply against the other, then both will not think about terminating a war except through the defeat of the other. (This dynamic also occurs if neither side's leadership can admit to itself or its public that it might not prevail and therefore seek ways to de-escalate.) Who among the military and political leaders on each side will dare to think *in advance* about the possibility that an escalatory process will not compel the other side to desist, and therefore one's own state must search for ways to end the conflict at lower levels of destruction and cost? This problem should be obvious, but scholars and military-security professionals who engage in this field of work tend to spend much more time and effort thinking about how to win the prosecution of war than they do about how to end it short of clear victory.[23]

One notable exception was a Swiss-born American, Fred Iklé, a long-time strategist at the RAND Corporation and defence department official in Republican administrations. In a short, incisive, historically rich book entitled *Every War Must End*, Iklé adduced insights that appear particularly apt today for readers concerned about war and peace in South Asia. '[W]ar plans tend to cover only the first act,' Iklé noted, so that leaders opting for war 'will in fact be choosing a plan without an ending'.[24] For example, Iklé wrote, 'The Pearl Harbor attack was one of the most successfully planned military operations in history.' Yet it started a chain of developments that ended in disastrous defeat for Japan. Similarly, the German campaign to use submarines to interdict US naval supplies to Great Britain in World War I was meant to coerce England to quit the war on Germany's terms. But Germany offered no political inducements to motivate the British government to make peace, and failed to account for the likelihood that the submarine attacks on shipping would bring the US into the war, which in turn would embolden Britain to fight on.[25] Pakistani planners in 1999 followed a similar pattern of tactical cleverness and strategic blunder when they successfully infiltrated forces to take Indian positions in the Kargil sector but failed to prepare capabilities and plans to deal with the responses by India and outside powers.

Iklé described a difficulty in ending war which seems particularly pertinent to India and Pakistan today: 'In a war where the enemy's forces invade the homeland, any government that tries to make peace with the enemy while facing military defeat will almost inevitably come apart at the seams.'[26] Pakistani leaders' historic reliance on irregulars, proxies, and jihadis to perpetrate low-level violence in India, rather than conduct large-scale military invasion, may reflect a belief that Indian leaders would respond with moderation. That assumption—if it in fact has existed—may be increasingly dubious insofar as the terror attacks of 2001 and 2008 have created a growing demand in India for resolute military response to any future aggression. In any case, Iklé's observation about the political vulnerability of leaders accepting defeat presents Indians with a double-edged sword. On one side, Indians may value the prospect that a major military retaliation against Pakistan following another terror attack could cause enough damage and humiliation to turn Pakistanis against their own military and intelligence services. However, on the other side of the sword is the possibility that the Pakistani government indeed could 'come apart at the seams'. In the ensuing internal struggle to govern Pakistan the most militant actors could prevail, hardly an outcome that Indian leaders would seek.

The Indian and Pakistani militaries—like military and national security professionals in other states facing major threats—seek doctrines and capabilities that will enable them to 'win' an exchange at any level of conflict. The alternative—accepting the adversary's superiority and/or avoiding conflict even when provoked—is professionally anathema. Moreover, the capacity to dominate at any level of conflict is seen as the best way to deter war in the first place and thereby engender stability. If the adversary has reason to assess that it cannot win, it will not aggress. The problem, of course, is that when each opponent thinks and acts this way and seeks escalation dominance, the result is a potentially unending competition that is inherently destabilizing. In the case of India and Pakistan, such conflict could end in nuclear devastation.

Possible Options

The preceding introductory comments establish the context for India's deliberation on options it might pursue to motivate Pakistani leaders to prevent a future conflict, or to manage one with restraint if it erupts. We have sketched some of the perspectives and impulses that experienced Indian military, diplomatic, and national security professionals bring to the current challenges. We have recounted recent crises that inform the ways in which Indians define the challenges and the imperatives of Indian policy. And we have identified and briefly analysed some of the conceptual and strategic problems that underlay the Indo-Pak challenge in ways unaccounted for in the strategic affairs literature and unprecedented in the experiences of other nuclear-armed competitors.

The first chapter describes the institutional setting and dynamics of Indian and Pakistani decision-making. It summarizes longstanding shortcomings in the Indian state's formulation and implementation of national security strategy and defence procurement and management. This includes failure to come to terms with Pakistan's basic strategy of using ambiguous threats of low-level violence (terrorism) to compel India to compromise on the two nations' disputes. In doctrinal and operational terms, special note is made of the challenge of integrating military expertise and perspectives into policymaking and execution, and the imposition of more professional oversight over defence procurement and intelligence agencies. Without a much improved apparatus for the development, debate, and implementation of national security strategy and development of military and intelligence capabilities to pursue strategy, analyses of options to affect Pakistani behaviour will remain disconnected from any material reality.

The ensuing chapters analyse five ideal-type options that India will likely evaluate. Our analysis considers the potential effectiveness and implications of each option in terms of the three basic, inter-related strategic objectives discussed: 1) How and in what directions does it motivate Pakistan to act? 2) What are the implications for escalation management? and 3) How does the conflict end?

Chapter 2 considers the option of enhancing capabilities and plans to conduct army-centric incursions into Pakistan along lines described in India as a 'proactive' strategy, perhaps better known as the 'Cold Start' doctrine. While the provenance and material realities of Cold Start provide much grist for discussion, pertinent durable questions must be addressed concerning whether and how effective ground-based incursions into Pakistani territory could be carried out without provoking early risks of Pakistani nuclear response. India remains far from possessing the military hardware, supplies, and deployed force posture and reconnaissance capabilities envisioned by proponents of army-centric operations against Pakistan. But even if and when India acquired the requisite means to execute such operations, grave doubts would remain about their strategic efficacy.

Chapter 3 analyses the logic and capabilities that would be involved in a strategy focusing on limited, airborne operations launched against targets directly associated with terrorist organizations and their presumed backers in the Inter-Services Intelligence apparatus. Recent American and Israeli use of air power against terrorist organizations and their state hosts heighten Indian interests in such operations. Yet, the capabilities the US and Israel possess compared to their adversaries are vastly different than those that India possesses relative to Pakistan. Assuming India did possess requisite capabilities, this chapter analyses the risks and opportunities that India could face in initiating conflict with Pakistan via various sorts of airstrikes, paying close attention to implications for escalation and war termination.

Chapter 4 explores whether, how, and to what effect India could concentrate on a more symmetrical covert strategy to deter and counter terrorism from Pakistan by fomenting insurgency and disorder in Pakistan itself. Symmetry and proportionality may enhance the deterrence and compellence effects of this option. Indeed, the threat of symmetrically balancing Pakistan's longstanding use of sub-conventional operations could open space for bargaining to achieve a more peaceful modus vivendi between the two antagonists. On the other hand, the use of covert operations carries risks. Imperfect operations can produce embarrassment. Successful ones can invite retaliation. Being perceived to conduct violent covert operations could jeopardize India's reputational advantage over Pakistan, leading actors in South Asia and the international community to conclude there is little difference between the two states' behaviour in this domain.

Chapter 5 addresses possible innovations India could undertake in nuclear doctrine and capabilities to complement either an army-centric strategy, or a precision-strike strategy, or prosecution of a conflict that escalated from Indian sponsorship of insurgents in Pakistan. An enhanced suite of nuclear capabilities and a revised nuclear doctrine would not substitute for the other forms of coercion analysed in prior chapters. Rather, it would complement any or all of these options by seeking to manage the risk of Pakistani counter-escalation through nuclear threats. In particular, we consider arguments for and against revising India's adherence to no first use, its eschewal of battlefield nuclear weapons, and its reliance on massive retaliation.

Chapter 6 draws on India's restraint following the 2001 and 2008 attacks to consider whether and how such restraint could be elaborated into a strategy of non-violent compellence that would leverage international outrage over another major terrorist attack into a campaign to isolate and punish Pakistan economically, politically, and morally. Such a strategy would spare India the risks and costs of war. If such a strategy could be optimized, Pakistan and, in particular, the agencies associated with groups involved in anti-India terrorism, would suffer ill-effects without reaping the benefits from Indian military responses that could have the adverse effect of unifying the Pakistani nation behind the military.

In the Conclusion, we summarize the analyses of the preceding chapters and hazard a few predictions regarding how India's policymaking apparatus and capabilities acquisition processes will evolve and which strategies and policies are likely to be pursued over the next decade. Based on an analysis of each option against the four Indian objectives described previously, we assess that limitations of capabilities, plus the precedence of other national priorities and the historically beneficial results of relative restraint in the use of force, will make Indian leaders most likely to respond to another major terrorist attack by conducting largely symbolic airborne attacks on terrorist-related targets in Pakistan-administered Kashmir. It is also likely that India will undertake covert operations to kill at least one major terrorist target, and increase covert financial support for groups that challenge the Pakistani establishment, especially in Balochistan and Karachi. India also will continue using routine diplomatic channels to urge other states to protest against Pakistan.

Though a significant change compared to India's prior responses, the relative restraint inherent in actions like these would reflect the basic balance of power that now exists between India and Pakistan at the sub-conventional, conventional, and nuclear levels of coercion. In the conclusion, we note analytically that such a balance creates an opportunity for leaders to stabilize and pacify the Indo-Pak competition through explicit agreements that clarify expectations and standards of behaviour. Such agreements—negotiated accommodations—could raise the stakes for any authorities that would subsequently violate them, and would facilitate Indian efforts as an aspiring great power to create an international coalition to hold Pakistan to account if it fails to prevent further attacks by Pakistani militant groups in India. However, considering the political challenges that confront leaders seeking to take peace-building approaches, we assess that leaders of India and Pakistan will not soon be willing *and* able to negotiate arrangements to stabilize the rough balance of power that has been created and, more broadly, to pacify their competition.

Notes and References

1. The discussion here, informed from many sources, draws most heavily on Pranab Dhal Samata, '26/11: How India Debated a War with Pakistan that November', *Indian Express*, 26 November 2010. Available at: http://archive.indianexpress.com/story-print/716240/. Participants in the 29 November meeting included the prime minister, his national security advisor, the defence minister, and the heads of the domestic and external intelligence services, in addition to the three armed forces representatives.

2. Authors' conversations with Pakistani military and civilian officials and experts in Pakistan and Washington, DC.

3. India has an interest in curtailing all terrorism in and emanating from Pakistan; this interest is shared by most Pakistanis. However, as a practical matter of policy, India focuses first on terrorists that target it directly. International norms and resolutions on terrorism also concentrate most clearly on interstate terrorism. Thus, throughout this book we emphasize the Indian objective of motivating Pakistani authorities to curtail terrorism directed against India.

4. Thomas C. Schelling, *Arms and Influence* (Yale University Press, 1966), 69–70.

5. Todd S. Sechser and Matthew Fuhrmann, 'Crisis Bargaining and Nuclear Blackmail', *International Organization* 67, no. 1 (January 2013): 173–95; Robert J. Art, 'To What Ends Military Power?', *International Security* 4, no. 4 (Spring 1980): 8–10. Sechser and Fuhrmann argue that nuclear deterrence is far more successful than nuclear compellence. Using quantitative analysis, they find that nuclear powers are not more successful than non-nuclear powers at compellence. Art similarly argues, 'Compellence may be easier to demonstrate than deterrence, but it is harder to achieve...compellent actions tend to be vaguer in their objectives than deterrent threats and for that reason more difficult to obtain.... In contrast to compellent actions, deterrent threats are both easier to appear to have ignored or easier to acquiesce to without great loss of face. In contrast to deterrent threats, compellent actions more directly engage the prestige and the passions of the put upon state.' For an early critical review of deterrence: Alexander L. George and Richard Smoke, *Deterrence in American Foreign Policy: Theory and Practice* (New York: Columbia University Press, 1974).

6. Angel Rabasa, Robert D. Blackwill, Peter Chalk, Kim Cragin, C. Christine Fair, Brian A. Jackson, Brian Michael Jenkins, Seth G. Jones, Nathaniel Shestak, and Ashley J. Tellis, 'The Lessons of Mumbai', (RAND Corporation, 2009), 16.

7. Interview with former foreign secretary, New Delhi, 22 October 2013.

8. Interview with retired Air Force officer, New Delhi, 24 April 2014.

9. Interview with BJP foreign policy advisor, New Delhi, 23 April 2014.

10. Interview with senior official, New Delhi, 25 April 2014.

11. 'Strong India Response Stuns Pakistan, Border Aggression Stutters', *Deccan Herald*, 10 October 2014.

12. Interview, New Delhi, 24 April 2014.

13. Daniel Byman, *A High Price* (Oxford University Press, 2011), citing Robin Wright, 203.

14. In a paper urging India to emulate this example, two associates of the Vivekananda International Foundation, which was directed by Ajit Doval before he was recruited to become National Security Advisor to Narendra Modi, reflect Indian enthusiasm for the Israeli military model. 'Irrefutably, it is the military Might that adds awe and aura to a nation's standing in the regional and international equations. Israel would simply not exist today if it were not so. Today its utterance and posturing shakes up the neighbourhood and makes the world sit up and listen to it—their consent or dissent just don't seem to matter.' Col. (ret.) Karan Kharb, 'State of Military Might of Resurgent India', Vivekananda International Foundation, 25 August 2014. Available at: http://www.vifindia. org/article/2014/august 25/state-of-military-might-in-resurgent-India. Maj. Gen. (ret) G.D. Bakshi devotes a whole chapter in his recent book, *Limited Wars in South Asia*, to lessons India should draw from Israel's use of force since 1967. Referring to the 2006 war against Hezbollah in Lebanon, Bakshi writes, 'The Israeli offensive provides an excellent military role model for a Cold Start that is initiated by air power and followed up by ground assault.' Maj. Gen. (ret.) G.D. Bakshi, *Limited Wars in South Asia: Need for an Indian Doctrine* (New Delhi: Knowledge Books, 2010), 71. A former senior officer in India's Integrated Defence Forces similarly invoked Israel in a 2014 interview: 'What has Israel done? They hit all the time. It hasn't necessarily stopped the terrorists, but their costs have gone way up.' Interview, New Delhi, 24 April 2014.

For more on India's desire to follow the Israeli model, see also: B. Raman, 'Can India Emulate Israel's Action in Gaza?' *Outlook*, 9 January 2009. Available at: http://www.outlookindia.com/article/ can-india-emulate-israels-action-in-gaza/239392; Anand Raj Singh, 'India Should Emulate Israel, Says Bhagwat', *New Indian Express*, 11 January 2010. Available at: http://www.newindianexpress.com/ nation/article221030.ece; 'Emulate Israel to Fight Terrorism', *New Indian Express*, 18 July 2011. Available at: http://www. newindianexpress.com/cities/chennai/article420425.ece; Air Commander Arjun Subramaniam, 'Air Power and Irregular Warfare in the Indian Context', *Indian Defence Review*, 19 August 2011. Available at: http://www.indiandefencereview.com/interviews/ air-power-irregular-warfare-in-the-indian-context/. On India-Israeli security cooperation, see Alvite Ningthoujam, 'India's Promising Israel Defense Ties', *The Diplomat*, 9 October 2014. Available at: http://thediplomat.com/2014/10/indias-promising-israel-defense- ties/; Pramit Pal Chaudhuri, 'No More Hiding in the Closet: 3 Reasons for PM Modi's Visit to Israel', *Hindustan Times*, 1 June 2015. Available at: http://www.hindustantimes.com/india-news/ why-modi-should-visit-israel-it-is-india-s-indispensable-ally/ article1-1353637.aspx; Jayita Sarkar, 'India and Israel's Secret Love Affair', *The National Interest*, 10 December 2014. Available at: http://nationalinterest.org/blog/the-buzz/india-israels-secret-love- affair-11831?page=2; Gilli Cohen and Reuters, 'India Buys $525m Worth of Missiles From Israel, Rejecting Rival U.S. Offer', *Haaretz*, 25 October 2014. Available at: http://www.haaretz.com/news/ diplomacy-defense/1.622677; Amos Harel, 'Israel-India Strategic Ties No Longer a Secret', *Haaretz*, 18 February 2015. Available at: http://www.haaretz.com/news/diplomacy-defense/1.643024. For a contrasting opinion, see: Nicolas Blarel, 'The Myth of India's "Shift" Toward Israel,' *The Diplomat*, 19 February 2015. Available at: http:// thediplomat.com/2015/02/the-myth-of-indias-shift-toward-israel/. For a discussion of social-ideological Indian-Israeli convergence, see Pankaj Mishra, 'India, Israel Start to See New Enemies from Within', 13 July 2015. Available at: http://www.bloombergview.com/ articles/2015-07-13/india-and-israel-start-to-see-enemies-within.

15. Jodi Rudoren, 'Amnesty International Says Israel Showed "Callous Indifference" in Gaza', *The New York Times*, 4 November 2014. Available at: http://www.nytimes.com/2014/11/05/world/middleeast/

amnesty-international-says-israel-showed-callous-indifference-to-gaza-civilians.html.

16. Amos Yadlin, 'The Strategic Balance of Operation Protective Edge: Achieving the Strategic Goal Better, Faster, and at a Lower Cost', in Anat Kurz and Shlomo Brom (eds), *The Lessons of Operation Protective Edge* (Tel Aviv: Institute for National Security Studies, 2014), 199.

17. Interview with retired Air Force officer, New Delhi, 24 April 2014.

18. Interview with former national security advisor, 25 April 2014.

19. Israel seeks to deter terrorism and compel state sponsors of terrorists to desist, but to date none of these states possesses nuclear weapons to counter Israel's ultimate recourse.

20. Robert Jervis, 'Political Implications of Loss Aversion', *Political Psychology* 3, no. 2 (June 1992): 195. For the original econometric explanation of Prospect Theory: Daniel Kahneman and Amos Tversky, 'Prospect Theory: An Analysis of Decision Under Risk', *Econometrica* 47, no. 2 (1979): 263–91; The Israeli philosopher Avishai Margalit aptly notes 'the asymmetry between the relative willingness to behave morally [with restraint in the use of force] in situations of gain and the relative unwillingness to do so in situations of loss'. Avishai Margalit, *On Compromise and Rotten Compromises* (Princeton University Press, 2010), 126.

21. Rupert Smith, *The Utility of Force* (New York: Vintage Books, 2008 edition), 198.

22. Forrest E. Morgan, Karl P. Mueller, Evan S. Medeiros, Kevin L. Pollpeter, and Roger Cliff, *Dangerous Thresholds: Managing Escalation in the 21st Century* (Santa Monica, CA: RAND Corporation, 2008), 15.

23. The field of conflict resolution may offer useful insights, but defence and national security establishments tend to be much less versed in this literature than in theories of escalation dominance and deterrence.

24. Fred Iklé, *Every War Must End* (New York: Columbia University Press, revised edition, 1991), 8.

25. Iklé, *Every War Must End*, 46–7.

26. Iklé, *Every War Must End*, 68.

1

THE DECISION-MAKING SETTING

In his recent encyclopaedic tome on the subject, Sir Lawrence Freedman defines strategy as 'being about maintaining a balance between ends, ways, and means; about identifying objectives; and about the resources and methods available for meeting such objectives'.[1] Strategy includes reconciling ends to means that are realistically available. Importantly, strategy is required in situations of actual or potential conflict where interests clash. Ultimately, Freedman writes, 'The challenge for the strategist—indeed, the essence of strategy—is to force or persuade those who are hostile or unsympathetic to act differently than their current intention'.[2]

India has a vital security need to motivate Pakistani decision makers—particularly in the Army and Directorate for ISI—to demonstrably prevent terrorist attacks against India. To achieve this objective requires a strategy and policies that befit India's real capabilities (today and in the future) and are likely to motivate and sustain desired changes in Pakistani behaviour. A strategy can be multifaceted, of course, combining diplomacy, military preparedness, doctrine, and international economic and political inducements or sanctions. And strategy can be segmented according to different time horizons—short-term, medium-term, and long-term. Thus, India could have a long-term strategy of encouraging democratization of Pakistan and normalization of relations, and a more near-term strategy of compelling the Pakistani security establishment to demobilize anti-Indian terrorist groups. Policies and capabilities to decisively punish Pakistan in the event of another major terrorist attack against India could serve both objectives, even as the longer-term strategy would emphasize other instruments of power and influence.

Remarkably, Indian authorities have not articulated any comprehensive strategy, nor rigorously analysed and debated the resources and methods they could feasibly acquire and deploy in order to motivate Pakistani leaders to curtail the terrorist threat.[3] As Manoj Joshi, a member of the 2012 Naresh Chandra Task Force on national security, reports: 'India has no overarching national security doctrine and, flowing from it [sic], no national security strategy that has a formal and considered approval of the political authorities.'[4] In the absence of a robust declared strategy and matching capabilities—or in lieu of subjecting the country to the expense and risks of pursuing them—Indian leaders since 1971 have enacted a de facto strategy of non-violent resistance to Pakistan. To be sure, Pakistanis do not perceive India's performance and capabilities this way. Still, compared with the violent provocations India has borne from (allegedly) Pakistani sources, Indian leaders have been remarkably restrained. The question is whether tomorrow's India, with forceful leadership, burgeoning global aspirations, and military capabilities, should or will conclude that more demonstrable applications of coercion are necessary to change Pakistani behaviour.

Indian strategists and policymakers are not operating in boundless circumstances. Several facts and factors condition their interests and potential choices. Most portentously, the possibility of nuclear war limits the location and scale of force India and Pakistan can apply to each other without self-destructing.[5] Given the nuclear constraint and India's overall conventional military size, Pakistani leaders will not initiate large-scale conventional military aggression against India. Thus, the scope of strategy towards Pakistan (as distinct from China) can be relatively narrow. It concerns the management of escalation of conflict that could ensue if Pakistani authorities fail to do all in their powers to prevent major terrorism against India, and India reacts in ways that Pakistani leaders answer with force. Within this scope, multiple assessments are necessary to inform a strategy: What interests and perceptions motivate Pakistani decision makers?

What can they reasonably be expected to do, first to demobilize anti-Indian elements on their territory, and second, if this fails, to bear Indian retaliatory punishment? What instruments does India possess now or in future that would predictably defeat Pakistani countermeasures and achieve desired effects on Pakistani behaviour? What are the likely costs to India of preparing for and conducting various plausible policies against Pakistan? These questions are difficult to answer with confidence, but they are not infinite. The government and expert community of a major power—especially a democracy with uncensored media—could reasonably be expected to proffer strategies and policies that derive from defensible answers to these questions.

The chapters in this book explore these questions by analysing plausible 'ideal-type' policies Indian leaders could choose in order to motivate Pakistani leaders to prevent further terrorist attacks on India. The key word is 'choose'. Policies for the use of force or other forms of coercion and inducement do not choose themselves. Choices are made by leaders. The decision-making process begins— or should begin—with the development of strategy, which in turn is influenced by history, strategic culture, bureaucratic habits and interests, personalities, information, capabilities, and trade-offs with other priorities. Assuming for the sake of our analysis that India and Pakistan will not achieve diplomatic breakthroughs leading to a stable peace, we focus here on policies regarding coercion, again reflecting the current emphasis of Indian policy debates. By 'policies' we mean a combination of capabilities and plans to apply them.

In an ideal world, great thinkers could imagine an appealing strategy and their state could then quickly produce the instruments necessary to implement it. However, in the real world, time, resources, and institutions limit how fully and quickly states can acquire the means to pursue strategic ends. This is especially true in a democratic union of diverse states with decentralized powers, such as India. Thus, before evaluating possible strategies, capabilities, and operational plans that India might choose to pursue, it is first necessary to describe the policymaking setting in which such decisions will be made.[6]

The Strategic Cultural Background

Indians and outside observers have long noted that the country lacks effective institutions and processes for making decisions about national security strategy, as well as the policies and material means to carry out such a strategy. After the Kargil conflict of 1999, the Indian Cabinet constituted a committee to 'look into this episode'. Headed by the legendary strategist, K. Subrahmanyam, the committee issued a wide-ranging report. It found 'many grave deficiencies in India's security management system'.[7] Since 1947, the report noted,

[t]here has been very little change...despite the 1962 debacle [in war with China], the 1965 stalemate and the 1971 victory [over Pakistan], the growing nuclear threat, end of the cold war, continuance of proxy war in Kashmir for over a decade and the revolution in military affairs. The political, bureaucratic, military and intelligence establishments appear to have developed a vested interest in the status quo. National security management recedes into the background in time of peace and is considered too delicate to be tampered with in time of war and proxy war. The Committee strongly feels that the Kargil experience, the continuing proxy war and the prevailing nuclearized security environment justify a thorough review of the national security system in its entirety.

Had the report been written after the terror attacks on the Parliament in 2001 and Mumbai in 2008, the authors no doubt would have encompassed these events in their lament over the inadequacies of national security strategy and policymaking.

Indeed, writing a decade after the Kargil conflict, Stephen P. Cohen and Sunil Dasgupta highlighted major deficiencies that remain in the Indian national security system. 'Over the last two decades', they wrote, 'the military threat to India has changed dramatically toward unconventional war, but the nation's armed forces and national security decisionmaking structure appear not to have made insurgency and terrorism the centerpiece of the military modernization effort'.[8] Unlike the mid-twentieth century warfare wherein military battle led to victory or defeat and a termination of conflict, confrontation with Pakistan is neither war nor peace, but rather a chronic contest of wills occasionally punctuated by bursts of violence.[9]

The military and strategic communities of India and Pakistan—like those in other countries—remain slow to transition from antiquated industrial-war mindsets and forces to the challenges of modern confrontation. Part of the problem is institutional. As Cohen and Dasgupta reported regarding India: 'There remains an imbalance among the services, and little or no serious integration of strategic planning, let alone operational coordination. The critical bottleneck, one unlikely to be remedied soon, is the lack of civilian expertise in defense and security matters, despite the proliferation of research centers and think tanks devoted to defense and security matters.'[10] In August 2014, a former Army officer and leader of one such think tank, Gurmeet Kanwal, highlighted these problems as a top priority for reform: 'The structures for higher defence management and the process of national security decision making in India need to be examined afresh.... The lack of adequate military inputs into decision making continues to remain the most significant lacuna.'[11]

Correcting these shortcomings would require much greater expertise and attention on the part of top political leaders, and improved integration of military leaders into policymaking deliberations. But neither change has ever been a priority of civilian leaders. Moreover, if the military's mindset is outdated—focused on mid-twentieth century industrial warfare—its inputs into policymaking will be unsuited for twenty-first century challenges.

The sources of India's strategic inefficiencies are deep. In a seminal 1992 study for the RAND Corporation, George Tanham reported that 'although India has, over time, developed elements of a defense strategy...it has produced little formal strategic thinking and planning.'[12] As Tanham noted, 'India's early prime ministers, particularly Nehru and his daughter, Indira Gandhi, thought out and managed foreign policies and strategies on their own, or with a small coterie of advisors. No serious strategic planning institutions, if they ever existed, have survived in independent India, and none exists today.' The ensuing decades and governments led by figures as diverse as V.P. Singh, Chandra Shekhar, Narasimha Rao, Deve Gowda, Inder Gujral, Atal Bihari Vajpayee, and Manmohan Singh brought little significant change in this domain.

Tanham traced the 'the lacunae in strategy and planning' to 'India's historical and cultural development'. He averred that

[t]he Hindu concept of time, or rather the lack of a sense of time—Indians view life as an eternal present, with neither history nor future—discourages planning.... Hindus consider life a mystery, largely unknowable and not entirely under man's control. In this view fate, intuition, tradition, and emotions play important roles, but how, how much, and when is never clearly known. Man's control over his life is thus limited in Hindu eyes, and he cannot forecast or plan with any confidence.[13]

Decades after Tanham wrote this, one prominent faculty member at Jawaharlal Nehru University reiterated the point in a discussion of Indian policy planning to deal with another Mumbai-like attack: 'In Hindu culture we believe in timelessness and reincarnation, so we are in no hurry to act.'[14] This cultural interpretation may seem strange, especially to Westerners, and it may be unwelcome to some Indians today. Yet, western governments' inabilities to manage recent international events ranging from the Russian interventions in Ukraine, the emergence of the Islamic State of Iraq and the Levant (ISIL) in Iraq and Syria, and the chaos in Libya suggest that even the most proactive governments are unable to predict and control events. Hubris regarding a state's capacity to control complex dynamics of groups, individuals, and events in other states can be just as dangerous as humility, if not more.

The Indian military's non-participation in the independence movement is one factor that Tanham and others cite to explain the military's exclusion from policy formulation.[15] Another factor is the determination of Nehru and his successors to preclude military coups that could threaten India's nascent democracy. A recently retired high-ranking military officer echoed this explanation for the military's exclusion from policymaking: 'The freedom struggle was nonviolent. The military wasn't part of it. If anything, the military was associated with the colonizers. So from the beginning the military was not on the inside, and was suspect.

Then there was the fear of coups, etc.'[16] It is remarkable that this perception of military trustworthiness persists almost 70 years after independence, with an established record of civilian primacy and military faithfulness to democracy.

Tanham's essay engendered controversy in India. However, no lesser figures than K. Subrahmanyam and former Army Chief of Staff K. Sundarji endorsed his basic conclusions. More recently, in April 2014, two former highly placed Indian officials—one a civilian who has operated multiple times at the apex of Indian security deliberations, and one a three-star military officer quoted above—volunteered without prompting, 'Tanham was right.' Indeed, the officer continued, 'I know it's controversial to say it, but he was right.'[17] The civilian was even more emphatic: 'It must be recognized that there's a complete lack of strategic view, and complete lack of understanding between civilian and military leaderships. It is a disaster.'[18]

Military integration into policymaking processes would not be a panacea, of course. In some respects, India has done better than most major powers in avoiding international security debacles and unaffordable defence spending, despite or perhaps because of the lack of military participation in policymaking. India's experiences combatting internal insurgencies offer insights into the complexities of 'irregular' confrontations. Bringing military leaders into decision-making would be necessary to enhance the information basis of strategy and policy formation, but it would not be sufficient. India ultimately would need civilian and military cooperation in undertaking institutional reform across the range of organizations involved in intelligence, national defence, and foreign policy.

The following sections sketch some of the major institutional shortcomings that Indian leaders must redress. As Americans we understand that readers in India and Pakistan may bristle at our description of flaws in their countries' national security policymaking structures and outcomes, even though we base this analysis on local sources. People naturally are more receptive to hearing criticism from within than from foreigners. All the more so when the authors hail from an exceptionally powerful and often interventionist state that has committed numerous strategic blunders which have harmed other people. Thus, we wish to be clear that the brief account of institutional shortcomings in India and Pakistan that follows here does not suggest that national security policymaking in the US or any other state is free from similar problems or others of greater or lesser consequence. We imagine that security professionals from other countries, including ours, will find much here that is familiar.

Analysis of Pakistan

In order to achieve their objectives toward Pakistan, Indian leaders should seek to understand what motivates relevant Pakistani actors and how these actors would most likely respond to possible Indian moves. Both calculations are difficult to obtain with confidence. Moreover, it is possible to understand Pakistani motivations without being able to predict whether and how possible Indian actions would change Pakistani behaviour. Still, in developing strategy, Indian officials must take into account Pakistan's interests and the character of its decision-making structure.

Pakistan is determined to win either sovereignty over the Muslim-majority area of Kashmir now held by India, or an arrangement for the governance of this area that would be acceptable to the Kashmiri Muslim population in ways that would validate the Pakistan Army's historic exertions (ostensibly) on their behalf. Pakistan thus seeks to compel India to negotiate forthcomingly on Kashmir as well as other disputes (including control over the Siachen glacier and Sir Creek). At a minimum, Pakistan aims to deny India the option of ignoring Pakistan's demands and interests, and to retain the international community's attention to disputes with India.

Pakistan's structure and culture of policymaking could hardly be more different from India's. In Pakistan, the military has been pre-eminent in shaping the policies and capabilities that the state has deployed against India. This influence has been most obvious when the military has directly ruled the country—nearly half of Pakistan's history. But even when civilians have headed the government, the military—including the ISI—has been the primary designer of capabilities, plans, and operations.[19] This role applies not only to land, air, and naval forces, but also to the longstanding cultivation and use of 'irregular' forces, as well as the Pakistani nuclear arsenal.

Military predominance has not produced effective national security strategies for Pakistan, even if it is unclear whether civilian leaders would have done better. Military leadership presided over the loss of East Pakistan in 1971. After 1979, the ISI cultivated militant organizations to wage jihad against the Soviet Union in Afghanistan and India in Kashmir, only to realize very late that such actors would sow violence and terrorism that now threaten Pakistan itself. Military leaders took advantage of the civilian Prime Minister Nawaz Sharif and conjured the Kargil incursion in 1999, but inadequately prepared for India's reaction to it. If Pakistan today faces severe crises of security (and economics and governance) then the military's priorities and strategic choices are largely responsible.

Still, in terms of competition with India, Pakistan's military-dominated security apparatus has yielded significant results which Indian officials must take into account. The Pakistani state has prioritized the development of military and paramilitary capabilities. The operators of forces have determined the procurement and development of the weapons they could use, adding to operational effectiveness and overall morale. They have ensured quicker and smoother procurement and modernization processes than those in India. The General Headquarters has command over the army, air force, navy, nuclear forces, and, through the ISI, sub-conventional assets. This, in theory if not always in practice, facilitates coherence in doctrine and command of operations. Military doctrine has been adapted with greater care, decisiveness, and dispatch. Pakistan's nuclear programme has been directed with military purposefulness and has grown and advanced technically with speed. While India has greater overall financial and technical resources to invest in military capabilities (broadly defined), Pakistan has mobilized its less ample resources with more resolve, purpose, and efficiency.

Whatever positive, long-term objectives it has, the Pakistani military does not want to lose another war with India or be humiliated. This leads to the use of proxies and sub-conventional tactics to keep conflict below the threshold of major warfare. Since 1947, the Pakistani military has cultivated and utilized irregular forces to challenge India in Kashmir, fight the Soviet Union in Afghanistan, and, more recently, counter Indian influence in Afghanistan and maintain pressure in Kashmir. Some of these groups morphed with varying degrees of Pakistani military direction and assistance into terrorists who have conducted attacks in the Indian heartland. The authorship of the violence projected by non-regular forces can be difficult to attribute to the Pakistani state.[20] Obscuring attribution can serve several strategic purposes for the Pakistani military.[21] Ambiguity of authority combined with the relatively small scale of violence that terrorists perpetrate complicates India's calculations in responding. Whom must India deter and/or compel to change Pakistan's behaviour? Is Pakistan's elected prime minister in charge? Does the Army high command control the actions of the groups and individuals most likely to attack India? Or, somewhat differently, could the Army leadership prevent such groups and individuals from attacking India? Does the authorship of significant terrorist plans and capacities now reside at lower levels in the Pakistani establishment, beyond the capacity of the Army leadership to control thoroughly? Are groups such as the Lashkar-e-Taiba (LeT) more or less autonomous? The answers to these questions should inform calculations regarding what threats or inducements will be most effective to change given actors' behaviours. But the uncertainty of answers creates strategic risks for India in managing the potential escalatory process that could flow from responses to another terror attack. This uncertainty, of course, is desired, or at least welcomed, by the Pakistani security establishment.

Pakistan's development and utilization of sub-conventional forces has over time created portentous consequences for itself, too. Pakistani military leaders know whether they ordered a group to conduct an attack or wittingly did not oppose it. These leaders may lie or tell the truth to India—hence ambiguity—but they know. Ambiguity may benefit Pakistan in the short term by giving India and other powers pause in holding Pakistan to account. Yet, strategically, if groups operating on Pakistani soil may attack India without authorization, the leadership in Rawalpindi and Islamabad has significant problems. The military high command, or some faction of it, may know that an attack was prepared and authorized, but the civilian leadership might be uninformed. Or, an attack may occur without explicit authorization from either the military or the civilian leadership, but involving a group that someone in the ISI knew was trained and supplied for such attacks. When it is not clear which leaders in a state—civilian, military, intelligence— have authority over the projection of violence from that state, or whether any state officials have the authority and capabilities to assert positive or negative control over the projection of violence, such a state lacks a basic attribute of modern statehood.

Since 2012, signs have appeared that the Pakistani military command recognizes that the state must reimpose a monopoly on violence perpetrated within and from Pakistani territory. In an unusually pointed Independence Day speech on 14 August 2012, the then Army Chief of Staff Gen. Ashfaq Pervez Kayani committed the Army, and by implication Pakistan, to war against extremism and terrorism. He dutifully noted that hostile foreign forces benefit from Pakistan's 'internal weaknesses', but rather than focusing on outside elements he said 'our efforts must be directed towards stabilizing the internal front'.[22] 'No state', Kayani said, 'can afford a parallel system of governance and militias'. In July 2014, after much deliberation and internal jockeying between the military and civilian leadership, the military launched a major operation—termed Zarb-e-Azb—to 'cleanse' the tribal belt between Pakistan and Afghanistan of militant forces that had been hitting targets in Pakistan. This operation continues through the time of our writing in October 2015. Independent reporting on its effectiveness (and its financial and human costs) is scarce.

Retaliatory militant violence in the Pakistani heartland, which had been much feared in the run up to the operation, generally has not occurred. Whether this is due to the prophylactic operations of police and military forces, militant incapacity, or other factors is not clear through public sources. Also in 2015, paramilitary forces began extensive operations to pacify Karachi. It remains difficult to ascertain the extent to which these efforts to impose control over violent actors includes those who target India. Knowledgeable Pakistanis point out that no major attack has occurred in India since November 2008.

Looking at this pattern, there are signs that the Pakistani security establishment increasingly recognizes the liabilities of external as well as internal terrorism. However, given past experiences and ongoing suspiciousness, Indian policymakers look for clearer evidence of this establishment's intentions and capabilities.

'It's a Rubik's cube—dealing with Pakistan,' a former Indian national security advisor offered in a November 2014 interview. 'You keep fiddling with the squares, and as you move one set, others are affected or become problems. You don't have a solution.'[23] Another exceptionally knowledgeable former Indian official volunteered a similar metaphor: 'the problem is to get sufficient information and feel about Pakistani decision making. To find the right keys on the keyboard. The keyboard keeps changing. You don't know which buttons to push.'[24]

Indian policymakers must try to affect Pakistan as it is; they also have an interest in motivating Pakistani authorities—both military and civilian—to achieve greater clarity of control over groups that could project violence from Pakistani territory. But it is difficult to know which authorities are amenable to this objective and what India could do to enhance their resolve and capabilities. It is even harder to understand how India could alter the calculations of groups that have the wherewithal to mount major attacks on India. Terrorist organizations and their sponsors do not need to 'win'. They do not expect to take control of Kashmir or other territory under Indian sovereignty. Nor can they break India apart or prevent massive India from achieving its larger aspirations over the long term. But as long as terrorist organizations and their supporters within the Pakistani state do not lose—as long as they continue to exist—they win, at least in their own eyes.

Three obvious factors confound efforts to motivate and enable Pakistani authorities to demobilize anti-Indian terrorists.

First, the Pakistani military has justified its dominant position in the state as necessary to contest threats from India. Elements within the military (and its intelligence service) can be expected to impede initiatives by civilian leaders to change the national narrative of hostility and seek diplomatic rapprochement with India. In 1999, when Prime Ministers Nawaz Sharif and Atal Behari Vajpayee were seeking to build on their path-breaking Lahore Declaration, a few Pakistani generals, led by Pervez Musharraf, initiated the Kargil incursion. In the summer of 2013, after Nawaz Sharif had been returned to power with a large electoral mandate to improve relations with India, Pakistani forces allegedly broke a ceasefire along the LoC when five Indian soldiers were killed in Kashmir. Pakistan denied responsibility for the attack; action–reaction processes in this area are difficult to analyse with forensic precision.[25] The 2014 campaigns by Imran Khan and Tahir-ul-Qadri to unseat the Nawaz Sharif government also appeared to reflect military interference.[26] (On the other hand , when the military exerted itself to gain civilian support for the operation along the border with Afghanistan, it garnered national and international applause.)

Second, as noted above, the Pakistani military leadership traditionally has seen an advantage in obscuring the links between it and the irregular/proxy/terrorist forces that have projected violence against India. Such murkiness gives the Pakistan government some measure of plausible deniability of responsibility, while also confounding Indian decision-making. To clarify these links would ease India's (and the world's) attribution of responsibility to the Pakistani state, and perhaps reduce India's inhibitions in responding to attacks.

Third, the Pakistani leadership may now lack confidence in its capacity to impose control over the most capable anti-India groups such as LeT. The Pakistani state is bedevilled by a proliferating number of groups exercising violence against the Army, other agencies of the state, Ahmedis, Shi'ites, and other groups within society. The authorities—military and civilian—do not feel they can effectively confront all of these militant actors at once, while also defending the Afghan and Indian borders. The advertised success of Operation Zarb-e-Azb does not necessarily mean that the security establishment will next seek to demolish or, more feasibly, pacify anti-India groups, such as LeT or its offshoots.

The most potent anti-India groups, including LeT, are based in Punjab. Punjabis, whose interests have always been privileged by the government, are especially loath to confront militants in their state for fear of inviting the sorts of insecurity and economic risks that roil Balochistan, Sindh, Khyber-Pakhtunkhwa, and the Federally Administered Tribal Areas. Moreover, as Christine Fair has astutely suggested, the LeT counters 'the violent agendas of the rival militant groups [that are] savaging Pakistan....By bolstering the organization's domestic legitimacy through the provision of social services, JuD makes LeT ever more effective at countering the competing narrative offered by Deobandi groups' that attack the Pakistani state itself.[27] Thus, even if the Army decided that Pakistan would benefit by eliminating groups such as LeT, the costs and risks of doing so could appear unbearable.

A former director general of the ISI summarized the problem this way in a late-2013 interview:

There's a limit to what we can do, due to public opinion. There are many 'Lashkars.' You and India focus on Lashkar-e-Taiba, but Lashkar-e-Jhangvi is the worst. Look at the United States: why don't you go after Jundullah? [There is a Jundullah group in Pakistan, associated with the Pakistani Taliban, and also one in Balochistan that conducts operations against Iran. The general was speaking of the one that operates against Iran, which presumably the US does not try to stop]. I will tell you: because they are hitting Iran. The US has priorities in who it goes after too! You have to prioritize. The LeT has not hit GHQ. You can't cite one significant LeT attack in Pakistan. We have our hands full. Besides, since the ceasefire in 2003, how many attacks have there been on India from here? They [the Indians] want zero attacks in India, but Pakistan is taking two per day! There is an over-reaction in Indian thinking. It's not proportionate. It needs to be proportionate.[28]

Indians—and others—naturally counter that the ISI brought this problem on itself by cultivating LeT in the first place.[29] But, looking forward, knowledgeable Indians increasingly recognize that Pakistan may be unable to control, let alone dismantle, formidable anti-Indian groups like LeT. A senior official in the Modi government acknowledged to us in an interview shortly before he took office that the ISI 'used to be able to control these groups reliably. Less so now. They can't control all of them at all. As bad as it is for us, it's worse for them!'[30] As a former chief of India's RAW put it, Hafez Saeed, the amir of LeT, 'is totally controlling the social-economic life of Pakistan. He originally was seen as an instrument of the Army, but now is much, much larger. He has money, many enterprises, lots of followers. He's very powerful. I don't think the Army will be able to control him again, whether they want to or not'.[31] A former foreign secretary who remains deeply involved in Indian policy circles said in another 2014 interview, 'Maybe Pakistan can't control these guys like before. The leadership may be controllable, but rank and file go back and forth between LeT and Tehrik-i-Taliban Pakistan (TTP). Pakistan has become much more diffuse. Controls have started to fray'.[32] This man concluded with a thought that in some ways summarizes the fundamental challenge here: 'There is little that we can do. We don't know how to influence things in Pakistan. We have to keep lines of communication open.'[33]

To make matters worse (which is always possible), leaders of the most potent terrorist groups may themselves feel that they cannot control their own fighters, or that to retain control they must authorize attacks against India that they would not otherwise conduct. Terrorist groups compete to build their brands and recruit new members. Dramatic attacks in India can be valuable for recruitment and brand building. The journalists Cathy Scott-Clark and Adrian Levy report in their account of the 2008 Mumbai attack that, after the 2007 Pakistani government assault on the Red Mosque in Islamabad, jihadis in the LeT had grown frustrated by the group's recent restraint. These jihadis felt that the LeT leadership was too beholden and too deferential to the ISI, which had eschewed major violent operations in the Indian heartland since the crisis following the 2001 attack on the Indian Parliament. Frustrated Pakistani jihadis now were tempted to link with Al-Qaeda or other more extreme groups. Perceiving this problem, according to Scott-Clark and Levy, the military commander of the LeT and his ISI handler felt the need for 'an operation that would bind everyone together'.[34] A dramatic attack on not just Indians, but also American, European, and Israeli enemies of Islam, could 'sate the desire' of disaffected fighters. Whether or not this explains the Mumbai attacks of 2008, a similar dynamic within the terrorist community may have occurred in August 2014, when Ayman al-Zawahiri, the leader of Al-Qaeda, announced the formation of 'Al Qaeda in the Indian subcontinent', just as ISIL was commanding global attention as the new leading force of jihadism.

For all of these reasons, the most that Indian policy could realistically seek from Pakistan is a genuine, concerted effort to prevent anti-India groups from conducting further attacks in the Indian heartland. Pacification, not destruction, would be consistent with the sovereign monopoly on the projection of violence that Pakistani leaders should want to establish for their own reasons. 'We don't expect them to be perfect,' the senior Modi government official previously referred to volunteered in April 2014.

They can't stop everybody. But we need to know they are trying. We need to know—whether it's through private communications or whatever—that they are taking measures against LeT and others. That they are actually acting against those who have done terror against India. If we know they are doing this, via signals we can mutually understand, then we can respond accordingly.[35]

Here the question arises, what can India do to motivate Pakistani leaders to take these steps and send these signals? Textbook assumptions about statecraft, unitary rational actors, compellence, and deterrence do not apply neatly here. The requirement is not only to devise ways and means to inflict costs on Pakistani forces and other assets the Pakistani military holds dear, but also more broadly to enable civilian actors in Pakistan to displace the military in the structure of Pakistani decision-making.[36] Indeed, India's overall strategic objective must be to promote real civilian authority over security affairs in Pakistan. This is a long-term goal that cannot be accomplished in one strike or battle. Indeed, as we discuss in Chapter 6, non-violent pressure may be more effective (and less risky) than force in motivating change in Pakistan, especially if it were paired with conflict resolution diplomacy. In any case, pursuing short-term policies, including the use of force, without keeping the longer-term objective in mind will subvert India's overall strategic purpose.

Pitfalls surround efforts to motivate political change in Pakistan. Some are easier to see than others. Pakistan's over-militarized state and outlook has led it to act in ways that are simultaneously threatening to India and to Pakistan itself. Increasing the salience of Indian military threats against Pakistan could strengthen the military's grip on power and control over Pakistan's national narrative, even if India would intend the projection of threats to deter the Pakistani military. Threats also could abet recruitment into militant groups.

India's potential internal pitfall is quite different. The Indian state—some would say—has been under-militarized. Yet, if Indian governance needed to become more militarized in order to compel the military authorities in Pakistan to change their mindsets and behaviour, would India ultimately weaken itself by pursuing such a course? To avoid this pitfall, Indian officials and opinion shapers would need to clarify those attributes of their national security apparatus that they do not want to lose, while devoting sufficient high-level time and attention to identifying new attributes they need to acquire.

Fred Iklé, again, provides insights here that deserve serious contemplation:

Fighting a war can cost more in blood and money than any other undertaking in which nations engage. And to wage war, governments develop more detailed plans, establish a more rigid organization, and institute tighter discipline than for any other national effort. Yet, despite all this elaborate and intense dedication, the grand design is often woefully incomplete. Usually, in fact, it is not grand enough: most of the exertion is devoted to the means—perfecting the military instruments and deciding on their use in battles and campaigns—and far too little is left for relating these means to their ends.

In part, this deficiency stems from the intellectual difficulty of connecting military plans with their ultimate purpose....In part, governments tend to lose sight of the ending of wars and the nation's interests that lie beyond it, precisely because fighting a war is an effort of such vast magnitude. Thus, it can happen that military men, while skillfully planning their intricate operations and coordinating complicated maneuvers, remain curiously blind in failing to perceive that it is the outcome of the war, not the outcome of the campaigns within it, that determines how well their plans serve the nation's interests.[37]

The Indian challenge now is to develop stronger and more dexterous military muscle, better intelligence capabilities, and more effective international coalition-building skills while retaining policy focus on the broader, longer-term national interest. It would be strategically self-defeating if India, in order to more effectively influence Pakistani military authorities, adopted the overly tactical mind-set and predilections of which Iklé warns and which Pakistan itself embodies.

Operational Intelligence

Finding an effective means to motivate desired changes in Pakistani policymaking and behaviour is more than an intelligence problem, of course. But the larger strategic objective will not succeed without better intelligence at the level of high policy discussed in the preceding paragraphs as well as at the operational level.

Regarding operational intelligence, Indian civilian and military leaders need confidence that they will receive warning of possible attacks. If attacks cannot be prevented, then intelligence is required on the character and location of targets for possible Indian retaliation. The more precise, real-time, and reliable the intelligence would be, the greater the range of options India would have in retaliating. And because India must then assume that

Pakistan could react militarily in turn, Indian leaders would need to know the most likely scenarios and elements of Pakistani counter-attack that Indian forces would need to be able to target. Most vitally, and often underappreciated, intelligence during a conflict would need to provide insights into the conditions under which Pakistani leaders would be most likely to terminate conflict, or conversely, to escalate it.

Such operational questions are easy to ask and difficult for all states' intelligence agencies to answer with confidence. Nonetheless, there are reasons to conclude that India's intelligence capacities are far from satisfactory. The Kargil Review Committee reported in 2000 on shortcomings of particular and systemic natures. In the former category, 'The critical failure in intelligence was related to the absence of any information on the induction and de-induction of battalions and the lack of accurate data on the identity of battalions in the area opposite Kargil during 1998.'[38] The systemic problems were graver. The committee bemoaned the lack of coordination among intelligence agencies and between these agencies and the Army.[39] Most broadly, the review committee concluded:

There are no checks and balances in the Indian intelligence system to ensure that the consumer gets all the intelligence that is available and is his due. There is no system of regular, periodic and comprehensive intelligence briefings at the political level and to the Committee of Secretaries. In the absence of an overall, operational national security framework and objectives, each intelligence agency is diligent in preserving its own turf and departmental prerogatives. There is no evidence that the intelligence agencies have reviewed their role after India became a nuclear weapon state or in the context of the increasing problems posed by insurgencies and ethno-national turbulences backed with sophisticated hi-tech equipment and external support.[40]

The intelligence situation evidently had not improved dramatically by November 2008, when the attacks on Mumbai occurred.[41] As Scott-Clark and Levy report, since August 2006, RAW had received 26 alerts of preparation for an attack on Mumbai, many shared by the Central Intelligence Agency

(CIA).[42] 'Eleven warnings suggested the plan would involve multiple simultaneous attacks. Six warnings pointed to a seaborne infiltration, which would be a first in India.' RAW would then be expected to pass such warnings to the Intelligence Bureau. Whether or not the CIA could have been more helpful in the warning process, there was a clear break down on the Indian side. This became still clearer once the attacks in Mumbai began, and India's security forces, including elite commandos, were utterly ill-prepared to respond.

The inadequacy of intelligence was not limited to warning of attack. It also seriously impeded options for militarily responding to the attacks. As Praveen Swami reports, at a top-level meeting on November 29, the Chief of the Indian Air Force (IAF) told the Prime Minister that India did not have adequate targeting data to conduct strikes against Pakistan.[43] A former RAW official echoed this, saying, 'We might have acquired precision munitions, but the data we have on the camps and infrastructure is not so accurate.'[44]

As we discuss in subsequent chapters, a serious Indian capability to target terrorists and their infrastructure in Pakistan would require much more than coordinates of fixed positions. It would require extensive human-source intelligence that could provide real-time information about the locations and activities of suspected enemies, and could help ensure that potential airborne ordnance does not hit misidentified civilian targets, which would be strategically counterproductive. Knowledgeable Indians say that their on-the-ground capabilities in Pakistan are poor.

Here, the current Indian attraction to the 'Israeli model' may be instructive. In the 2014 war in Gaza, Israeli forces occasionally hit misidentified targets, but generally displayed an outstanding capacity to know precisely where Hamas targets were and then to deliver kinetic force to destroy them. Israeli forces killed 500 children in the process, though it is difficult to say how many of those were the result of mistakenly targeted strikes and how many were 'collateral damage' of accurately targeted weapons. Leaving aside the conclusion of many Israeli and other observers that Israel did not achieve a meaningful victory,[45] from the operational point of view, Israeli intelligence was impressive, as was the integration of intelligence with tactical operations by the armed forces. As Daniel Byman reports, the Israelis learned from successive incursions into Gaza how important it is to integrate the Shin Bet intelligence service and its information gathering into the Israel Defense Forces so that there is a constant feedback process between them.[46]

As we discuss in chapters on precision air strikes (Chapter 3) and covert operations (Chapter 4), India has nothing remotely resembling this sort of operational intelligence capability. For example, according to an *Indian Express* report in December 2014, India's RAW suffers from a 40 per cent shortage in authorized personnel, with particular deficits in critical technology positions.[47] These observations suggest that India must undertake and achieve major institutional reform, technological improvement, and human agency recruitment if its intelligence services are going to enable the effective conduct of any of the policy options discussed in this book. In all major states it is tempting for national security-*wallah*s to fantasize about things that new doctrines and weapons can accomplish. But if the intelligence provided to leaders is inadequate—at the strategic level as well as the operational—the destruction of targets will not necessarily translate into victory.

Engagement with Pakistan for Intelligence/Relationship Management

It would be reasonable to expect that Indian leaders would seek opportunities for their own military and civilian officers to meet and exchange views with Pakistani counterparts. Such exchanges provide opportunities to benignly gain intelligence and to cultivate mutual understanding of competing perspectives and interests. For these reasons, exchanges have been relatively common in US–Russian, and US–Chinese relations, albeit with interruptions.[48] Military-to-military engagements cannot be expected to resolve underlying tensions or normalize relations, but this limitation merely bounds the utility of military-to-military engagement rather than negating it.

Indian political leaders traditionally are reluctant to authorize direct interaction between their military officers and counterparts in Pakistan. This stems largely from the belief that the Pakistani military is the principal cause of Indo-Pak tensions and the risk of violent conflict, and that India should not legitimize the Pakistani military's power by engaging with it. Indian leaders, sometimes backed by pundits and political elites, seem to feel that by confining official interactions to civilians, they simultaneously signal protest of military domination and advocacy of democracy. So much the better if this conveys the moral–political superiority of India's democratic governance.

The righteousness of this stance comes with costs, though. As a former leader of India's RAW put it in a 2014 interview, 'The Indian political establishment refuses to deal with the Pakistani military. Even though we know the military is in charge, our people say we can't meet with them and treat them as the leaders. It's a sort of one-upmanship about democracy, but it's unrealistic and maybe not effective. It's not as if we don't know who matters.'[49]

Pakistani military leaders mirror this observation. In discussing Pakistan's possible production and deployment of battlefield nuclear weapons with a retired senior Pakistani military officer, we noted the risks of escalation that could arise if there were another terrorist attack on India, and New Delhi responded with major conventional operations against Pakistan. The *threat* of escalation could be valuable to Pakistan's deterrence strategy, just like the threat of major conventional operations could be valuable to India's strategy, but both sides would seem to have an interest in avoiding inadvertent escalation. To reduce risks of inadvertence and miscommunication, perhaps it would be useful for Pakistan's Strategic Plans Division to explore these issues with their Indian counterparts? This officer responded, 'Yes, it would be good to do, but who is my counterpart in India? And would he be allowed to have such a discussion?'[50]

Instead of direct interactions between currently serving military leaders, India and Pakistan rely ambiguously and indirectly on Track II dialogues that include retired military officers and diplomats. Such dialogues are better than nothing, and they seem to reflect some acknowledgement of the benefits of communication. But would not more be gained in terms of intelligence and understanding if serving officers were to meet? Similarly, given the growing problem of terrorism within and between both countries, exchanges among leaders of the ISI and RAW could be mutually beneficial. (Here, Pakistan may be the more reluctant party.)

Ultimately, Indian interests require efforts both to promote the authority of civilian leadership and institutions in Pakistan and to interact directly with the Pakistani military and intelligence services. Indian and Pakistani officials would need to determine creatively how this could be done, perhaps under the aegis of each prime minister's office. But the effort will not be made unless both heads of government make it a priority.

Integration of the Military into Policymaking

To the extent that India needs sound political–military strategy toward Pakistan that incorporates informed assessments of India's and Pakistan's present and future military capabilities and the dynamics between them, Indian military professionals must be integrated into the policy-forming process. This would require major change. A recently retired high-ranking leader of the Integrated Defence Staff posed the problem:

The bureaucracy would rather keep the military out, too, for their own reasons. Political leadership is invariably attuned not to look at the military as part of national strategy. They don't think proactively and strategically. The sense is only when we are attacked will they then look and see what we can do. But if it stays this way, there will be a crisis. We could really face a crisis and not be prepared.[51]

Indeed, the Kargil conflict in 1999 provided an object lesson of the risk. In Rajesh Basrur's words,

an important lesson of Kargil was that the management of national security policy required revamping. Besides the failure to integrate the political and military dimensions of intelligence, the Kargil Review Committee emphasized that the armed forces ought to have more than an 'operational role' in the formulation of decision-making. As a result of the traditional practice, the military lacked a 'staff culture', policymaking was deprived of military inputs, and comprehensive planning suffered.[52]

Fifteen years later, an eminent strategist with extensive experience at the apex of the Indian system lamented that

[a]mong politicians there is a complete lack of understanding of the military. None. Politicians always prefer to manage the military through civilians in the bureaucracy. And that bureaucracy has contempt for the military. Politicians sort of fob the military off by extending terms, giving small raises, and so on. They don't give them what they really want and need, which is better procurement and real strategy and input. They just throw them perks and extensions and they accept it and stay quiet.[53]

The problem extends beyond relations between cabinet-level politicians and the military. The Ministry of Defence (MoD) itself does not effectively integrate military inputs into its work. As Raja Mohan wrote in August 2014, the MoD 'views its role in terms of control over the armed forces. The MoD has, over the decades, shunned the responsibility of developing and implementing a defence strategy for India'.[54] Indian military leaders perceive a caste-like divide between themselves and the civilian defence leadership. As a knowledgeable observer explains, 'protocol dictates that a civilian secretary in the MoD outranks any military officer, so in meetings a parade of secretaries who may have little expertise or competence enters the room before the service chiefs. This symbolism rankles.'[55] India's traditional reliance on administrative service generalists throughout the MoD has deprived it of the historical, military, technical, and financial expertise of professional defence experts that other major powers have found necessary to employ in their establishments.

All of this has implications for India's internal development of policies, capabilities, and operational plans, as well as for India's engagement with the defence establishments of allied states, and China and Pakistan. Thus, in Raja Mohan's words, the MoD 'has created no institutional capacity within the ministry to engage foreign defence establishments'.[56]

Of course, military inputs into the policy formulation process would not necessarily yield more effective policies, especially if military leaders have not adapted to the current nature of the Indo-Pak confrontation. Results would depend on the quality and coherence of military expertise and recommendations, and on the blending of these with contributions from intelligence officials, diplomats, and political leaders. Yet, there is plenty of evidence that excluding the military has produced ill-effects. When military leaders expect that their views will not significantly affect policy decisions, they tend not to think as carefully and comprehensively as they would if they knew their advice could be acted upon. This reinforces an unhealthy cycle: politicians exclude the military because they (the military) are perceived to be reckless and don't consider all the necessary implications; having been excluded from decision-making, the military feel little need to consider implications of force, and are tempted by the satisfaction of expressing toughness and derring-do.

For decades Indian military leaders, civilian defence experts, and a few attentive political leaders have recognized this problem. Since 1990, at least four high-level commissions have been tasked to assess the state's national security apparatus and recommend reforms. Arun Singh, the state minister for defence in Rajiv Gandhi's government, led a Committee on Defence Expenditure in 1990. K. Subrahmanyam chaired the Kargil Review Committee in 2000. This was followed by a Group of Ministers Task Force on Defence Management in 2001, also led by Arun Singh, who was then an advisor to the Vajpayee government. In 2011, the Congress-led United Progressive Alliance (UPA) government created a commission to review national security, chaired by Naresh Chandra, a former cabinet secretary.

Of these commissions and task forces, only the Kargil Review Committee's findings (in a declassified version) were made public. Yet, enough is known about the other studies to conclude that they all made similar recommendations. They all called for more information sharing and higher-level coordination amongst civilian and military intelligence agencies. They all called for more involvement of military professionals in policy deliberations and for greater inter-service coordination. The 2001 Group of Ministers Task Force on Defence Management recommended creation of a Chief of Defence Staff position, whose occupant should oversee planning and operation of nuclear forces. Eleven years later, the Naresh Chandra Task Force repeated this recommendation because it still had not been adequately implemented, and urged that the incumbent in the Chief's position serve for a full two-year term. This task force endorsed a prior recommendation of the Standing Committee of the MoD to place military personnel in the hierarchy of the defence secretary's office and to incorporate civilian officers in the Integrated Headquarters of the military services.[57] The Chandra Task Force also urged requiring the defence ministry, with military inputs, to annually submit a classified report on India's military readiness to the Cabinet Committee on Security. Such a report could highlight shortcomings in procurement, defence research, and development, among other things, to help generate political pressure to implement reforms.

Notwithstanding awareness of these problems and the recommendations of these commissions, relatively little has been done to improve the situation. As a person exceptionally knowledgeable about governmental deliberations on the issue of creating a full-term ('permanent') chairman of the Integrated Defence Staff explained, 'Politicians don't want to push for a real chairman. They fear that if they have a high-profile general at the top, and for a significant term, it will be like Pakistan. India will start to look like Pakistan, and they worry that a general could then lead to a military take over.'[58] In early 2015, the new defence minister, Manohar Parrikar, said the appointment of a Chief of

Defence Staff was 'a must', but as of October 2015 this still had not occurred.[59]

We cannot say what actions by which individuals would be *sufficient* to achieve the most promising reforms, but we can say that sustained exertion by the prime minister for a period of years would be *necessary* to provide India the military policies, doctrines, and forces it needs. The seven prime ministers of India between 1990 and 2014 found other priorities to be more pressing. It remains to be seen whether Narendra Modi will be different in this domain.

Inter-Service Cooperation

It is well known that the Indian military services—the Army, Navy, Air Force, and more recently the Strategic Forces Command—have resisted cooperation or 'jointness' in elaborating military doctrine, coordinating procurement, and conducting military operations. In the words of Manoj Joshi, 'There is no harmonization of the doctrines of the three military services.'[60] The former chief of the Indian Navy, Admiral D.K. Joshi (no relation) confirmed this: 'India has services' doctrines, but these lack credibility and weight because they do not represent a comprehensive view of national priority.'[61] The US and other large military powers also experienced great difficulties in achieving jointness. Each service has its own history and culture, its own desire to be independent, its own favourite roles and missions. Yet, advances in reconnaissance technology, precision-targeting, and other technologies of warfare, along with increased global norms on the minimization of civilian casualties, have placed a premium on inter-service cooperation, especially between armies, air forces, and special forces.

In India, as in Pakistan, the Army historically has been the most important and influential service. There are many reasons for this. Among them, the government has depended on the Army to deal with insurgency and other potential internal security requirements, beyond conflicts with Pakistan and China. Whatever the causes, the Army's central role in interfacing with civilian leaders and planning and conducting war in 1965, 1971, and the Kargil conflict in 1999 denied India the benefits that would have come from greater inter-service cooperation. As Benjamin Lambeth reports in his estimable study of the Kargil conflict, India initially suffered a 'near-total lack of transparency and open communication between the Indian Army and the IAF with respect to the gathering crisis. Without question, the onset of the Kargil confrontation revealed a lack of effective air-ground integration in India's joint arena at the most senior leadership level'.[62] Lambeth, an experienced fighter pilot and RAND Corporation expert on air power, adds that the Army, in first seeking to counter the Pakistani incursion alone, 'failed to honor the reasonable proposition advanced four years earlier in the IAF's first published air doctrine that "wars are rarely won...by a single component of military force".'[63]

The imperative of real cooperation among the military services still had not been appreciated by 2004 when the Indian Army pronounced a new proactive strategy, nicknamed the 'Cold Start doctrine'. As will be discussed more fully in the next chapter, Cold Start was portrayed as a new military doctrine featuring smaller, quickly deployable ground forces that would conduct rapid, limited thrusts into Pakistan-controlled territory, abetted by support from the IAF. Yet, the IAF was not fully involved in the development of Cold Start and, after the new doctrine was (unofficially) publicized, did not subscribe to its assumptions about the Air Force's role in it. (The fact that the Indian political leadership did not officially endorse Cold Start is another matter.) Nor is it apparent that the Navy was brought into the development of Cold Start, even though a sound military strategy would need to plan for Pakistan's countermoves and the likelihood that naval forces would be needed to quarantine Pakistani naval forces and ports to limit the potential for protracted escalation of conflict.

Informed Indians understand the need for greater interoperability among the services. Yet, naturally, the Navy and Army still want to be self-sufficient in light air power, with their own helicopters, pilots, and other assets. They do not want to rely on the Air Force to provide support, and the Air Force does not want to be an appendage to the Army and Navy. The Air Force reasonably takes precedence in acquiring and operating heavy aircraft, bombers, and deep strike systems, which are highly specialized systems. But in a major war, the Army and the Navy would want to have control over such air assets too. The resulting problems are circular and will not be straightened out and addressed without determined, informed, and sustained political leadership emanating from the prime minister.

More recent still, the planning of Indian nuclear operations also lacks inter-service cooperation. This is important because even if Indian leaders chose to respond with limited military force to a future terrorist attack attributed to Pakistan, India would still need to prepare for escalation of an ensuing conflict. If escalation mounted, most portentously through the projection of Indian ground forces into Pakistan, Pakistan could counter by preparing to conduct battlefield nuclear operations. In that event, the Indian Army, Air Force, and Navy would need to coordinate not only their conventional military actions, but also their roles in potential nuclear retaliation to Pakistan. Yet, as Iskander Rehman finds in a study of India's nuclear submarine programme, 'There is little intellectual cross-pollination in-between the Strategic Forces Command (SFC), and the Integrated Defence Staff, let alone between the different services. Furthermore, no higher defence learning institution imparts any substantive form of education to military officers on nuclear strategy and operations, and service headquarters continue to plan primarily for conventional war.'[64]

The Army's traditional pre-eminence among the Indian military services is particularly problematic in the current situation with Pakistan and the shadow that nuclear weapons cast over it. The Army's interest is to project ground forces into Pakistan. But, as will be discussed in Chapter 2, putting Indian boots onto Pakistani territory in response to sub-conventional attack could be escalatory in ways that would invite Pakistani nuclear threats. Compared with airborne precision strikes, covert operations, and fomenting of insurgency within Pakistan, armoured force projection may be less advisable. But if the other military and intelligence services do not gain more influence and resources relative to the Army within the Indian system, the liabilities of Army-centrism in the current environment will remain uncorrected. Moreover, even if and when the Air Force and Navy gain resources and influence, the challenge of interoperability will remain.

If Indian leaders conclude that air-centric options are better suited for retaliating to another major terrorist attack, the service-cooperation problem would arise in a different way, as discussed in Chapter 3. The RAW and the Air Force would identify targets and plan precision strikes, aware that Pakistani leaders could respond with ground operations. Thus, the Indian Army would need to plan and deploy as a facet of what would be intended as limited, precise air operations. The Air Force, in turn, would then need to dedicate some of its capabilities to protecting the Army deployment and potential operations. The cooperation and coordination required would not be trivial.

If the inadequacies of inter-service cooperation are well known, the real question is why this dysfunction persists. Arun Singh, one of India's most experienced defence officials and observers, offers a succinct explanation and prescription:

> If you want jointness, which we need, you find that others can kill it by saying that the services won't agree. That's true, but that just means the [prime minister] would have to impose his will and make it happen. But if you say the services will resist, then people decide it's too much trouble and so they let it drop. To impose jointness and other reforms, politicians would have to take a *decision*. They haven't felt it was important enough to do that and enforce it.[65]

Time is of the essence, because if US experience is indicative, even with determined political leadership and legislative mandate, achieving effective inter-service cooperation takes many years.

Procurement of Forces and Other Capabilities

The inadequacies of India's defence-related procurement process are famous (or infamous) by now. Thousands of pages have been written about them, including the 2012 volume by Stephen P.

Cohen and Sunil Dasgupta, *Arming without Aiming*.[66] There is no need to rehearse here the analyses of the procurement problems or recommendations for redressing them. Basically, notwithstanding the fact that today India is the world's top importer of arms, with an expenditure of approximately $21 billion in constant 1990-value dollars between 2010–14, the Indian Army, Navy, Air Force, and strategic forces lack the quantity and quality of weapons, supplies, and enabling technologies that they, in principle, are supposed to have acquired.[67]

'[T]he situation is dismal,' begins a typical litany regarding the Army in 2014.

The armour and mechanized infantry remain equipped with obsolete or no night fighting capabilities. Only a small number of units have adequate night fighting capability. Deficiencies in armour ammunition including war wastage reserve have already reached critical levels. With no gun inducted ever since Bofors (in the late 1980s), artillery is ageing fast too. With no spares available, requirements are being met by 'cannibalizing'... The state of army air defence is even worse...Air Defence missile units are equipped with [long obsolete systems]. Army Aviation is similarly carrying on with obsolete Cheetah and Chetak helicopters. New acquisition of 197 helicopters is stuck even four years after trials and re-evaluation of Russian Kamov 226 and Eurocopter AS 550 models.[68]

The situations with the Navy, Air Force, and Strategic Forces Command are not dissimilar.

Part of the problem is an epically long-lasting hangover from the Bofors procurement scandal that erupted in the late 1980s over kickbacks involved in the $1.3 billion purchase of 410 155mm field howitzers for the Indian Army from the Swedish firm, Bofors. Media reportage of the alleged corruption created a scandal that led to the defeat of Rajiv Gandhi in the 1989 elections. Ever since, the Indian procurement process has been bedevilled both by allegations of corruption and by reluctance to complete procurements for fear that such allegations will be made. Ironically, the 1985–9 period was the most effective in India's history in terms of acquiring military equipment. India bought MiG-29s, T-90 tanks, and submarines from the Soviet Union. The IAF purchased the Mirage 2000 fighter from France. The Indian Navy acquired diesel submarines from Germany.[69] The ensuing years have left the military services (and the country) facing mounting shortfalls in authorized acquisitions of weapons, equipment, and reconnaissance assets. As a former high-ranking Integrated Defence Forces officer explained when asked in late 2014 about India's reconnaissance and targeting capabilities to threaten terrorist targets in Pakistan, 'We know what we want to acquire to do these things, but the political problems are huge. Politicians ask, "how does this acquisition affect my political career?" This is the number-one consideration.'[70]

The lack of technical and military expertise in the Indian civilian defence bureaucracy also is a well-known problem, as alluded to above. So, too, is the influence of India's state-owned defence enterprises that for understandable parochial reasons contest procurement from foreign sources even when such sources offer higher quality at competitive costs. 'Our MoD is the most incestuous organization you can imagine,' a member of the Naresh Chandra Task Force observed. 'They give obvious preference to state-owned ordnance factories—there is no focus on efficiency.'[71]

If these and other causes of India's acquisition shortfalls are widely understood, they persist because they have deep roots in the Indian political economy. The ideology and economic and political interests that oppose imports and prefer domestic production cannot be easily dismissed or overcome in a democracy. And the resulting preferences remove competitive incentives for domestic producers to improve quality and timeliness of delivery, as we discuss immediately below. As with service integration, it will require enormous sustained effort to address this deficiency.

Indigenous Defence Research/Development/Production

Multiple competing interests shape India's acquisition of technologies that could enable it to pursue military strategies and operations against Pakistan (and other states). India has long desired to increase the role of indigenous technology development and defence production in its forces. This befits an aspiring great power with many talented scientists and engineers and a clear interest in the employment and other economic benefits of indigenous production. On the other hand, advanced militaries today rely on proven suppliers of complicated technologies to produce the sorts of weapons and enabling capabilities that India's military wishes to acquire. The Indian defence research, development, and production complex often has been unable to provide such capabilities. The tension between aspirations for indigenous design and production and the superiority of foreign-supplied capabilities is exacerbated by the reluctance of foreign suppliers to license and share state-of-the art technology with India and by the inefficiencies of India's procurement processes. Frictions among India's interests and institutional players, and between them and the interests of foreign suppliers, create a dissatisfying situation in which India's acquisition of intelligence, surveillance, reconnaissance systems and weapon systems lags behind what would be needed to undertake the sorts of precise, rapid military operations that Indian military leaders see the US, Israel, and other states conducting.

Indian military research and development is centred in the Defence Research and Development Organisation (DRDO) whose headquarters occupy a shiny new building complex adjacent to South Block in the heart of Lutyens' New Delhi. Over the years, DRDO has promised to produce state-of-the-art indigenous weapons that would serve as mainstays for the Army, Air Force, and Navy. Two illustrative examples are the Indian Small Arms System (INSAS) assault rifle and the Light Combat Aircraft (LCA). The lure of national self-sufficiency and technological development made these weapon systems attractive. But in each case, after long delays and cost overruns, when the DRDO-designed systems finally arrived, their performance has been so inadequate that the military services could not rely upon them.

The assault rifle saw its first large-scale use in the Kargil conflict in 1999. Soldiers complained of jamming, magazines cracking, oil spurting into their eyes as they fired, and other problems.[72] Some paramilitary units such as the Rashtriya Rifles decided to purchase

AK series rifles or other alternatives instead. In December 2012, the Indian Army requested proposals for a new assault rifle to replace the INSAS. Firms from the Czech Republic, Israel, Italy, the US, and Switzerland have entered the competition.

The Tejas LCA programme began in 1983 and similarly has been plagued by delays, cost overruns, and performance problems. The IAF took delivery of the first iteration—the Mk1—in January 2015, although the plane failed to meet the Air Force's qualitative requirements.[73] There is some hope that by the mid-2020s an improved, Mark II variant may enter service. However, in August 2015, *Jane's Defence Weekly* reported that the builder, Hindustan Aeronautics Limited (HAL), notified the Air Force that the start of production of the Mark II would be delayed further, beyond 2024.[74]

Indian military leaders and security experts frequently bemoan the shortcomings of the defence production and procurement systems. Complaints about indigenous defence research and development tend to be made less publicly. A brave exception was a June 2014 article by Lt. Gen. (ret.) B.S. Nagal in the journal *Force*. Nagal—a tall, serious, reserved man—was the commander of India's nuclear forces from 2008 to 2010, after which he was tasked with establishing a nuclear planning cell in the Prime Minister's Office. With irony he noted: 'A unique feature of nuclear deterrent signalling has been the role of DRDO scientists in speaking on strategy, development and employment philosophy.'[75] The prominence of DRDO scientists—rather than political or military leaders—in public signalling of Indian strategy and doctrine would be less intolerable if the scientists' chest-thumping claims were true. Unfortunately, as Nagal reported, the scientists' advertisements of delivery systems usually are premature and 'later become embarrassing when time lines are overshot/delayed... Subsequent delays then become capability denial'.[76]

Nagal then listed shortcomings in a host of weapons and intelligence-surveillance-reconnaissance systems. 'There is a deficit of long range bombers with a capability to deliver cruise missiles or nuclear capable standoff air to surface missiles,' he wrote. 'The SSBN [Nuclear Powered Ballistic Missile Submarine] is the most challenging and complex, and this is where India's capability has been found most wanting.... Other aspects for future development are improved guidance systems, miniaturization, bigger SSBNs [to carry longer-range missiles], anti-satellite capability, space based sensors, earth penetrating systems and host of new technology required to overcome protection/defensive systems.'[77] While this list of deficits pertains mainly to strategic nuclear systems, the problems Nagal highlighted extend to intelligence, surveillance, reconnaissance systems, and weapons platforms that would be needed for precise conventional military operations too.

Nagal ended with a plea that other senior military officers have made privately for years: 'Our programme for weapons delivery platforms has not fully delivered at the pace required by national security, and a detailed performance audit is required to address the shortcomings and deficiencies, and bring about structural changes in the way strategic programmes are organized.... [W]e need to introspect and appraise the performance of DRDO, where required change must be made.'

Other veterans of high-level service in national defence do not expect political leaders to heed the call of Nagal and other frustrated military experts. 'DRDO is a complete farce,' a former apex MoD leader exclaimed. 'Why do politicians play along with this? The reason DRDO gets away with it is there is no strategic culture in the system and media. The public doesn't know anything about these matters. We make all this noise about corruption in procurement, etc., and meanwhile the Army has no towed howitzers!'[78]

Prime Minister Modi, who came to office with no experience in national defence matters, seems to have gotten the word. In January 2015, he essentially fired the head of DRDO, Avinash Chander, who previously had led the Agni missile programme. He also assigned the position of Scientific Advisor to the Minister of Defence, which formerly was held by the Director General of DRDO, to a separate scientist, creating the potential for greater independent evaluation of DRDO's work and recommendations.

While these steps appear positive, it remains to be seen whether the Prime Minister will sustain his attention to these matters to the degree necessary to achieve fundamental change. The problems of indigenous research, development, and production of advanced military capabilities have no easy solution. Historically—and still today—Indian leaders and interest groups understandably desire to build indigenous capabilities instead of buying foreign equipment. Yet, this also has encouraged wishful thinking and reality-denial that has enabled DRDO to continue to underperform. A recent publication from the Vivekananda International Foundation, which is closely aligned with the Modi government, illustrates the political difficulty. 'Cleaning up the mess, cobwebs and dirt surrounding the defence procurement procedure should be the top most priority of the Narendra Modi led Government,' wrote Radhakrishna Rao.[79] 'Of course,' he continued, 'this should be followed by vigorous and multi-faceted efforts to acquire self-reliance in all aspects of defence research development and production.... Services should be told in no uncertain terms that there is always a home grown alternative to the "glitzy fighting equipment" touted around in the global defence market.' 'Make In India'—a new Indian national marketing slogan—is a laudable public relations campaign and economic goal, but the military services know the gaps in quality and timeliness that result in 'home grown alternatives'. Military preparedness continues to suffer because politicians, pundits, and DRDO leaders refuse to acknowledge them.

Joint technology development and production with entities with proven track records in building effective weapons, guidance systems, and reconnaissance platforms and networks could be helpful. Yet, facilitating such cooperation will also require reforms in India, and foreign suppliers will always be reluctant to share their most advanced know-how. The government's April 2015 decision to buy 36 off-the-shelf Rafale jets from France in a government-to-government agreement reflected the two countries' mutual frustration after three years of unresolved commercial negotiations between Dassault and the Indian government for supply of 126 Rafales. The framework of the original negotiations called for Dassault to build 108 of the planes in India, to invest at least 50 per cent of the contract value in India, and provide technology transfer to, among other things, improve the Indian Tejas programme. But the April 2015 government-to-government agreement does not involve any production in India. Finalization of this agreement subsequently was stalled over India's insistence that Dassault invest at least 30 per cent of the contract value in India, and Dassault's doubts about the feasibility of doing this, especially at the price India is willing to pay for the planes. According to Amit Cowshish, a former advisor on arms purchases to the Indian Defence Ministry who tracked the negotiations, 'This issue has become bigger than the procurement' itself.[80] Meanwhile, satisfying the Air Force's requirement for 126 new fighters looks like an increasingly distant prospect that, for now, would depend on adding 90 indigenous Tejas planes to the proposed 36 Rafales.

By shaking up the DRDO leadership and pushing through the Rafale/Tejas deal with France, Prime Minister Modi indicated that he recognized the need for change in India's defence technology sector. But, as the subsequent hang ups in the Rafale negotiations suggested, this is the beginning of the beginning of what would necessarily be a long, intense reform struggle. The leadership of DRDO can be changed, but will it embrace reviews and audits of its designs and tests by independent scientists and military experts? Will DRDO leaders desist from prematurely advertising unproven technologies, and be held to account if they do? Will efforts to integrate proven technologies from multiple foreign suppliers into Indian platforms yield effective weapons systems, as the new fighter agreement with France envisions? Reforming and disciplining this system will take sustained, close attention from the top of the Indian government. Given the range of economic, political, and internal security priorities that any prime minister must pursue, it will be interesting to see how this sector ranks over time.

Mobilizing New Non-Violent Capabilities

Sometimes it is easier to create new institutions or enlist non-governmental agencies to develop and implement policies than it is to reform existing governmental bodies. India would need innovative communications techniques to mobilize the international community and actors in Pakistan and elsewhere to press Pakistani leaders to uphold international norms against interstate terrorism.

The twenty-first century is being defined (thus far) by the individuals, groups, and businesses that are most innovative in the use of information technology to motivate large numbers of people to do as these individuals, groups, and businesses want them to. Exemplars of this skill are widely recognized: popular entertainers and sports stars such as Amitabh Bachchan, Sachin Tendulkar, Lady Gaga, and Taylor Swift; corporations such as Apple, Google, and Airtel India; politicians, including Narendra Modi and Barack Obama; and even groups like the 'Islamic State'. These actors use communications media to induce people to buy things, to listen to music and watch films and amusing videos (and then buy things from advertisers), to 'like' things or people or causes, to join movements (including terrorist ones), to attend protests, and to boycott products and vendors.

India and like-minded states and society have an interest in raising the costs to Pakistani leaders of failing to implement the legally binding, Chapter VII requirement of UN Security Council Resolution 1373, to 'take the necessary steps to prevent the commission of terrorist acts' and to 'deny safe haven to those who finance, plan, support, or commit terrorist acts, or provide safe havens'.[81] Holding states accountable to these obligations is a form of soft power, as we elaborate in Chapter 6. India will be better able to do this if it enhances its capacities to mobilize public opinion in countries that Pakistani leaders depend upon and in Pakistan itself. This includes the US, which provides significant security assistance and aid to Pakistan, as well as other influential states that seek outstanding relations with India, including those in the European Union (EU), Japan, Australia, Iran, and the United Arab Emirates (UAE), among others.

The mobilization of national and international civil societies can help motivate state leaders to exert pressure on their counterparts when they might otherwise prefer not to. The capacity to conduct such mobilizations requires a combination of clear and persuasive foreign policy objectives, state-of-the-art technology and expertise in its use, and networks of individuals and organizations prepared to mount campaigns. Existing governmental institutions in India are ill-suited for this purpose (as in other countries too). The Indian foreign service is too small and set in traditional patterns of operation and communication. The external intelligence service lacks the requisite capabilities and, in any case, would be inappropriate for the political purposes envisioned. Rather than create new bureaucracies, Indian leaders could invite effective private sector consultancy enterprises and civil society organizations to design strategies, messages, and capabilities to mobilize international protests against the Pakistani government in the event it fails to fulfil its obligations to prevent major interstate terrorism. This may seem quixotic, but as Indian leaders know from their own (sometimes exaggerated and ill-conceived) reactions to the exertions of civil society in India, such campaigns have effects. Pakistan's security establishment may be less susceptible to popular pressure than the Indian government is, but Pakistan remains a relatively open society and this establishment is not immune to national and international opinion. Moreover, a central purpose of such twenty-first century non-violent campaigns would be to mobilize other influential governments to exert pressure on the Pakistani leadership.

* * *

India's decision-making context—in particular the various shortcomings described here in the institutions and processes of devising national security strategy and acquiring the means to implement it—is well understood by the Indian security establishment. The need for serial commissions on defence and security reform and the consistency of their recommendations invites the question: why have these recommendations not been implemented? With a sigh and wry smile, one long-time defence official explained:

If all the reform commissions were put end to end, you'd need another commission just to read them. Arun Singh, Subhramanyam, Naresh Chandra—they all did good work, but nothing has come of it. A prime minister could implement these reforms. If he wanted to, he wouldn't need a commission. Commissions are what you create when there's a problem you don't want to act on.[82]

A member of the 2012 Commission offered a similar conclusion:

Task forces are retired officers who, unlike serving officers, do not have to defend the status quo. But someone has to act. On national security, the politicians always take the lazy, easy way out. They say, 'we need a consensus'. But there never will be a consensus. You have to decide and then push for change, even if many people might not like it. If you say 'consensus', nothing will happen.[83]

For his part, Arun Singh said simply, 'No one cares about these commissions or their recommendations. Political leaders don't care. The closest we came was when the BJP was in. There was agreement to move, but then Vajpayee backed away'.[84]

Much could be said about all of this. For the purposes of this book, the central point is that the Indian government will not be able to develop a sound strategy for accomplishing its objectives vis-à-vis Pakistan, and then evaluate possible realistic means for pursuing such a strategy, if the above-mentioned flaws in state institutions are not corrected. India may be able to interdict terrorist operations or inflict losses on Pakistan after an attack, but it will not improve the strategic environment in any durable, fundamental way without significant reforms in the ways that strategy and the tools to implement it are developed. In the absence of major improvements in India's national security apparatus and capabilities, it will be counterproductive for Indian leaders and pundits to advertise bold new doctrines and threats of military action against Pakistan. Doing so merely reinforces unwelcome political dynamics within Pakistan and justifies the military's continued expansion of its conventional and nuclear capabilities. Without major changes in capabilities, India's traditional approach of minimizing risks and costs of military action against Pakistan will be superior to ill-prepared alternatives.

Notes and References

1. Lawrence Freedman, *Strategy* (Oxford University Press, 2013), xi.
2. Freedman, *Strategy*, 627.
3. In an April 2015 article, the eminent, well-sourced journalist, Shekhar Gupta, conveyed the absence of Indian strategy and doctrine by relating an episode in 1994 when Jaswant Singh, the erstwhile BJP defence expert, slipped Gupta a note on a scrap of paper while the two men were participating in a conference in Austria. 'I headed the parliamentary committee to examine India's military-strategic doctrine,' wrote Jaswant Singh. 'We concluded there was no strategy and no doctrine.' According to Gupta, in 2015, 'There is zero evidence this has changed.' Shekhar Gupta, 'Fear of Buying', *India Today*, 16 April 2015. Available at: http://indiatoday.intoday.in/story/rafale-jets-modi-indian-air-force-order-of-battle-mig-iaf-shekhar-gupta/1/430556.html.
4. Manoj Joshi, 'The Credibility of India's Nuclear Deterrent', in Michael Krepon, Joshua T. White, Julia Thompson, and Shane Mason (eds), *Deterrence Instability and Nuclear Weapons in South Asia* (Washington, DC: Stimson Center, 2015), 48.
5. This limiting condition of potential mutual destruction obtains as long as India and Pakistan have survivable, second-strike nuclear weapon capabilities.
6. Harold Saunders correctly notes that 'too often, political scientists make the mistake of treating policymaking and decisionmaking as synonymous.... Policymaking is itself the process of determining which moral principles or strategic objectives to prioritize'. Decision-making involves choices of action or inaction at a specific moment, which may or may not reflect policy. Decision-making often does not involve a process as rational and deliberative as policymaking is supposed to be. Saunders, 'What Really Happened in Bangladesh', *Foreign Affairs* (July/August 2014): 41.
7. Kargil Review Committee Report, 1990, 197.
8. Stephen P. Cohen and Sunil Dasgupta, *Arming without Aiming* (Washington, DC: Brookings Institution, 2012), xi.
9. For a compelling, practically informed analysis of modern warfare, see Rupert Smith, *The Utility of Force* (New York: Vintage Books, 2008 edition), 183–4.
10. Cohen and Dasgupta, *Arming without Aiming*, 144.

11. Gurmeet Kanwal, 'National Security Decision Making: Overhaul Needed', IDSA Comment, 26 August 2014.
12. George K. Tanham, *Indian Strategic Thought* (RAND, 1992), 50.
13. Tanham, *Indian Strategic Thought*, 50.
14. Chatham House Rule seminar, Jawaharlal Nehru University, 11 November 2014.
15. Tanham, *Indian Strategic Thought*, 70.
16. Interview with former military officer, New Delhi, 24 April 2014.
17. Interview with former military officer, New Delhi, 24 April 2014.
18. Interview with former policymaker, New Delhi, 23 April 2014.
19. See C. Christine Fair, *Fighting to the End* (New York, Oxford University Press, 2014); Aqil Shah, *The Army and Democracy: Military Politics in Pakistan* (Cambridge: Harvard University Press, 2014); and Husain Haqqani, *Pakistan: Between Mosque and Military* (Washington, DC: Carnegie Endowment for International Peace, 2005).
20. It is difficult to attribute state responsibilities for proxy and/or terrorist groups in other settings too, including Lebanon, Syria, Iraq, and Ukraine.
21. Recent uses of cyber-technology and know-how to conduct attacks against states and commercial entities demonstrate the value of attributional uncertainty to attackers and the dilemmas this poses to defenders.
22. Gen. Ashfaq Pervez Kayani, Speech at Pakistan Military Academy, Kakul, 14 August 2012. Available at: https://lubpak.com/archives/227063.
23. Interview with former Indian national security advisor, New Delhi, 10 November 2014.
24. Interview with former Indian official, New Delhi, 11 November 2014.
25. Tim Craig, 'Concerns Grow in Pakistan and India over Border Violence', *Washington Post*, 23 November 2013. Available at: https://www.washingtonpost.com/world/concerns-grow-in-pakistan-and-india-over-border-violence/2013/11/23/633519fc-4d15-11e3-bf60-c1ca136ae14a_story.html.
26. For a summary of allegations surrounding the military's machinations see Zahid Hussain, 'The Plot Thickens,' *Dawn*, 19 August 2015. Available at: http://www.dawn.com/news/1201279/the-plot-thickens.
27. Fair, *Fighting to the End*, 259.

28. Interview with former director general of ISI, Rawalpindi, 22 October 2013.

29. This blame game can be extended back in time by arguing that the US and Pakistan seeded the jihadi movement when they recruited, funded, armed, and trained militants to drive the Soviet Union from Afghanistan. Responsibility can then be shifted to the Soviet Union for invading Afghanistan, and so on.

30. Interview with senior official, New Delhi, 25 April 2014.

31. Interview with former chief of RAW, New Delhi, 26 April 2014.

32. Interview with former foreign secretary, New Delhi, 24 April 2014.

33. Interview with former foreign secretary, New Delhi, 24 April 2014.

34. Cathy Scott-Clark and Adrian Levy, *The Seige: 68 Hours Inside the Taj Hotel* (New York: Penguin, 2013), 53. The authors here rely on testimony from David Headley, the American convicted for his role in the Mumbai attack.

35. Interview with senior official, New Delhi, 25 April 2014.

36. Israel is an interesting, albeit always controversial case in point. The prowess of all branches of its military is widely recognized. Former military leaders also figure heavily in Israeli politics (especially compared to many other democracies). Yet, the primacy of civilian authority is definite. A passage from a recent article by former Prime Minister Ehud Olmert defending the conduct of the 2006 war in Lebanon makes this dynamic clear: 'I spoke with the commanders, I explained my position to them, and I added that I was proud of the soldiers and commanders who wanted to enter Lebanon, but that the political leadership has a broader view, which includes additional considerations that it must weigh, and it is the leadership that will decide if and when to act.' Ehud Olmert, 'In Retrospect: The Second Lebanon War', *Military and Strategic Affairs* 6, no. 1 (March 2014): 13. It is impossible to imagine today a civilian Pakistani prime minister speaking with such authority.

37. Iklé, *Every War Must End*, 2–3.

38. Kargil Review Committee Report, 190.

39. Kargil Review Committee Report, 199.

40. Kargil Review Committee Report, 203.

41. See, for example, James Glanz, Sebastian Rotella, and David E. Sanger, 'In 2008 Mumbai Attacks, Piles of Spy Data, but an Uncompleted Puzzle', *New York Times*, 22 December 2014.

42. Scott-Clark and Levy, *The Siege*, 25.

43. Praveen Swami, 'Shooting Ourselves in the Foot', *Indian Express*, 23 October 2014.

44. Interview with former RAW official, New Delhi, 24 April 2014.

45. See, for example, Assaf Sharon, 'Failure in Gaza', *New York Review of Books*, 25 September 2014. Available at: http://www.nybooks.com/articles/archives/2014/sep/25/failure-gaza/; David Shulman, 'Gaza: The Murderous Melodrama', *New York Review of Books*, 20 November 2014. Available at: http://www.nybooks.com/articles/archives/2014/nov/20/gaza-murderous-melodrama/.

46. Daniel Byman, *A High Price* (Oxford University Press, 2011), 369–71.

47. Praveen Swami, 'India's Spy Agencies More Toothless Than Ever', *Indian Express*, 1 December 2014. Available at: http://indianexpress.com/article/india/india-others/indias-spy-agencies-more-toothless-than-ever/.

48. To be sure, such exchanges commonly are cancelled or postponed when one side or the other seeks to express displeasure over an unwelcome turn in overall relations.

49. Interview with former RAW official, New Delhi, 26 April 2014.

50. Interview with retired Pakistani officer, Rawalpindi, 25 October 2013.

51. Interview with retired military officer, New Delhi, 24 April 2014.

52. Rajesh M. Basrur, 'The Lessons of Kargil as Learned by India', in Peter M. Lavoy (ed.), *Asymmetric Warfare in South Asia* (Cambridge University Press, 2009), 318.

53. Interview with former senior official, New Delhi, April 23, 2014.

54. C. Raja Mohan, 'An Indefensible Posture', *Indian Express*, 8 August 2014.

55. Interview, New Delhi, 12 November 2014.

56. Mohan, 'An Indefensible Posture'.

57. Joshi, 'The Credibility of India's Nuclear Deterrent', 53. Joshi was a member of the Naresh Chandra Task Force.

58. Interview with former senior official, New Delhi, 11 November 2014.

59. Gurmeet Kanwal, 'Military's Voice is Missing in National Security Decision Making Process', *Hindustan Times*, 9 April 2015. Available at: http://www.hindustantimes.com/analysis/national-security-military-s-voice-missing-in-decision-making-process/article1-1335318.aspx

60. Joshi, 'The Credibility of India's Nuclear Deterrent', 48.

61. Quoted in Pravin Sawhney, 'Whither Our War Preparedness?', *The Pioneer*, 4 June 2015. Available at: http://www.dailypioneer.com/

print.php?printFOR=storydetail&story_url_key=whither-our-war-preparedness&section_url_key=columnists.

62. Benjamin Lambeth, *Airpower at 18,000': The Indian Air Force in The Kargil War* (Washington: Carnegie Endowment for International Peace, 2012), 36. Lambeth also notes that the Pakistani Air Force was left out of planning for the Kargil incursion.

63. Lambeth, *Airpower at 18,000'*, 36.

64. Iskander Rehman, *Murky Waters: Naval Nuclear Dynamics in The Indian Ocean* (Washington: Carnegie Endowment for International Peace, 2015), 38.

65. Interview, New Delhi, 23 April 2014.

66. Cohen and Dasgupta, *Arming without Aiming*. For an illustration of the enduring nature of this issues, see also, Chris Smith, *India's Ad Hoc Arsenal: Direction or Drift in Defence Policy?* (New York: Oxford University Press/SIPRI, 1994).

67. Stockholm International Peace Research Institute, 'SIPRI Arms Transfers Database'. Available at: http://armstrade.sipri.org/armstrade/html/export_toplist.php, accessed 1 September 2015.

68. Col. (ret.) Karan Kharb, 'State of Military Might in Resurgent India', Vivekananda International Foundation, 25 August 2014. Available at: http://www.vifindia.org/article/2014/august/25-state-of-military-might-in-resurgent-india.

69. Sunil Dasgupta and Stephen P. Cohen, 'Is India Ending its Strategic Restraint Doctrine?', *The Washington Quarterly*, Spring 2011, 166.

70. Interview with retired high-ranking officer, New Delhi, 24 April 2014.

71. Interview with member of Naresh Chandra Task Force, New Delhi, 12 November 2014.

72. Col. (ret.) Karan Kharb, 'State of Military Might in Resurgent India', Vivekanada International Foundation, 25 August 2014: 'For the infantry soldier, the indigenously designed INSAS rifle has proved to be inferior to the modern assault rifles being acquired by our adversaries.'

73. Dilip Kumar Mekala, 'For A Better Future', *FORCE*, 2014, 35: 'Indian Air Force has ordered 40 LCA aircraft knowing they do not meet the qualitative requirements.'

74. Rahul Bedi, 'Delay to Tejas Mk 2 could push IAF into accepting modified Mk 1s', *IHS Jane's Defence Weekly*, 17 August 2015. Available at: http://www.janes.com/article/53674/delay-to-tejas-mk-2-could-push-iaf-into-accepting-modified-mk-1s.

75. Lt. Gen. B.S. Nagal (ret.), 'Checks and Balances,' *FORCE*, June 2014. Available at: http://www.forceindia.net/Checks_and_Balances.aspx.
76. The gap between DRDO boasts regarding programmes such as ballistic missile defence systems and actual capabilities are doubly injurious to Indian interests. Pakistani military leaders use the inflated Indian 'capabilities' to justify expansion of their own countervailing capabilities. For example, Pakistani strategists can argue that if India is on the verge of producing a brilliant missile defence system, or MIRVed (multiple independently targetable re-entry vehicles) missiles, then Pakistan must produce more fissile materials and more nuclear weapons to balance India.
77. Nagal, 'Checks and Balances'.
78. Interview with former senior defence official, New Delhi, 23 April 2014.
79. Radhakrishna Rao, 'Need to Clean Up the Augean Stables of Defence Acquisition', Vivekanada International Foundation, 27 May 2014. Available at: http://www.vifindia.org/article/2014/may/27/need-to-clean-up-the-augean-stables-of-defence-acquisition.
80. Sanjeev Miglani, 'Latest Indian, French Rafale Deal Runs Into Problems—Sources', *Reuters Business News*, 12 August 2015. Available at: http://in.reuters.com/article/2015/08/12/india-france-rafale-idINKCN0QH0P320150812.
81. United Nations Security Council, Resolution 1373, 28 September 2001.
82. Interview with former senior defence official, New Delhi, 24 April 2014.
83. Interview with member of the Naresh Chandra Task Force, 11 November 2014.
84. Interview, New Delhi, 23 April 2014.

2

PROACTIVE STRATEGY

After the 1998 nuclear tests, Indian strategists quickly recognized the need to rethink military strategy for the South Asian nuclear age. One of the early advocates of a shift toward limited war, perhaps surprisingly, was Gen. K. Sundarji, the author of India's then-extant Army doctrine. Writing in February 1999, prior to the onset of the Kargil conflict, Sundarji argued, 'If conventional hostilities become inevitable, Indian conventional counter offensives against Pakistan should be modulated in scope and depth of penetration into Pakistan territory, so that ingress can stop before Pakistan resorts to the use of nuclear weapons.'[1] No longer could the Indian Army contemplate major conventional conflict, as Sundarji previously had, in which it would bring to bear the full weight of its Strike Corps for deep penetration into Pakistan to seek victory over the Pakistan Army. The risk of nuclear escalation erased that possibility.

The dynamics of limited war appeared during the 1999 Kargil conflict after Pakistani forces had secretly taken Indian positions. In order to mitigate the potential for the conflict to escalate, the Indian government specifically limited its counteroffensive to Indian territory. Though India did raise the level of violence through use of air power, New Delhi opted not to attack Pakistani logistics or supply lines across the LoC, nor did it seek to open a second front that would redirect the Pakistan Army. After the conflict, in January 2000, then Chief of Army Staff Gen. V.P. Malik observed: 'We were able to keep Kargil war limited primarily due to nuclear as well as conventional deterrence.' But, foreshadowing how lessons from Kashmir might inform development of a limited war doctrine, he suggested that 'strategy adopted for Kargil, including the Line of Control constraints, may not be applicable in the next war'.[2]

The next war has not yet arrived, fortunately, but the 2001–2 crisis, which at several points might have escalated to war, provided stimulus for the Indian Army to speed development of a limited-war concept. On 13 December 2001, five gunmen attacked the Indian parliament building in New Delhi. Though major bloodshed was avoided, the attacks caused great shock. Indian officials accused Pakistan's ISI of supporting the militant groups that conducted the attack, identified by India as LeT and Jaish-e-Muhammad.[3] (Pakistani officials denied the charges and instead claimed that the attack was staged by India's own intelligence services to frame Pakistan.[4]) According to the then Indian National Security Advisor Brajesh Mishra, the Cabinet Committee decided 'that Pakistan must be given a very serious warning…We debated, we talked, and we came to the conclusion that the threat of military action should be held up'.[5] Indian leaders ordered the military to launch Operation Parakram, mobilizing more than 500,000 Army troops (as well as the Indian Navy) and threatening war if Pakistan did not forcibly shut down the jihadi groups involved in attacking India and transfer to India a number of high-profile terrorists. Pakistan countered by mobilizing several hundred thousand of its own forces to the border, and testing nuclear-capable ballistic missiles to signal the nuclear potential of the crisis.[6]

The denouement of the 2001–2 crisis came 10 months after it began. Despite several tense periods, Indian leaders did not attack across the border, finding it infeasible to launch a major conventional war that could risk escalation across the nuclear threshold. Amid the long Indian mobilization, the US and other outside powers brokered enough conciliatory promises and gestures from Pakistan's President Pervez Musharraf to make a massive Indian military campaign politically untenable. The Indian mobilization served a compellent purpose—to force the

US and others to pressure Pakistan to take steps to curtail militant operations in Kashmir—but effected no punishment on Pakistan for its perceived support of the militants that conducted attacks in India, beyond the unenforceable concessionary banning of militant groups including Jaish-e-Muhammad and LeT. This anti-climax frustrated many in India, especially the armed forces.[7]

During the two years following Operation Parakram, military strategists—primarily from the Army—and think tank analysts in India sought to develop an operational concept that would redress the problems perceived through the course of the 2001–2 crisis. Particular concern focused on the very slow Army mobilization. The strategy and forces that India had developed since the 1980s envisioned massive armoured assaults on Pakistan across the international border. Yet, as the recent experience showed, this force was too big, cumbersome, and slow-to-mobilize to be viable in response to a terror attack. In the time required for preparation, Pakistan could counter-mobilize and take political and diplomatic steps to confuse the regional and broader international context of the crisis. Outside powers, particularly the US, could then intervene to complicate the political, economic, and diplomatic calculus of Indian decision makers, militating against large-scale use of force. The spectre of nuclear war would loom larger, adding pressure on Indian leaders not to take steps that could appear to escalate the risk of major conflict.

To remove these constraints, some Indian strategists concluded that India needed a 'proactive strategy' backed by armed forces equipped, organized, trained, and postured to be able to launch punitive attacks on Pakistani military and terrorist targets within days. These forces needed to be operational before Pakistan could mobilize its defences and take easily reversible steps to redress the outrage over the instigating terrorist act—like the promises to crack down on militant groups that it had offered during the 2001–2 crisis. Rapidity was also necessary to enable India to impose military pain on Pakistan before the US and other outside actors could intervene to try to prevent an escalation of fighting. Finally, to diminish the perceived risks of nuclear war, Indian forces would need to be postured, supplied, and operated so as to demonstrate limited military aims that would not pose a great enough threat to warrant Pakistani use of nuclear weapons.

With these desiderata, the Indian Army produced in April 2004 what became known as the 'Cold Start' doctrine. 'Cold Start' was not a formal name, rather a term apparently coined by journalists to whom information about the new doctrine and the concomitant proactive strategy was leaked. Nevertheless, the catchy term stuck and ultimately was embraced by the Army. As the name implies, the Army sought to develop a capability for 'swift mobilization starting from a "cold start," instead of slow mobilization'.[8]

Proponents of Cold Start called for reorganizing the existing Holding and Strike Corps into a more nimble structure. The defensive Holding Corps would become 'Pivot' Corps, which would be able to undertake limited offensives from defensive positions to create a shallow bridgehead into Pakistani territory. These would be augmented by division-sized armoured combat units, called 'integrated battle groups' (IBGs), able to attack along different axes to advance into Pakistani territory.[9] Meanwhile, the deeper-based Strike Corps would be integrated with close air support capabilities provided by the IAF to create a concentration of firepower. These forces would be backed by conventionally-armed ballistic and cruise missiles able to strike targets deeper in Pakistan as needed. The objective was to be ready to retaliate into Pakistani territory within just a few days of a precipitating terror attack on India.

To avoid risks of triggering Pakistani nuclear retaliation, the Indian forces would be designed and ordered to penetrate only 'short' distances into Pakistani territory, 10–15 kilometres or more along the International Border, perhaps deeper in the desert.[10] With a quick mobilization and some element of surprise, Indian forces could gain and hold Pakistani territory before outside actors could pressure both governments to pull back. Indian forces would hold captured territory as leverage in subsequent negotiations to compel Pakistani authorities to genuinely and effectively uproot the groups conducting terrorism against India. Or, Indian forces could withdraw after having taught Pakistani authorities a lesson sufficiently punitive to motivate them to eschew future attacks on India.[11]

From the mid-2000s, Cold Start engendered considerable enthusiasm in both speech and print in India. Many Indian military analysts and retired officers, writing in defence journals associated with government-affiliated think tanks, described Cold Start as if it were official doctrine being implemented by the Indian Army.[12] A series of combined forces military exercises in the mid-2000s buttressed this contention.[13] The Indian Army began to re-organize its force structure to enhance mobility and readiness, both of which are necessary conditions to execute a Cold Start-style operation.

Yet, within the Indian armed forces and the government more broadly, there appears to have been no consensus on Cold Start. This resulted in the concept vastly exceeding the actual military capabilities being deployed.[14] The IAF in particular was sceptical of being cast in a secondary, close-air-support role. Retired Air Vice Marshal Kapil Kak, then deputy director the IAF-affiliated Centre for Air Power Studies, stated in 2009, 'There is no question of the air force fitting itself into a doctrine propounded by the army. That is a concept dead at inception.'[15] According to defence journalists Pravin Sawhney and Ghazala Wahab, the draft doctrine was never blessed by the MoD, let alone the Cabinet Committee on Security.[16] Reconfiguring and relocating Indian Army forces was occurring slowly. And, as discussed in Chapter 1 and further later in this chapter, procurement of equipment to update and replace obsolete kit lagged, leaving the Army short of the equipment and materiel needed to execute Cold Start. Enhancement of intelligence and communication capabilities and their connectivity between fighting units, commands, intelligence agencies, and the three armed services barely improved, despite efforts to resolve these issues in major field exercises.[17]

The gap between concept and actual policy and capabilities was borne out in 2008 when Mumbai was attacked by terrorists from LeT. India did not respond by mobilizing its military forces, let alone unleashing them in ways envisioned by proponents of Cold Start. As the well-informed journalist Manoj Joshi reported, the Army had to acknowledge that it would take 'several weeks before it could prudently commence operations'.[18] This in turn precluded naval or air strikes on Pakistani targets, as such action would have been foolhardy without Army readiness to blunt possible responses by Pakistani ground forces. While the Indian government's restraint then was wise, and ultimately Pakistan suffered significant internal and external damage to its reputation, the 2008 attack did raise questions about the viability of Cold Start. For all the talk about this new doctrine, six years after Operation Parakram, there was no readiness to implement it.

The enunciation of Cold Start without first developing the capabilities to back it up was self-defeating in at least two ways. First, India was touting a concept and capability that it did not actually possess and that the political leadership had never officially embraced. Or, more accurately, *some Indians* in the Army, the strategic affairs community and the media were projecting a Cold Start doctrine, echoed by commentators elsewhere, while the Indian political leadership did not deign either to embrace and resource the doctrine or to reject it and pose an alternative. Thus, when India was attacked by terrorists or insurgents from Pakistan, it would not be able to conduct the game-changing retaliatory operations that had been advertised. The credibility of a proactive strategy for deterrence by punishment was also thereby undermined. Second, while Cold Start's deterrent effects on Pakistan were ambiguous at best, it did provide a handy justification for Pakistani military leaders to call for more intensive production of nuclear weapons with a new emphasis on battlefield systems that could counter India's putative proactive capabilities and doctrine.[19] As a leading BJP foreign policy figure put it in April 2014, 'Cold Start was genuinely defensive, meant to be a deterrent. It's not offensive. There's nothing we want in Pakistan. But if we are attacked from there, then this was a limited, clearly limited, defensive way to respond. But the Pakistanis played it up as an offensive strategy and proof that India wants to break up Pakistan.'[20] To deter this perceived existential threat from India, Pakistan could justify recourse to battlefield nuclear weapons.

Even before the Mumbai attacks, the Indian Army seemingly had begun to shift away from the Cold Start terminology, though it continued to pursue a proactive strategy. In September 2010, for example, then Army Chief V.K. Singh stated,

There is nothing called 'Cold Start'. As part of our overall strategy we have a number of contingencies and options, depending on what the aggressor does. In the recent years, we have been improving our systems with respect to mobilization, but our basic military posture is defensive.... I think that 'Cold Start' is just a term bandied about by think tanks and media. It is neither a doctrine nor a military term in our glossary.[21]

Whether the Army had internalized some of the criticism of Cold Start, or felt that it had achieved the deterrence effect against Pakistan, Cold Start was a dead letter, at least as a term embraced officially by the Indian Army.[22]

Still, the desire for quick mobilization and proactive options remains among many analysts and military officers, who continue to favour the proactive strategy as a means to provide punitive options for deterrence and compellence in case of a future sub-conventional attack. And the Indian Army continues to conduct exercises involving the Pivot and Strike Corps that indicate sustained interest in rapid manoeuvre warfare.[23] Recalling a waggish quip that 'anything not worth doing is not worth doing well', we analyse the strategic dilemmas raised by an army-centric strategy before we consider the capabilities India would still need to acquire in order to implement a proactive strategy. The core question concerns the objective of putting Indian boots on Pakistani territory in response to anything less than a large-scale military aggression by Pakistan, and whether this objective can deliver the promised punishment sufficient to compel change in Pakistan and/or deter Pakistan from escalating in response to Indian action.

Deterrence by Punishment

There is no official statement of the strategic objective(s) a proactive strategy would serve, not least because the Indian government never officially embraced or enunciated such a strategy. The lack of official clarity created space for proponents to posit any number of aims for India's proactive strategy. Indian Army Colonel-turned-scholar Ali Ahmed argues variously that the strategy seeks to force Pakistan to 'cease its offensive strategic posture at the sub-conventional level', to coerce Pakistan into ending sponsorship of anti-Indian terrorists, and to reinforce deterrence by showing resolve through military action.[24] Brig. Arun Sahgal (ret.) thinks of it as an ability for 'seizing early initiatives in any confrontation'.[25] Brig. Gurmeet Kanwal (ret.), the former director of the Army think tank Centre for Land Warfare Studies, offers what may be the maximalist view: 'The overall aim would also be to destroy the Pakistan Army's war waging potential through the application of asymmetric firepower.'[26]

The lesser of these outlined objectives is 'deterrence by punishment'. As a matter of military strategy, deterrence has a simpler, more defensive logic than compellence. That is, a credible threat of punishment can be sufficient to dissuade an enemy from taking a certain action, thereby preserving the status quo. But to compel the enemy to change its overall policy, rather than merely refrain from a course of action, requires a higher level of resolve to carry through on a threat by instigating military action. From Pakistan's perspective, as a matter of intelligence, law enforcement, and border patrol, it is presumably possible to take observable measures to restrain groups that desire to infiltrate and attack India, as Pakistan claims it has done since the 2008 Mumbai attack. (Proponents of the proactive strategy submit this as evidence of its success as a deterrent, arguing that it has induced caution and defensiveness in the Pakistan Army.[27]) It would be far more daunting to dismantle those groups, which is a compellence objective that some proactive strategists also posit.

Most immediately, a strategy of meting punishment could help satisfy the need to maintain domestic confidence and support for the government in case of another attack. More ambitiously, the capability to punish can serve as a deterrent if it causes an adversary to abstain from the triggering behaviour. But these two possible benefits will emerge only if the plausible chain of actions and reactions that follow from the triggering event would impose greater costs on the instigator than the punisher. This, of course, depends on whether escalation of conflict ensues and how it ends. Indeed, as the aforementioned former US undersecretary of defence Fred Iklé cautioned in *Every War Must End*, 'Inflicting "punishment" on the enemy nation is not only an ineffective strategy for ending a war, it may well have side effects that actually hasten the defeat of the side that relies on such a strategy.'[28]

Calibrating punishment is a significant challenge. Tit-for-tat as a strategy works in game theory, but evidence from neuroscience and social psychology indicate that punitive actions often have greater-than-intended effects on the recipient.[29] For instance, in a crisis simulation administered by the US Naval Postgraduate School, an Indian decision to escalate a crisis with a naval blockade was seen as an inherently escalatory step by the Pakistani team, while the Indian team had seen it as a punitive but clearly limited retaliatory measure.[30] Thus, satisfying a desire for punishment but executing it in ways that do not contribute to escalatory steps by Pakistan, and which terminate the exchange on terms favourable to India, will be a real challenge for Indian decision makers. Too little punishment will not inflict sufficient costs on Pakistan, while too much punishment might lead to escalation.

India may calculate that the Pakistan Army would seek to avoid escalation and thus not respond to an Indian ground incursion. But it is difficult to see how Pakistan Army commanders could under any circumstance accept Indian boots on Pakistani territory. Given the primacy of India as a threat in Pakistani military logic and doctrine, Pakistan's Corps Commanders would face high pressure from both politicians and junior officers to evict the invading forces, or to respond with a counterattack across the border, even if they calculated that the costs to Pakistan would be greater than for India.[31] The asymmetry in the stakes of a conventional military conflict on Pakistani territory thus places additional demands on India to make punishing deterrent threats credible.

Proponents of the proactive strategy have wrestled with the 'how much punishment' question. Fearing potential for escalation, some have suggested a deliberately more limited option—what Ahmed terms 'Cold Start and stop'—in which an Indian incursion is framed as a prelude to diplomacy, rather than as the opening salvo of a broader campaign of attrition.[32] As Cold Start fell out of favour and the proactive strategy was challenged by Indian officials and analysts, other Indian scholars proposed that the strategy be targeted only at Pakistani Kashmir, which is a contested territory, rather than the International Border—Katoch, for example, urges punitive attacks on Pakistani military outposts that support infiltration in Indian Kashmir, while Sawhney and Wahab see this strategy as a way to re-draw the LoC in ways that would limit incursion routes.[33] Of attacking non-military targets in Kashmir, though, Ahmed cautions, 'This would punish, but contrary to expectation, could place the population firmly behind the military.'[34] In any case, such analyses tend to discount the potential difficulties that India might encounter in achieving a quick defeat of dug-in Pakistani forces in Kashmir, as well as the possibility that Pakistan would escalate the conflict in ways that complicate an Indian exit. Nor are they clear on how military operations, specifically holding Pakistani territory for bargaining, will facilitate diplomatic objectives, a topic taken up further in this chapter.

Proactive Compellence

Compellence is based on a credible threat of military action to force the enemy to do something different than 'he' has been doing. Compellence is widely viewed in academic literature as a much more difficult objective to achieve than deterrence.[35] In a nuclearized environment, in which threats to bring down political regimes or inflict total defeat are practically ruled out, exercising compellence is an exceedingly difficult objective. The record to date of successful compellent threats involving states with nuclear weapons is poor.[36]

For a compellent strategy, its conductors presumably should have a theory of how the proposed military operation would result in punishment and victory (through a potential escalatory process) that would be suitably frightening to the Pakistan military, but would not cross nuclear redlines that could cause escalation to total war. Indian proponents also need to articulate how that victory would in turn motivate and enable Pakistani authorities to curtail the operations of anti-India groups such as LeT, and ultimately reject proxy warfare in the future.

Indian scholarship is clear on the specific compellent threats to deliver: India will defeat local Pakistani forces and take territory until Pakistani authorities act to demobilize violent anti-India groups. However, Indian scholars offer relatively few ideas about exactly how and why limited conventional operations on Pakistani territory would motivate Pakistani authorities to change their policy and demobilize anti-India groups rather than escalate the conflict.

Territory as a Bargaining Chip

The most common compellent threat associated with the proactive strategy is to seize and hold Pakistani territory for use as leverage in post-conflict bargaining. This is different from a deterrent threat to take Pakistani territory for the purpose of inflicting punishment on the Pakistan Army. In order to serve as a compellent threat, holding conquered territory would seem necessary in order to exert diplomatic leverage on Pakistan to demobilize anti-India militants. In essence, 'If you want your land back, do what we tell you to.'

The requirement to hold territory as a bargaining chip raises a number of thorny issues. Among them, the topology and population density of Pakistan are important. Relatively flat and unpopulated desert territory across the International Border in Rajasthan, for instance, would presumably be easier for invading Indian forces to seize and hold. But if Indian forces did manage to break through Pakistani defences and seize territory, how long could they remain before they would experience a significant increase in insurgent attacks? Indian proponents do not say why or how the presence of Indian troops on Pakistani soil would not spur recruitment of militants from Pakistan, Afghanistan, and elsewhere to fight the occupiers and mount terrorist attacks in Kashmir and the Indian mainland. Ahmed drily suggests: 'Controlling [seized land] for any duration of time may not be feasible given the Iraq-style asymmetric war that could be the inevitable counter.'[37] Vijay Shankar, a former commander of India's strategic forces, more bluntly suggests: 'The US experiences in Afghanistan, Iraq and Syria suggest exactly how despairing it can be when conventional forces are pitted against jihadists.'[38] One potential means for avoiding an inevitable escalation in asymmetric warfare against Indian forces would be to target less populated territory, such as in the Rajasthan desert. But such territory would have diminished utility as a demonstration of resolve to carry through on compellent threats.

If Indian occupation of Pakistani territory would activate militant resistance, would a weakened Pakistani state retain the means to demobilize militant groups as demanded by India? Presumably the now-damaged Pakistan military would face a still more difficult challenge in imposing order (even if they were motivated to do so). Here it should be recalled that groups that practice terrorism often seek to provoke the adversary to overreact, in order to intensify their members' commitment and rally the wider nation to the justness of their cause.[39]

Some proponents of a version of proactive strategy recognize the paramount problems associated with holding territory. Lt. Gen. B.S. Pawar (ret.), for example, writes: 'The Indian Army will no longer concentrate on capturing and holding Pakistani territory as leverage for post-war negotiations.'[40] Though a quick withdrawal after victory may satisfy punishment objectives, it fails to answer whether and how Pakistani authorities would then be compelled to act to preclude future jihadi attacks on India.

Capturing legally disputed territory in Pakistani Kashmir, on the other hand, in theory would provide India with a real option to retain re-captured 'Indian' land, which would have much greater value as a compellent threat given the symbolic importance of Kashmir to the Pakistani military and state.[41] But capturing and holding well-defended, mountainous territory in Kashmir presents difficult operational challenges too.

Attrition of the Pakistan Army

A second clear compellent threat contemplated by proponents of the proactive strategy is attrition of the Pakistan Army's 'war waging ability'. The logic for carrying out this threat is actually tied closely to the issue of holding territory. As Ahmed writes,

The capture of significant territory is in order to entice enemy military reserves into reacting, thereby exposing them to destruction by ground and air action. This meshes with the second aim of inflicting attrition on the enemy forces....The idea is to make the pivot corps get past the first obstacle [and capture territory], so that the strike corps keep their powder dry for the more pertinent deep battle.[42]

Thus, the proactive strategy explicitly envisions capturing territory to invite escalation so that India is justified to launch stronger firepower to destroy the Pakistan Army. Of course, execution of this strategy would take it beyond the realm of limited conflict.

The logic of attrition-through-escalation raises serious questions about how and why it might produce the desired compellence effect. If the existence of the Pakistan Army as a fighting force was reasonably threatened by the Indian military's superior conventional capability and strategy, Pakistan Army commanders conceivably could consider demobilizing militant groups whose actions could trigger a conflict. But in an escalating conflict, as discussed above, India could expect that militant groups would join the cause, carrying out attacks on Indian forces both in Pakistan and in the Indian mainland. Far from seeking to break up militant groups, the Pakistan Army might welcome their efforts to repel Indian invaders.

Inviting escalation in order to destroy the Pakistan Army also brings into play Pakistani nuclear threats. Indians might assess that Pakistan would not use nuclear weapons on the battlefield to stop an initial armoured thrust, but if the Pakistan Army is facing defeat it might also perceive a use-or-lose dilemma with nuclear weapons. Could Indian leaders be reasonably confident that Pakistan would not consider nuclear use as a last-ditch measure to avoid defeat?

Assuming for the sake of argument that Indian forces were reconfigured, re-equipped, and retrained as envisioned by champions of proactive strategy, and then succeeded in 'destroying the combat potential of the Pakistan Army and its war-fighting capacity', then by what means would the Pakistan Army and the ISI become motivated *and* able to compel LeT and other groups to demobilize?[43] The Pakistani establishment today is not sufficiently strong to keep the Federally Administered Tribal Areas clear of militants and 'take on' LeT (if it chose to do so). It is further unlikely that Pakistan simultaneously could manage the political-security backlash this would create in the Punjabi heartland and elsewhere, while also contending with the disorder sown by the Pakistani Taliban, Baloch insurgents, and sectarian violence in Karachi. It is at least reasonable to question whether and how a defeated Army would pursue this objective. Pakistani police forces for the foreseeable future will simply lack the capabilities to take on an organization as large, well-resourced, and well-trained as LeT, especially if the ISI would not share their determination to do so. The Pakistan Army and the ISI would seem to be necessary instruments in dismantling or at least compelling militant groups to abandon terrorism against India.

These problems reveal some of the gaps in the logic offered by proponents of the proactive strategy, as well as what might be called 'magical' thinking. For instance, Ahmed acknowledges, 'Expecting weaker civilian politicians today to eclipse the military after a defeat in conflict may be to credit them with greater strength and wisdom than warranted.' Yet, he then elides this problem to reach the conclusion that 'even if the military remains in power, it may come round to seeing its policy as dysfunctional and change it, with the civilians providing it with "face saving" cover'. However, Ahmed does not explain why the military would conclude this. Finally, he suggests, 'With the military's power whittled, the new regime would be more amenable to changing Pakistan's India policy.... Attrition of the military would be a direct way to degrade their post-conflict hold over the Pakistani state and society. It would open up space for democratic forces to reclaim Pakistan at long last.'[44]

Well-informed Indian civilian experts doubt the feasibility of the proposed strategy. As one put it in a 2014 interview, 'There is no theory of how Cold Start or any other military action would compel the Pakistanis to dismantle the terrorist infrastructure. You have to negotiate with the Pakistanis to close the camps.'[45]

Escalatory Effects on Pakistan

Even if army-centric operations against Pakistan are implausible to compel the Pakistani security establishment to demobilize anti-Indian terrorist groups, such operations could satisfy a domestic Indian desire to punish Pakistan. However, for such punishment to be effective, India would have to prevent or else win any escalatory conflict that ensued. Otherwise, if Pakistan fought back in ways that inflicted serious harm on Indian interests, the net effect could be negative for India both strategically and in terms of domestic opinion. Thus, it is necessary to assess how Pakistan would likely react to Indian employment of the army-centric proactive strategy, and how India could then attempt to deter or defeat escalation.

In order to keep conflict limited, both sides must observe limitations in the means of violence. India seeks to communicate that it intends a capability to sustain only shallow incursions, not the total defeat of the Pakistan Army and/or dismemberment of the Pakistani state. Yet, even if Indian forces could readily achieve such incursions in one or more areas, which we discuss later in the chapter, the question arises whether this would appear 'limited' to Pakistan. On one hand, the penetration distances envisioned by the proactive strategy are well in excess of the 10–15 kilometres that Indian troops covered across the International Border into Pakistani territory in the 1965 and 1971 wars. Pakistani canals and other fortifications have been designed to stymie just such an Indian advance, which would suggest that thrusts greater than 15 kilometres are perhaps more than optimistic, and yet clearly not limited in historical context.[46] On the other hand, two major Pakistani cities in Punjab—Lahore and Sialkot—are just 25 kilometres and 15 kilometres from the border, respectively, meaning an Indian advance of the minimum distance suggested by proactive strategy supporters could potentially threaten both cities. Threats to major cities would also not connote limited objectives. Assessing this problem from the Pakistani perspective, Mansoor Ahmed, a scholar at Quaid-i-Azam University, argues,

A shallow maneuver by India, close to ten to fifteen miles of Lahore, would be tantamount to triggering Pakistan's spatial thresholds and thus also impinging on the country's military thresholds [for nuclear use]. A loss of territory in the desert areas might not be seen as a threat to the country's survival or at least that of its conventional forces, but acceptability even for limited territorial losses would be very low.[47]

Some Indian analysts seem to appreciate the challenge of first conveying and then sustaining the use of limited means for limited objectives, and why it presents a perception problem for Pakistan. Kanwal, one of the most unabashed proponents of the Cold Start doctrine, acknowledges that Pakistani analysts see Cold Start as 'inherently escalatory'. He continues,

Its major disadvantage [in terms of strategic stability] would be that it provides India a viable option for launching low risk shallow-thrust offensive operations ['to capture a long swathe of territory almost all along the international boundary'] in the plains in response to a grave provocation .... While India's initial military response would probably be limited to the areas across the LOC in Jammu and Kashmir, should Pakistan choose to escalate the situation by launching retaliatory strikes in areas across the international boundary, India may be forced to implement its Cold Start doctrine immediately by launching several divisional-size IBGs into Pakistani territory all across the Western front.[48]

Kanwal is correct that Pakistani analysts have concluded that an Indian proactive strategy is escalatory, precisely because of the writings of Indian strategists like Kanwal who have suggested that the strategy aims 'to destroy the Pakistan Army's war waging potential'.[49] Given such ambitions, even if held only by some more hawkish elements in India's strategic community, it is difficult to believe Pakistan would not assume the worst. Thus, it is imprudent to expect that the Pakistan Army, militant groups, and citizens would consider Indian penetration even as shallow as 10–15 kilometres into Pakistan a limited incursion, so as not to warrant the exertion of all of Pakistan's military (and jihadi) capability to resist. Brig. (ret.) Javed Hussain writes, for example,

For Pakistan the dimensions of time and space assume paramount importance as it lacks territorial depth, is opposed by a larger adversary and lacks the resources to fight a protracted war.... The fact that the Pakistani Army can occupy their wartime locations earlier than the Indian army confers on it the ability to pre-empt Cold Start; failure to do so could lead to firing of low-yield tactical warheads at IBGs as they cross the start line or even earlier. Cold Start would be a portent of escalation, and inevitably a disaster for both.[50]

Whatever India's initial intentions, it could be driven to escalate for reasons advocates of proactive strategy prefer not to discuss. Presumably, Pakistani forces would be intensely resisting Indian advances. If they were successful early in the conflict, India would seek to direct more firepower at them, or else risk the humiliation of failure (recalling India's need for clear victory to achieve political objectives). As India added weight to its attack, in the fog, dust, and smoke of war its aims could appear less-than limited; it might also be forced to bring to bear means of warfare, such as the Strike Corps, that break its initial self-imposed capability restraints. Conversely, if India's attacking forces were succeeding according to plan, Indian military leaders would be tempted to press on—or at least Pakistani authorities would assume that Indian leaders would act upon this temptation.

Arun Singh understands these challenges. He was India's Minister of State for Defence under then Prime Minister Rajiv Gandhi and, together with Army Chief of Staff Gen. K. Sundarji, devised and conducted the massive Brasstacks exercise in December 1986. Singh was called back into government service by the BJP-led government in 1999 to help prosecute the Kargil War and then, afterward, to help reform Indian defence policy.

'Cold Start?' Singh sighed, in an April 2014 interview.

How does anybody think this is going to work? How will the Pakistanis believe you will stop? You say you only have limited objectives, and somehow, therefore, the Pakistanis will recognize this. But how? What makes you think they will? And what if they don't? What if the General on the ground doesn't want to stop? Regional commanders in India have considerable autonomy. And if they don't have confidence that the General will stop, how do you give them that confidence?[51]

Another veteran Indian defence official, P.R. Chari, was similarly rueful. 'In the real world it's hard to stop an advancing Army which has a goal that has been agreed. Try stopping generals and an Army half way. You have to accept that your Army Chief will disagree. And how do you convince the other side that you will stop? Do you say you will shoot your general if he disagrees?'[52]

Nuclear Shadow

An army-centric strategy to put Indian boots on Pakistani ground bumps against the central effect of nuclear weapons. Nuclear weapons have proved relatively useless for compellence, for defeating insurgencies, and for deterring terrorism.[53] Their real value is to deter other states from committing aggression into a nuclear-armed state's territory on a scale that threatens existential interests. An Indian strategy that centres on moving troops and armour into Pakistani territory invites a relatively credible threat of Pakistani nuclear retaliation against those forces. This is particularly true if those troops are crossing over the International Border into Punjab or Sindh, which as discussed earlier is more likely to be interpreted in Pakistan as anything but a limited attack.

Indian proponents theorize that Pakistani leaders would not exercise their nuclear threat because they would recognize the limits of India's military aims and would accept the posited less-than-existential defeat rather than initiate use of nuclear weapons which would invite 'massive retaliation' by India. Indian proactive strategy, therefore, assumes that Pakistani nuclear thresholds are sufficiently high to permit limited conventional responses. Further, many Indian analysts posit that Pakistani decision makers would be deterred by the Indian threat of massive nuclear retaliation. However, this optimistic dismissal of Pakistan's nuclear options depends on two dubious assumptions: first, that in the midst of an intense war, Pakistani leaders would perceive and appreciate that India's aims were limited; and second, that Pakistani leaders would accept India's victory by allowing India's threat of massive retaliation to deter them even if Pakistan could reciprocate by launching its surviving nuclear forces against Indian cities. We addressed above the unreliability of the first assumption. In Chapter 5, we analyse the deterrent credibility of threatening massive nuclear retaliation in response to Pakistan's potential use of nuclear weapons against invading Indian forces on Pakistani territory. Here it is sufficient to say that Pakistani leaders—and perhaps much of Pakistani society—would view Indian combined armed attacks on the Pakistani heartland a grossly disproportionate response to a terrorist attack on India. While India would begin operations with the commitment of a defender responding to a terrorist aggression, if the Indian response was seen as excessive, Pakistanis would then feel the psychology of the defender, with all that entails for the dynamics of commitment and escalation in a nuclearized environment.

Even if Pakistani leaders believed India's military objectives were as 'limited' as proponents of proactive strategy purport, they would still deem the Indian action as excessive and warranting an all-out Pakistani defence. (Indeed, some champions of Cold

Start, such as Kanwal and Sahgal, volunteer that the Indian action *should* be disproportionate.[54]) If Pakistan's conventional forces were not stymieing Indian advances, or if they were succeeding and India then intensified its attacks, Pakistani military leaders would see the use of battlefield nuclear weapons as necessary and justified to compel India to stop what Pakistanis would perceive to be India's offensive action. Pakistan would be defensively shifting the burden of escalation back on to India, in this view. Indian leaders would then have to decide whether to counter with massive nuclear retaliation, as called for in India's current doctrine, knowing that Pakistan could then retaliate with nuclear attacks on Indian cities. The escalatory nature of the proactive strategy indicates a problematic disjuncture between India's conventional and nuclear doctrines.[55] Specifically, a victory-seeking offensive conventional doctrine with significant escalatory potential is at odds with a defensive nuclear doctrine that aims to avoid war. (One way to resolve this is by developing limited nuclear options that join the conventional and nuclear conflict spectrum, which is explored further in Chapter 5.)

A terrorist attack on an Indian city, however horrible and unconscionable, would be small-scale compared with the consequences *to India* of an escalation process that resulted in massively destructive nuclear exchanges. If nuclear escalation is thus assumed in the proactive strategy, does that not essentially ensure self-deterrence by India, given the asymmetry in stakes in an escalating conflict? And, if India has a strong interest in reducing the salience of nuclear weapons in Indo-Pak relations, then how would an army-centric strategy with the escalatory potential of Cold Start serve that interest? In broader strategic terms, India ultimately wants to see Pakistan transition to genuinely democratic civilian governance with the Army withdrawn from politics and foreign policymaking. Positing a doctrine that threatens to take Pakistani territory plays directly into the Army's preferred narrative and helps justify its predominance within Pakistan.

To their credit, some Indian strategists and political leaders have addressed these questions. One such group, the authors of *Nonalignment 2.0*, noted that under Cold Start, 'capture of significant amounts of Pakistan's territory continues to be the primary military objective underpinning the doctrine and organization of the Indian armed forces'. However, these authors concluded, 'The capture of significant amounts of territory is no longer a valid proposition, owing to the nuclear equation.'[56] Ahmed concurs, arguing that 'the escalatory potential of limited war makes it a less than appealing option for the political decision maker when confronted with live situations, as occurred during Mumbai 26/11'.[57]

Capabilities for a Proactive Assault

Today—and so long as Indian efforts to reform its military procurement system do not succeed—the greatest risk is not that Indian forces will be so overwhelming that the Pakistani military would have to fear multi-pronged penetration of their heartland. Rather, the near-term problem is that if Indian leaders authorize a proactive response to another terrorist attack, the Indian forces are unlikely to achieve the quick splendid victory that proponents of the strategy imagine. This is partly due to the difficulty of combined forces operations in an environment of enduring inter-service rivalry.[58] But the more significant issue is the general state of hardware capability and readiness of the Indian Army and Air Force.

Conventional wisdom over the last decade held that India had attained conventional military advantages over Pakistan, which permitted it to develop the force concentrations and mobility necessary for the manoeuvre warfare envisioned by the proactive strategy. But recently this conventional wisdom has been challenged by several analyses that indicate a military balance not as advantageous to India as imagined.[59] Sawhney, for example, wrote in the January 2014 issue of *FORCE*:

There is a belief that India has a conventional superiority over Pakistan. This is not true, because this perception is based on bean-counting of assets of both sides. The Pakistan Army scores over the Indian Army in strategic command, control, coordination and higher directions of war. However much the Indian Army may shorten its mobilization time, it is impossible to beat Pakistan Army's advantage of operating on internal lines. Thus, at the operational level of war, the two armies are nearly matched.[60]

The growing obsolescence of Indian military hardware, complicated by a broken procurement system beset by scandal after scandal, is perhaps the most significant, non-structural aspect of this problem. This problem derives from public policy issues in India and has nothing to do with the capability and terrain advantages of the Pakistan Army. Most of the indications of this issue come from frustrated Indian Army officers. For example, an Army briefing to a parliamentary committee in 2009 stated that the Army's 'modernization plans were so far behind schedule that they would meet their current targets only by 2027'.[61] The towed artillery and tank fleets are 1970s and 1980s vintage, and suffer from lack of spare parts and upgrade equipment. Another critical report indicated a lack of self-propelled 155mm howitzers, multiple rocket launch systems, and surface-to-surface missiles.[62]

Perhaps the most striking airing of this problem came in May 2012, when retiring Army Chief Gen. V.K. Singh wrote a letter to the then Prime Minister Manmohan Singh declaring that the Indian Army was not prepared to fight a war. According to reports of his letter, he indicated an 'alarming' state of readiness among the major fighting divisions. Among his complaints: the Army's tank fleet is 'devoid of critical ammunition'; the air defence is '97% obsolete'; infantry has 'deficiencies of crew served weapons' and possesses no ability for night fighting; and 'large-scale voids' in surveillance capability.[63] These deficiencies are echoed by Sawhney, who argued that the 'Indian Army may not have ammunition to fight the next war (with Pakistan, not to mention China) beyond three to five days.... Stockings for artillery (70 percent [of] fuses needed for firing are unavailable) and armoured fighting vehicles' ammunition are unlikely to last beyond four to five days of intense war.' Reserve ammunition stocks for most categories of weapons did not exist. Sahwney went on, 'The artillery is obsolete and inadequate; air defence is antiquated; armour is unreliable due to regular barrel accidents caused by mismatch between indigenous barrels and ammunition; and night fighting devices are insufficient.'[64] In August 2014, the *Times of India* reported that India did not possess enough ammunition for an intense fight beyond 20 days.[65] Numerous other reports detail capability problems in multiple areas critical to the success of a proactive operation.[66]

Cold Start is an army-centric concept, but it depends significantly on support from the Air Force. However, here, too, capabilities lag in at least two ways. First, as discussed in Chapter 3, the IAF itself suffers from shortages of front-line aircraft and other necessary enabling assets. Second, the Air Force apparently continues to resist having its role and doctrine subordinated to the Army. Like other modern air forces, the IAF defines its primary mission as defeating the Pakistan Air Force and targeting the enemy's strategic assets. Focusing air operations on defending ground forces and opening pathways for their advance is not a priority. Moreover, the IAF rejects the Army notion of air-ground operations and the need to associate air assets to particular ground units, preferring instead to leverage its numerical superiority over the Pakistan Air Force.[67] The result is that the Air Force neither desires to nor is prepared to provide close air support to a proactive offensive. By extension, the IAF presumably prefers to practice air-to-air tactics and strategic targeting rather than honing its skills in destroying dug-in defensive ground positions. Thus, as in the 1999 Kargil conflict, the IAF likely faces a steep learning curve if it were called upon to support an Army offensive.[68]

Despite these manifest challenges, it is clear that the Indian Army continues to develop and exercise a proactive strategy. In 2015 it held two major field exercises involving its Southern and Southwestern Commands.[69] Pakistani interlocutors also report that India continues to build new cantonments and road infrastructure close to the border, essentially turning its old war-time positions into new peace-time positions. It is unclear the extent to which the political leadership in New Delhi and the Air Force command leaderships have embraced the Army's continued pursuit of something like Cold Start. In Pakistan, however, the existence of Cold Start essentially is perceived as a cold, hard fact. Critical analyses that downplay the Indian threat are viewed as naïve or, worse, perfidious to the extent they are coupled with arguments that Pakistan need not develop tactical nuclear weapons.

Notwithstanding Pakistani claims about Cold Start, it is fair to assess, as many Indian analysts do, that the IAF are not equipped to execute a successful proactive operation. It is also fair to assess that the manifest bureaucratic and procurement challenges facing the Indian military make the acquisition of all necessary capabilities unlikely in the near term. However, if and when the Indian government overcomes the severe impediments to resourcing, organizing, training, and deploying the combined ground and air forces required for Cold Start, the aforementioned problem of convincing Pakistani leaders that India's objectives are limited would become central. And, here, the shadow of nuclear weapons darkens the prospect.

* * *

Writing one year after the Mumbai attack, Manoj Joshi pronounced a fitting judgement on the Army's proactive strategy. 'So, the military grumbles that the politicians lack the will to order a strike, and our politicians complain that the military does not have the capacity to deliver a decisive outcome. Were it not pathetic, it would seem that it is a well-scripted drama to fool the public.'[70]

The logical flaws and challenges revealed by India's experimentation with a proactive, army-centric strategy have clearly dampened any enthusiasm for it that existed among India's civilian leadership. Many military analysts have also become less sanguine about the strategy. Major Gen. (ret.) G.D. Bakshi, for instance, acknowledges that the proactive strategy 'suffers from some inherent constraints. Land wars generate far greater levels of the "fog of war." They are difficult to control and calibrate. A land-centric start does not even give the Air Force adequate time to gain a favourable air situation and forces it to concurrently fight the air battle and support the surface forces.'[71]

But the strategic challenge has not gone away, nor the desire for robust military options to motivate Pakistan to prevent future major terrorist attacks in India. The Indian Army seemingly has moved on from Cold Start, but still retains a desire for punishing options. Bakshi suggests that

[a] mass casualty terrorist strike could be first responded to by precise and calibrated Air/Special Forces strikes on the originators, their control centres and headquarters, their leaders and critical infrastructures... Such attacks need not be confined to targets across the LoC alone, as the triggering attacks have been on the Indian mainland...Partial mobilisation could be concurrently ordered to cater for any Pakistani move to further escalate the situation.[72]

Similarly, Ahmed assesses, 'The window that appeared to exist between the sub-conventional and nuclear planes is not as wide as was first thought. This re-evaluation may result in a decisive move away from limited war to short, sharp military engagements not amounting to war. This may be more in keeping with war avoidance, critical in the nuclear age.'[73]

The following chapters explore these alternative means of punishment, including those involving precise airborne and, possibly, special forces strikes on Pakistani targets. Of course, as Bakshi foreshadows, airborne strikes (and special force operations) would have to be backed up by ground forces prepared to respond to Pakistani countermoves, with the attendant implications discussed above.

Notes and References

1. K. Sundarji, *Vision 2100: A Strategy for the Twenty-first Century*, (Delhi: Konark, 2003), 147.
2. Swaran Singh, 'Indian Debate on Limited War Doctrine', *Strategic Analysis*, 23, no. 12, 2000: 2180.

3. Polly Nayak and Michael Krepon, 'US Crisis Management in South Asia's Twin Peaks Crisis', Stimson Report 57, second edition, 16 September 2014. Available at: http://www.stimson.org/images/uploads/research-pdfs/Twin_Peaks_Crisis-FINAL-WEB.pdf.

4. Celia W. Dugger, 'India Rebuffs Pakistanis over Inquiry into Attack', *New York Times*, 18 December 2001. Available at: http://www.nytimes.com/2001/12/18/world/india-rebuffs-pakistanis-over-inquiry-into-attack.html.

5. Steve Coll, 'The Stand-Off', *New Yorker*, 13 February 2006. Available at: http://www.newyorker.com/magazine/2006/02/13/the-stand-off.

6. Coll, 'The Stand-Off'; Polly Nayak and Michael Krepon, 'U.S. Crisis Management in South Asia's Twin Peaks Crisis', in Zachary S. Davis (ed.), *The India-Pakistan Military Standoff: Crisis and Escalation in South Asia*, (New York, NY: Palgrave Macmillan, 2011), 163.

7. Frustration was intensified by the accidental deaths of nearly 800 Indian personnel in the mobilization itself, and its estimated cost of $1.2 billion. See Gurmeet Kanwal, 'Lost Opportunities in Operation Parakram', *Indian Defence Review*, 13 December 2011. Available at: http://www.indiandefencereview.com/spotlights/lost-opportunities-in-operation-parakram/.

8. '"Cold Start" to New War Doctrine', *Times of India*, 14 April 2004. Available at: http://timesofindia.indiatimes.com/india/Cold-Start-to-new-war-doctrine/articleshow/616847.cms.

9. Walter C. Ladwig III, 'A Cold Start for Hot Wars? The Indian Army's New Limited War Doctrine', *International Security* 32, no.3 (Winter 2007/08), 164.

10. For more details, see: Ladwig, 'A Cold Start for Hot Wars?', 165; Pravin Sawhney and Ghazala Wahab, 'Not a Myth', *FORCE*, December 2011; Gurmeet Kanwal, 'India's Cold Start Doctrine and Strategic Stability', Institute for Defence Studies and Analysis, 1 June 2010. Available at: http://www.idsa.in/idsacomments/IndiasColdStartDoctrineandStrategicStability_gkanwal_010610; Gurmeet Kanwal, 'Cold Start and Battle Groups for Offensive Operations', *Strategic Trends* 4, no. 18 (June 2006).

11. See: Ladwig, 'A Cold Start for Hot Wars?'; Ali Ahmed, *India's Doctrine Puzzle: Limiting War in South Asia*, (Routledge, 2014), 58–9; Kanwal, 'India's Cold Start Doctrine and Strategic Stability'.

12. For example: Dr Subhash Kapila, 'Indian Army Validates Its Cold Start Doctrine', *Intellibriefs*, 7 June 2005. Available at: http://intellibriefs.blogspot.com/2005/06/indian-army-validates-its-cold-start.html.

13. Arun Sahgal, 'Cold Start: New Doctrinal Thinking in the Army', *CLAWS Journal* (Summer 2008). Available at: http://www.claws.in/images/journals_doc/1370052420_ArunSeghal.pdf; Kanwal, 'Army Doctrine Undergoes Change in Nuclear Era'; Ladwig, 'A Cold Start for Hot Wars?'

14. For three outstanding analyses of Cold Start, see Ladwig, 'A Cold Start for Hot Wars?'; Shashank Joshi, 'India's Military Instrument: A Doctrine Stillborn', *Journal of Strategic Studies* 36, no. 4 (2013): 512–40; and Ali Ahmed, *India's Doctrine Puzzle: Limiting War in South Asia* (New Delhi: Routledge, 2014).

15. As quoted in Pinaki Bhattacharya, 'Army and IAF Face Off over New War Plan', *India Today*, 14 December 2009. Available at: http://indiatoday.intoday.in/story/Army+and+IAF+face+off+over+new+war+plan/1/74898.html.

16. Sawhney and Wahab, 'Not a Myth'.

17. See discussion in Ladwig, 'A Cold Start for Hot Wars?'; Ahmed, *India's Doctrine Puzzle*; Jaganath Sankaran 'Pakistan's Battlefield Nuclear Policy', *International Security* 39, no. 3, (Winter 2014/15); Christopher Clary, 'Deterrence Stability and the Conventional Balance of Forces in South Asia,' in Michael Krepon and Julia Thompson (eds), *Deterrence Stability and Escalation Control in South Asia*, (Washington, DC: The Stimson Center, 2013): 135–60.

18. Manoj Joshi, 'Was the Indian Army Ready for War?', *Mail Today*, 17 January 2009. Available at: http://mjoshi.blogspot.com/2009/01/was-indian-army-ready-for-war.html.

19. Pakistani military leaders probably would have moved in this direction without the stimulus provided by Cold Start, but the latter enabled them to deflect internal questioning and international pressure by putting the onus on India.

20. Interview with senior Indian foreign policy expert, New Delhi, 24 April 2014.

21. Manu Pubby, 'No "Cold Start" Doctrine, India Tells US', *Indian Express*, 9 September 2010. Available at: http://archive.indianexpress.com/news/no--cold-start--doctrine-india-tells-us/679273/2.

22. Sawhney and Wahab, 'Not a Myth'; Ahmed, *India's Doctrine Puzzle*; Dhruv C. Katoch, 'Combatting Cross-Border Terrorism: Need for a Doctrinal Approach', *CLAWS Journal* (Winter 2013) 6. Available at: http://indianarmy.nic.in/WriteReadData/Documents/combattingcrossborder.pdf.

23. Ali Ahmed, 'The Strange Silence Surrounding an Indian Military Exercise', *Diplomat*, 2 November 2015. Available at: http://thediplomat.com/2015/11/the-strange-silence-surrounding-an-indian-military-exercise/.

24. Ali Ahmed, 'Towards a Proactive Military Strategy: "Cold Start and Stop"'; *Strategic Analysis*, 2011, 404.

25. Arun Sahgal, 'Cold Start: New Doctrinal Thinking in the Army'.

26. Gurmeet Kanwal, 'India's Cold Start Doctrine and Strategic Stability'.

27. Katoch, 'Combatting Cross-Border Terrorism', 7.

28. Iklé, *Every War Must End*, xi.

29. Nicholas D. Wright, 'Knowing How Your Adversary Thinks: Influence in International Confrontations', Carnegie Endowment for International Peace, 18 October 2013. Available at: http://carnegieendowment.org/2013/10/18/knowing-how-your-adversary-thinks.

30. Feroz H. Khan and Ryan W. French, 'South Asian Stability Workshop: A Crisis Simulation Exercise', NPS PASCC Report No. 2013-008, October 2013, 12. Available at: http://www.nps.edu/Academics/Centers/CCC/PASCC/Publications/2013/2013%20008%20South%20Asian%20Stability%20Workshop.pdf.

31. Fair, *Fighting to the End*, 6–7; Shah, *The Army and Democracy*, 38, 207; Haqqani, *Pakistan*, 319.

32. Ahmed, 'Towards a Proactive Military Strategy'.

33. Katoch, 'Combatting Cross-Border Terrorism', 11; Sawhney and Wahab, 'Not a Myth'.

34. Ahmed, 'Towards a Proactive Military Strategy', 406.

35. See discussion in Todd S. Sechser, 'Militarized Compellent Threats, 1918–2001', *Conflict Management and Peace Science* 28, no. 4 (2011): 377–401.

36. Sechser and Fuhrmann, 'Crisis Bargaining and Nuclear Blackmail', 173–95.

37. Ahmed, 'Towards a Proactive Military Strategy', 405.

38. Author e-mail correspondence, 19 August 2015.

39. The authors of *Nonalignment 2.0* warn that if India captured 'significant amounts of [Pakistani] territory...we could find ourselves ensnared in a costly counter-insurgency campaign'. The authors do not define what are 'significant amounts' of Pakistani territory, and therefore what amounts would be less-than-significant and thereby avoid this danger. See: Sunil Khilnani et al., *Nonalignment 2.0: A Foreign and Strategic Policy for India in the 21st Century* (New Delhi: Centre for Policy Research, 2012): 108.

40. B.S. Pawar, 'Time to Warm Up: Is India's Cold Start Doctrine a Myth or Reality?', *FORCE*, August 2013.

41. Ahmed, 'Towards a Proactive Military Strategy'.

42. Ahmed, 'Towards a Proactive Military Strategy'.

43. Pawar, 'Time to Warm Up'.

44. Ahmed, 'Towards a Proactive Military Strategy', 406.

45. Interview with former senior official, New Delhi, 24 April 2014.

46. Sankaran, 'Pakistan's Battlefield Nuclear Policy'.

47. Mansoor Ahmed, 'Proactive Operations and Massive Retaliation: Whither Deterrence Stability,' *South Asian Voices*, 11 September 2013. Available at: http://southasianvoices.org/proactive-operations-and-massive-retaliation-whither-deterrence-stability/.

48. Kanwal, 'India's Cold Start Doctrine and Strategic Stability'.

49. Kanwal, 'India's Cold Start Doctrine and Strategic Stability'.

50. 'A Challenging Doctrine', *Dawn*, 8 February 2010. Available at: http://www.dawn.com/news/846285/a-challenging-doctrine.

51. Interview, New Delhi, 23 April 2014.

52. Interview, New Delhi, 24 April 2014.

53. See for example, Sechser and Fuhrmann, 'Crisis Bargaining and Nuclear Blackmail'.

54. Sahgal, 'Cold Start: New Doctrinal Thinking in the Army'; Kanwal, 'India's Cold Start Doctrine and Strategic Stability'.

55. See discussion in Ali Ahmed, 'Cold Start: The Life Cycle of a Doctrine', *Comparative Strategy* 31, no. 5 (2012): 462–5.

56. See Khilnani et al., *Nonalignment 2.0*. The authors continue in a more robust vein, asserting that 'the capability that India should acquire is one that enables us to make shallow thrusts that are defensible in as many areas as feasible along the international border and the LoC. This will require significant restructuring of the India's [*sic*] strike capability' (109). Thus, while seeming to reject

one possible version of Cold Start, the authors seem to embrace another version proffered by some of the doctrine's proponents. The authors do not acknowledge that the 'capability' they recommend actually entails a long list of capabilities and reforms that are still not on the horizon. Nor do they define the difference between taking 'significant' amounts of Pakistani territory, which they reject, and making and holding 'shallow' thrusts, which they support. Further, they do not address whether and how India's definition of 'shallow thrusts' would be shared by Pakistan, and by what means, over how much time, India would defend the territory that would be taken.

57. Ahmed, 'Cold Start: The Life Cycle of a Doctrine'.

58. Over the course of multiple exercises, Ladwig finds that the Indian Army and Air Force 'consistently failed to integrate their actions'. Ladwig, 'A Cold Start for Hot Wars?', 182–3.

59. Walter C. Ladwig, 'Indian Military Modernization and Conventional Deterrence in South Asia', *Journal of Strategic Studies*, 2015, 32–3.

60. Pravin Sawhney and Ghazala Wahab, 'At the Crossroad', *FORCE*, January 2014.

61. As quoted by Manoj Joshi, 'Who is afraid of Cold Start? Certainly Not Pakistan', *Mail Today*, 17 February 2010. Available at: http://mjoshi. blogspot.com/2010/02/who-is-afraid-of-cold-start-certainly.html.

62. Gurmeet Kanwal, 'India's Military Modernization: Plans and Strategic Underpinnings', National Bureau of Asian Research Policy Brief, September 2012. Available at: http://www.nbr.org/downloads/ pdfs/Outreach/NBR_IndiaCaucus_September2012.pdf.

63. Saikat Datta, '"DNA" Exclusive: Gen VK Singh Tells PM Some Hard Truths', *DNA*, 28 March 2012. Available at: http://www.dnaindia. com/india/report-dna-exclusive-gen-vk-singh-tells-pm-some-hard-truths-1668283.

64. Pravin Sawhney and Ghazala Wahab, 'Armed Without Ammunition', *FORCE*, January 2013.

65. Rajat Pandit, 'Army's Ammunition Won't Last 20 Days of War', *Times of India*, 25 August 2014. Available at: http://timesofindia. indiatimes.com/india/Armys-ammunition-wont-last-20-days-of-war/articleshow/40862131.cms.

66. Sankaran, 'Pakistan's Battlefield Nuclear Policy'; Gurmeet Kanwal, 'Modernisation Plans Need a Major Boost', *CLAWS Journal*, Winter 2010. Available at: http://www.claws.in/images/journals_

doc/1397562852Gurmeet%20Kanwal%20%20CJ%20Winter%20 2010.pdf; Gurmeet Kanwal, 'Artillery Modernisation: Need for Firepower', IDSA Comment, 27 November 2014. Available at: http:// www.idsa.in/idsacomments/Artillerymodernisation_gkanwal_ 271114.html; V.K. Kapoor, 'Indian Army—A Perspective on Future Challenges, Force Development, and Doctrine', *USI Journal* 134, no. 3 (July–September 2004): 355–75; Pinaki Bhattacharya, 'Army and IAF Face Off Over New War Plan', *India Today*, 14 December 2009. Available at: http://indiatoday.intoday.in/story/Army+and+IAF+face +off+over+new+war+plan/1/74898.html; Y.I. Patel, 'Dig Vijay to Divya Astra: a Paradigm Shift in the Indian Army's Doctrine', *Bharat Rakshak*, 12 October 2006. Available at: https://bharat-rakshak.com/ ARMY/today/324-a-paradigm-shift.html.

67. Ladwig, 'Indian Military Modernization and Conventional Deterrence in South Asia', 32–3.

68. Lambeth, *Airpower at 18,000*.

69. Ali Ahmed, 'The Strange Silence Surrounding an Indian Military Exercise'; and Ali Ahmed, 'What This Year's Maneuver Season in India Tells Us', *Foreign Policy Journal*, 12 May 2015. Available at: http://www.foreignpolicyjournal.com/2015/05/12/ what-this-years-maneuver-season-in-india-tells-us/.

70. Manoj Joshi, 'We Lack the Military that Can Deter Terrorism', *Mail Today*, 26 November 2009.

71. G.D. Bakshi, 'Mumbai Redux: Debating India's Strategic Response Options,' *Journal of Defence Studies* 3, no. 4 (2009): 22–3.

72. Bakshi, 'Mumbai Redux', 23.

73. Ahmed, 'Cold Start', 464.

3

AIR POWER

Indian military analysts increasingly recognize the risks of even limited ground operations, notwithstanding initial excitement over the more finely calibrated plans proffered by proponents of the so-called Cold Start doctrine, as discussed in Chapter 2.[1] Doubts about army-centric plans to retaliate to another Mumbai-like attack lead analysts to search for alternatives they find less risky. Airborne strikes are appearing more attractive: they are plausibly less escalatory than ground operations and sufficiently punitive and visible to satisfy Indian leaders' political needs. As retired Air Vice Marshal Manmohan Bahadur remarked, air power will attain 'prima donna' status in Indian doctrine because of its 'reach, flexibility, fire-power, and quick response capability in the complete spectrum of conflict'.[2]

In his illuminating, albeit sanguine, book, *Limited Wars in South Asia*, Indian Major Gen. (ret.) G.D. Bakshi reflects this new enthusiasm:

Responding with air power first would enable India to carefully calibrate its responses to terrorist attacks and ensure escalation dominance...Just and proportionate air strikes...would serve as a shot across the bow that would place the onus of further escalation on the enemy.... Their high level of optical visibility serves to dramatically and emphatically highlight that such terrorist attacks are not acceptable any more. At the same time, air power does not hold ground or capture territory. To that extent, its initial use may be less of an existential threat to the Pakistanis than a full-fledged ground assault that captures and holds territory.[3]

Limited punitive air strikes also would put India into a league with the US and Israel as 'hard', militarily capable democracies determined to combat terrorism and to punish states that do not fulfil their obligations to curtail terrorists' operations. This has appeal to strategists and politicians in today's India.[4] 'In the modern era of warfare the Israelis have been pioneers in the use of air and space assets to prosecute a campaign against non-state actors like the Hamas and Hezbollah,' wrote Air Commodore Arjun Subramaniam in 2009. 'Though their strategy has met with limited success and evoked widespread international condemnation, it has certainly opened new vistas for the employment of air power at the lower end of the spectrum of conflict.'[5]

Yet, India does not possess offensive capabilities remotely comparable with those of the US and Israel. Moreover, Pakistan possesses air defence capabilities far greater than those confronted by US and Israeli pilots and drone operators, as well as other air and ground capabilities backed by nuclear weapons. Beyond these substantial differences in capabilities, the US and Israeli experiences show that punitive air strikes often have not solved the problems they were meant to address. In Iraq in the 1990s, Afghanistan in the 1990s as well as the ongoing war, and Lebanon and Gaza in 2006, 2008, 2009, and 2014, air strikes degraded adversaries' capabilities and won immediate political support for the governments that authorized them, but they did *not* produce durable strategic gains.[6]

Moreover, the US and Israeli experiences indicate that air power does not obviate the need for ensuing ground operations. Indian (and Pakistani) military strategists understand this. Ground forces must be readied both in order to deter the opponent's escalation and also because air strikes alone may prove insufficient to compel the adversary to demobilize, if not dismantle terrorist organizations. For these reasons, then, one should evaluate air strike options first as a stand-alone concept of military operations, and second as a stage in a conflict that could escalate to major land warfare—by plan or due to action–reaction processes.

In this chapter, we puzzle through the dilemmas involving Indian use of limited air power against Pakistan, including the potential benefits, risks, and escalation potential of selecting certain targets, and the need for ground mobilization to back up an air power option. We then assess the capabilities that India currently has and would need to prosecute effective airstrikes against Pakistan.

Kashmir or Heartland?

In selecting kinetic options to punish Pakistan and motivate its leaders to demobilize anti-India terrorist groups, Indian decision makers would begin by determining the location and category of targets to strike in Pakistan. Sorting through the logic of targeting choices reveals the complexity of executing a retaliatory strike in a way that furthers India's strategic objectives.

A threshold question would be whether air strikes should be conducted against targets in Kashmir, which is the scene of regular cross-border violence, or in the Pakistani heartland of Punjab and Sindh. It is notable that both Indian and Pakistani defence officials and experts consider attacks on non-state targets in Kashmir as inherently less provocative. As a foreign policy advisor to the BJP put it in an April 2014 interview, 'India must react if there is another Mumbai-like attack. The only option is to do some sort of surgical strike in POK [Pakistan-occupied Kashmir]. This is territory that is legally disputed, that both sides acknowledge is disputed.'[7] By focusing action in Kashmir, India would demonstrate that 'terrorism is not cost free and that our military's hands have been untied', while putting the burden of further escalation onto Pakistani leaders, he said. If Pakistan then retaliated by expanding the conflict beyond Kashmir, India would then be seen as justified in mounting wider operations in Pakistan.

The differences between attacks in Kashmir and in the heartland point to strategic dilemmas for Indian decision makers. Attacking targets in Kashmir with air power, and not merely artillery as is normally done, would be somewhat escalatory. Yet it also would signal a measure of restraint, as compared with attacking targets in Pakistan's two eastern provinces. Striking targets in Pakistani Kashmir would convey an Indian interest in meting out visible punishment against Pakistan, which could satisfy Indian public opinion and political imperatives for the government. Indian leaders also would consciously signal a greater willingness to risk escalation than was evident after the terror attacks on New Delhi in 2001 and Mumbai in 2008. But confining the targets of Indian strikes in this way could unintentionally lead Pakistani decision makers to feel that the price they were paying for the instigating terror attack against India was not so great as to require a change in Pakistani support or tolerance of anti-India terrorist groups. After all, the Pakistani heartland would have been spared.

Indian air attacks on the Pakistani heartland would be much more punitive and provocative. Such attacks could reinforce the compellence message Indian leaders would wish Pakistan to receive. This could motivate Pakistani decision makers to act more decisively against terrorist groups, as India wants. In attacking terrorist-related targets in the Pakistani heartland, Indian leaders could reasonably feel and argue that they were responding symmetrically and proportionately to terrorist attacks against India's heartland. On the other hand, attacking the heartland could cause Islamabad to fight back more intensively to defy New Delhi and signal that Pakistan cannot be coerced.

Attacking targets in Punjab or Sindh also raises another troubling asymmetry. The government in New Delhi would unambiguously authorize the Indian strikes, unlike the initial terrorist attack imputed to Pakistan. If India (or other governments' intelligence agencies) did not have unmistakable proof that the leaders of Pakistan authorized the initial terrorist attack, an asymmetry in responsibility could be perceived. Pakistani leaders and society could feel that their homeland was being attacked unjustifiably—an act of aggression rather than of retaliation in self-defence. This would create strong motivation for Pakistan to respond militarily, opening the way to cycles of escalation. In a war that escalated on this basis, regional and international attention would shift from the original act of terrorism perpetrated on India to the mutual responsibility of Pakistan and India for the ensuing destruction and carnage. Such a shift would be a net loss for India.

Of course, if India could demonstrate clearly to Pakistanis and the world that the original terrorist attack was the responsibility of Pakistani authorities, the legitimacy of Indian counter-strikes on terrorist-related targets in Pakistan would be difficult to deny. Then the question would be effectiveness and what ensued next. Striking targets in the heartland of Pakistan would show India's willingness to take risks to compel Pakistani leaders to dismantle terrorist organizations and infrastructure, but, to repeat, it could also impel Pakistani military leaders to demonstrate their own resolve and capabilities to deny India any claim of victory. Otherwise, the standing of whomsoever in Pakistan was held responsible for the situation—be they military or civilian leaders— would be jeopardized in the inevitable domestic recriminations which would ensue.

Camps, Leaders, or State Targets?

Beyond the strategic logic and escalatory dynamics entailed in choosing where to conduct air strikes, different categories of targets present varying potential benefits and risks at the operational level. The least escalatory option would be to target terrorist camps and other infrastructure in Kashmir. Yet as noted above, few Indians or Pakistanis believe that attacking terrorist targets in Kashmir would cause Pakistani officials to change their policies or mobilize Pakistani civil society to press for such change.

There are operational challenges and risks, too. Terrorists and their installations can move easily. It is difficult to know in real time whether suspected camps are occupied. If a targeted site were empty, or women and children were harmed, Pakistani authorities would project the resultant images on television and other media to make India look dastardly, inept, or both. The former acting director of the US CIA, Mike Morell, recounts in his memoir that the United States' cruise missile attacks in 1998 on Osama bin

Laden in Afghanistan and a suspected chemical weapons plant in Sudan turned into important victories for Al-Qaeda. By surviving the onslaught of 75 cruise missiles, bin Laden gained more status. And, according to Morell, the mistaken destruction of 'an aspirin factory' in Sudan embarrassed the US in ways that 'no doubt' emboldened its enemies.[8]

Interviews with Indian interlocutors with extensive government experience highlighted these challenges. 'We might have acquired precision munitions, but the data we have on the camps and infrastructure is not so accurate,' said one former intelligence officer. 'We have sent people with GPS to locate the camps precisely, but then these camps can be moved easily.'[9] A BJP foreign policy advisor added, 'The terrorist infrastructure in POK may be ramshackle. These may be camps that could easily be rebuilt, so it's true, we could hit them one day and they could reappear soon after. Also, there is a risk that strikes could kill civilians and create a propaganda bonanza for Pakistan and the terrorists.'[10]

A second category of potential targets would be the Pakistani military and intelligence infrastructure in Kashmir, which India might select if it believed such installations to be associated with infiltration of militants into India. While few international observers would find such targeting to be unjustified if there were clear evidence of Pakistani state complicity in the preceding terrorist attack on India, the Pakistani military leadership likely would take a different view. International pressure, if applied sharply and immediately on Rawalpindi, could complicate Pakistani decisions to respond militarily against India. However, Indian leaders could not count on such pressure being adeptly mobilized in time, nor could they be confident that international pressures would restrain Pakistani leaders.

The anti-India militants who prepare for and conduct operations from Pakistan's side of Kashmir are merely foot soldiers. Leaders of groups such as LeT, and of the Pakistani security establishment who support them, are based in Punjab and Sindh. These leaders and the infrastructure that surrounds them would represent a more strategically important target of Indian retaliatory strikes. This third category of potential targets could include the 200-acre LeT complex at Markaz-e-Taiba, near Muridke, about 30 kilometres from Lahore.

The attractiveness of targeting well-known headquarters of groups such as LeT is obvious at one level—at least obvious both to Indians and Pakistanis.[11] These headquarters are symbolically important even if they are not necessarily where terrorist organizations plan and orchestrate operations against India. Indeed, immediately after a high-profile terrorist attack on India, the leaders and operatives of the groups allegedly responsible would take the precaution of staying away from well-known facilities, such as the campus in Muridke. Still, attacking such locations could give India the satisfaction of visibly holding the sponsoring organization accountable. Indian officials could proclaim that Pakistani authorities' failure to uphold their international obligations under UN Security Council resolution 1373 (to actively combat terrorists operating in and from their territory) left India no choice but to strike in self-defence.

Yet, the LeT campus at Muridke also reportedly contains a madrassa, hospital, market, residences, and farms, making it very likely that a strike would also kill non-combatants. It is improbable that the LeT keeps large stores of arms or other instruments of violence there, making it harder for India after the attack to demonstrate this was a legitimate target. Furthermore, Muridke is just 30 kilometres from Lahore; millions of non-militant Pakistanis probably would feel that India was striking too close to home. Indian leaders could hope that striking on the outskirts of Lahore would bring the costs of Pakistan's sub-conventional conflict to the heartland and motivate Pakistanis to tell their own government 'enough is enough'. Israeli officials offer a similar purpose behind the massive bombardment of Gaza—to turn non-combatant residents against Hamas. Yet, as has been the case in Gaza at least to some extent, and so too perhaps in Pakistan, attacks near Lahore could just as well rally Pakistanis against India.[12]

A former top-level officer of Pakistan's ISI Directorate put it this way when asked what would happen if India struck the LeT headquarters:

They talk of hitting Muridke. It's in the middle of a town! We know their capabilities. If a strike hits the outskirts of Lahore, in central Punjab, it would be a severe escalatory step. We'll strike back. We could hit camps where they work with the Baloch. Our argument would be the same as Indians argue. We don't want it to be escalatory, but it must be commensurate to what they did. If they kill 20, we can't just drop bombs in a field. We would claim we imposed *more* casualties than they did. It may be true or not, but the media will report it. An attack on Muridke will also lead to a mobilization on both sides. We would move troops to the border, as they will. We will move from the Eastern border—forget the war on terror. Fighting India would become the priority.[13]

Such comments may be self-serving and blustery, but it would be reckless to discount them entirely.

A fourth category of targets for precision strikes could be leaders of a group (or groups) that conducted the next major terrorist attack on India. Targeting individual terrorist leaders is operationally much more demanding than attacking headquarters and other facilities used by their organizations. (We discuss other, covert means of targeting individuals in the next chapter.)

Targeting specific leaders requires exceptionally precise intelligence and equally precise and quickly deliverable means of attack. If remote weapons were intended to make the kill, Indian officials would need to know exactly when and where targeted individuals are located, and that they would remain there for as long as the prescribed ordnance would take to reach the target. To minimize political backlash—in Pakistan, India, and internationally—Indian weaponry also would need to be aimed and scaled precisely enough to severely limit civilian casualties. Alternatively, India could seek to recruit one or more insiders who would have occasion to be near the target and to help guide the airborne attack.

To target individuals effectively while minimizing damage to non-targeted individuals and property, India would need constant and exact intelligence on targets' locations and surroundings.

In the cases of the US and Israel, this intelligence comes from expansive state-of-the art electronic surveillance, overhead imagery from drones and satellites, and networks of informants on the ground. The combination of technical and human intelligence is extremely difficult and expensive to acquire. Then, to deliver strikes in a timely and precise way, the US and Israel rely on drones and plane-delivered weaponry that are able to loiter over a potential target until a propitious moment to strike and then to put ordnance exactly on an aim-point. This generally is possible only in uncontested airspace.

The value of going after specific leaders depends on the retaliator's theory of how the target's death would affect the future. For example, would killing the leader of LeT, Hafiz Muhammad Saeed, motivate the surviving members of the organization to desist from further attacks on India? Would it motivate the Pakistani security establishment to do more to prevent the organization from conducting further attacks? Would killing an individual terrorist leader (or leaders) significantly degrade the organization's capacity to mount anti-India operations, and if so, for how long? How would Indian assassination of prominent jihadi leaders affect broader Pakistani political dynamics? Would it facilitate broader public support for government efforts to combat militant groups within Pakistan, or the reverse?

The answers to these questions are not obvious. The US has systematically targeted leaders of al-Qaeda in Afghanistan, Pakistan, Iraq, and Yemen from the air. Israel famously has conducted long assassination campaigns against leaders of Hamas's military wing. Pakistan itself recently has targeted leaders of the Pakistani Taliban with air-delivered ordnance. The impulse to do so is intuitively sensible. Among other things, killing known terrorist leaders may at least somewhat satisfy the desire for vengeful justice within the polities that these leaders' organizations have terrorized. This in turn may provide irresistible political benefits for the leaders of the retaliating governments, who otherwise could be accused by opponents of 'not doing enough'.

The challenge in evaluating the effects of targeted assassinations is even greater when a potential target plays multiple roles within their organization and society. A bomb-builder or operational planner is clearly a belligerent. Members and followers of their group, as well as of international society, expect that such people may be targeted as de facto combatants. But the wisdom of targeting a person such as Hafiz Saeed is less clear, for he is seen in Pakistan as a spiritual and political leader of a broader movement that promotes political change and social welfare (at least for its followers) in addition to jihad on behalf of Kashmiri Muslims.

While few reasonable people could doubt that his organization, LeT, has perpetrated attacks on non-combatants in India, Saeed's broader role in Pakistan makes him appear to be more than a combatant. Jamaat-ud-Dawa—or JuD, the political parent of LeT that Saeed heads—has functioned as a charity, providing free schools and hospitals as well as relief to those affected by natural disasters in the region. The US State Department's decision to sanction the group in the summer of 2014 was met with defiance by the Pakistani government. The JuD released an official statement afterward announcing that State Department sanctions 'always helps us get more support in Pakistan'.[14] Additionally, the JuD clearly liaises with Pakistan's ruling Pakistan Muslim League Nawaz (PML-N) party, which governs Punjab province, and politicians from mainstream political parties have shared the stage with Saeed at JuD rallies. Thus, people would view the killing of Saeed in a different light than, say, killing a terrorist commando at a camp where he is preparing followers for missions in India.

Indians might get deeper satisfaction from removing a figure of Saeed's stature, but strategically, the result could make it more difficult for Pakistani authorities to compel LeT followers to desist from further attacks on India.[15] It is thus wise for Indian leaders to ask whether an Indian attack on LeT infrastructure or targeted against its leadership in Punjab would reinforce the ISI's restraint of the organization or, instead, motivate both the LeT and the ISI to retaliate. A long-time Indian intelligence specialist on Pakistan offered a plausible answer: 'Taking out Hafiz Saeed would be bigger to the Pakistanis than when the United States took out Osama bin Laden. It would be a big blow to the Pakistan Army if he were killed. So they would be motivated to strike back.'[16]

President Barack Obama made the extremely rare decision to order the killing of an American citizen on foreign territory when he authorized a drone strike on the charismatic imam-cum-terrorist Anwar al-Awlaki in Yemen in 2011. Since then, as Scott Shane reports in a 2015 book, investigators have discovered that almost all of the terrorists conducting attacks in the US have been inspired by Awlaki.[17] Shane notes that 'Awlaki's pronouncements seem to carry greater authority today than when he was living, *because* America killed him.' As Mohamed Elibiary, a conservative Republican security consultant, told Shane, 'If you're trying to fight a martyrdom culture, you don't go make martyrs....In that world [of terrorists] you find that they're convinced that Anwar al-Awlaki is a good guy and a martyr....What seals the deal for them is that he was killed by the United States.'[18] If you substitute 'India' for the 'United States' in imagining the effects of airborne assassination strikes on charismatic militants in Pakistan, the results probably would not be very different.

None of the scholars who study the subject argue that killing leaders of organizations that conduct terrorism solves the strategic challenges of counterterrorism.[19] At best, targeted killing is sometimes an effective tactic that can in limited ways contribute to a larger strategy. If assassinating terrorist leaders were strategically decisive, though, Israel presumably would not have felt the need to keep doing it for five decades. The US drone and special operations assassinations in Afghanistan would not have gone on for 13 years with no end in sight. This is not to say that sparing the lives of leaders of groups that practice terrorism would yield better results. But the gains of targeted killings clearly are insufficient to accomplish strategic objectives.

The more telling explanation for Israeli and US continued reliance on targeted killing is that this tactic acquires a momentum of its own and political leaders see more short-term benefits in persisting with it than in questioning long-term implications and sustainability. At least they are doing something. Voters appreciate this. And it is easier for leaders of terrorized states to authorize targeted killings than to explain why they would eschew them.

Assessing Airpower Operations

Use of fighter-bombers or missiles across the LoC in Kashmir would represent the most daring projection of Indian military power into Pakistani territory since the 1971 war. Attacking the Pakistani heartland, of course, would represent bolder action still. During the Kargil Conflict in 1999, the Vajpayee government ordered the IAF not to cross the LoC in conducting operations.[20] This injunction, along with the Pakistan Air Force's non-involvement in the planning and conduct of the Kargil incursion, helped enable the IAF to contribute importantly to India's victory without creating escalatory pressures. In a scenario where the IAF's objective would be to strike targets in Pakistan, the risks of escalation would be greater, as would be the signal of India's forceful resolve.

Operationally, the IAF would need to contend successfully with Pakistani air defences if strikes were to be delivered by Indian aircraft operating in Pakistani airspace. Pakistan's air defences, reportedly, have been significantly upgraded since the 2011 US raid on Osama bin Laden's compound revealed considerable gaps.[21] Some Indian analysts have signalled concerns about the lack of stealthy aircraft that could penetrate such defences.[22] Without stealth capability, standard procedures would call for India initially to conduct missile or bomb attacks on air defence installations and other capabilities to open corridors for follow-up attacks on the primary targets. If and when India possessed cyber or other non-kinetic means to disable Pakistani air defences, the scope and scale of kinetic action required to conduct air strikes on targets in Pakistan could be reduced. This could in turn reduce the escalatory risks of such attacks. Yet, cyber threats against Pakistan's command and control systems would cause Pakistan's military to take countervailing precautions which could increase risks of intentional or inadvertent escalation. For example, they could plan to launch conventionally-armed missile attacks on Indian military air bases and other fixed targets in the event that Pakistani air defences were shut down or corrupted.

In any case, the air defence assets that India would target, including air bases and intercepting fighter planes, would be owned and operated by the Pakistani military, not terrorist groups. Some Pakistani Air Force planes and pilots presumably would survive initial Indian attacks and stay in the air to repel Indian attackers. Thus, although India's primary targets would be terrorist-related, the Pakistani military also would be attacked directly. This, again, has clear implications for escalation.

If aircraft were used to conduct precision strikes, there is a risk that Pakistani air or ground defences could interdict them, creating the spectacle of wrecked Indian aircraft and dead or captured pilots. All of this could diminish the political support within India that the government would have intended the attack to produce. (Fear of pilot loss or capture is one reason why the US and Israel rely so heavily on drones and missiles to conduct strikes.)

Instead of using aircraft to strike Pakistan, India could opt to use ground-launched ballistic or cruise missiles armed with conventional ordnance to strike terrorist targets, similar to the US attack on al-Qaeda camps in Afghanistan in 1998 using 75 Tomahawk cruise missiles. Missile attacks would not require engaging Pakistani air defences, which could reduce the risks of casualties on both sides. India's ballistic missile arsenal is showing signs of slow improvement, and the 290-kilometre BrahMos cruise missile—co-developed with Russia—has undergone numerous operational tests and is reportedly in service.[23] (India's ballistic and cruise missile capabilities are discussed in greater detail in Chapter 5.)

Yet, Indian use of cruise or ballistic missiles would establish a new precedent in Indo-Pakistani conflict. Given the number and types of missiles Pakistan possesses and is developing for production, Indian leaders presumably would want to take great care before lowering the threshold for the use of these weapons. Moreover, India would want some confidence that Pakistani officials would not perceive that incoming missiles from India carried nuclear weapons, given that many ballistic and cruise missiles are capable of carrying both types of warheads with no visible distinguishing features between them. Otherwise, India could invite Pakistani nuclear counter-strikes.

As discussed further below, in all scenarios of limited, precise counter-strikes, Indian decision makers would have to prepare for Pakistani responses. India would have to mobilize elements of its Army and other services to deter and/or blunt reprisals by Pakistani forces. This mobilization would add time between the initial terrorist attack on India and even limited, punitive Indian air strikes on Pakistan. India's mobilization also would warn Pakistan, attenuating the element of surprise.

Air Strikes as Precursor to Ground Operations

Punitive airstrikes could have an appeal even if only to produce vivid pictorial images of Indian kinetic strength being visited upon Pakistani targets. However, Indian strategists and decision makers would be mistaken not to work through how limited air strikes could merely act as the first phase of a wider, longer war which would involve ground and naval forces, too.

The transition from air strikes to major ground warfare could come about for at least three reasons. First, Indian decision makers could conceive of air strikes as the first phase of a major air–land offensive into Pakistan, or at least Pakistani leaders might believe so. Second, notwithstanding Indian intentions merely to punish Pakistan with limited air strikes, Pakistan could respond more forcefully than India expected, thereby requiring India to counter-escalate with major ground operations. Third, India's limited air strikes, wherever and whatever their targets, could fail to compel Pakistani authorities to act against anti-India terrorist groups, leading Indian officials to conclude they must raise the compellence pressure by introducing ground forces, or else be seen to stop short of their objectives.

Indian and Pakistani officials and experts understand that significant ground forces would be mobilized by both sides in the event of Indian air strikes on Pakistan. This would occur whether or not the leaders of either state would initially plan to engage in ground warfare beyond the sorts of artillery exchanges which they routinely undertake across the LoC. In Bakshi's words, even limited air strikes 'must be accompanied by a partial or complete mobilization of the armed forces to cater for [sic] any Pakistani response'.[24]

'We have war-gamed this', a recently retired high-level Pakistani military strategist explained in a late-2013 interview. 'Air strikes are an option India has in response to something like Mumbai. But it cannot be separated. Indian air strikes will be answered by Pakistan. And there will be ground forces to back it up. So, the risk of escalation is there. You can separate air strikes from a ground war by three or four days but not longer.' This retired general grinned dismissively: 'It's different for the [United States]. When you go striking other countries, it is one-sided. The other side does not have an air force. There is an air vacuum. But not here.'[25]

A former Director General of the ISI responded similarly when asked why India should not find it more practical to use air power to respond to another attack like the one on Mumbai in 2008. 'India is not Israel,' he said, 'and we are not the Palestinians. It's not so one-sided. If India conducts air strikes on Pakistan, there will be serious escalation. Even after an LeT strike, if India used air strikes to hit an LeT camp, people here would react passionately. They would say India is acting like the US, like with Salala. Pakistan would have to retaliate.'[26]

Predictably, Indian advocates of air power downplay the risks of escalation. 'It's time to move away from "don't use air power because it is escalatory,"' exclaimed a recently retired high-ranking air force officer. He said India could minimize collateral damage with air power. With the correct and up-to-the-minute intelligence, India could strike at the right time. Unfortunately, this former officer intoned, 'Our political system will not allow this. There is a phobia that air power is escalatory. This should have changed after Kargil. Nuclear deterrence is very stabilized.

The only way to address subconventional aggression is with air power.'[27] This optimistic view may or may not be warranted. From India's perspective, the question would be how to plan to successfully manage possible escalation from air strikes into major combined-arms conflict, while retaining some clear idea about the means and potential decision points for terminating the conflict.

One of the more serious discussions of this challenge appears in the recent volume by Bakshi quoted earlier in the chapter. Bakshi is clearly on the hawkish side of the retired Indian officer corps, as a current high-level national security official in the Modi government volunteered somewhat dismissively in an interview.[28] Yet, extreme or not, Bakshi has thought and written more seriously than most commentators about the challenges addressed here. Hence, it is instructive to quote him at length and then analyse the implications of the scenario he envisions.

Should Pakistan choose to escalate further [following limited Indian air strikes], air and naval power would be used to set the stage for a well synergized air-land offensive designed to heavily raise the costs for Pakistan's adventurism. The objectives of these air-land battles would be force-oriented and not terrain-oriented. Air power was used to launch an 'inside out attack' on the concentric rings of target systems in Iraq. At the innermost ring was the political leadership. It was repeatedly struck. Though it survived, it was kept so preoccupied with survival, that it was rendered dysfunctional for the command and control functions. The communication, control and transport infrastructure was significantly destroyed. The fielded forces were then attacked and disabled significantly. This comprehensive air attack set the stage for the 100 hours ground war. The land forces had but to exploit the phenomenal success of the air campaign ...The rest was a foregone conclusion.[29]

Thus, in envisioning a 'limited war' against Pakistan, Bakshi and others not only underestimate the transitional challenges from limited strikes to combined-arms warfare, but also insist that the latter 'would only be necessary if Pakistan wishes to fight on to defend its non-state actors, who have routinely been wreaking havoc in India'.[30] This misstates the issue in several ways. If and when India struck targets beyond individuals and facilities directly related to terrorist organizations such as LeT, Pakistani leaders would be defending themselves, their territory, their institutions, and their people. Such would clearly be the case if limited air strikes transitioned into combined ground and air operations in Pakistan. The more profound misstatement of the issue derives from the fact, unrecognized by many Indian commentators, that India seeks to motivate Pakistani authorities not merely to cease defending 'its non-state actors'. India's objective is also for Pakistani security agencies to take active measures to disband these actors or at least deny them the capacity to attack India.

If precise, airborne Indian strikes could destroy enough anti-Indian terrorists and their supporting infrastructure to render them impotent or sufficiently demoralized to give up their violent struggle, then this option would be strategically attractive. But if strikes could not obtain this result, or in the process also destroyed non-terrorist targets in ways that caused Pakistan to escalate and thereby widen the war, then it is difficult to have confidence that the tidily idealistic scenarios of the sorts offered by proponents of precision air power would come to pass. India could imagine achieving a splendid military victory like the US did in Iraq, but still not accomplish its strategic purposes vis-à-vis Pakistan.

The foregoing analysis suggests that if India were to undertake punitive limited air strikes, it should take pains to prevent escalation to major ground warfare. Whether and how this could be done *while still* compelling Pakistani authorities to demobilize anti-India terror groups remains a daunting challenge whose solution has not yet been presented in credible ways by Indian or outside analysts.

Escalation under the Nuclear Shadow

The assertion that air strikes would 'ensure escalation dominance' also deserves more careful analysis.[31] In a contest between states that do not possess weapons of mass destruction, the state with effective advantages in ground, air, and sea power can enjoy some confidence that it can win at whatever level of violence the adversary is willing to fight. In a confrontation between roughly balanced armed forces backed by approximately matched nuclear arsenals, few sober analysts would say that escalation dominance can be 'ensured'. Between states with a conventional power asymmetry, nuclear weapons change the dynamic because the weaker side still can inflict enough damage on the stronger to render victory meaningless.

The central issue is not that Pakistan would use nuclear weapons in response to limited Indian air strikes on Pakistan. Rather, it is that Pakistan could be emboldened to engage India in an escalation spiral that would create risks far in excess of the damage done by the initial act of terrorism. India could increase the intensity and scope of conventional conflict to prevail over Pakistan's conventional manoeuvres, but at some point, Indian battlefield victories could drive Pakistan to use nuclear weapons to compel India to stop, or else force India to risk mutual nuclear devastation.

Recognizing this, decision makers should be expected to ask not only for best-case scenarios of moves and counter-moves that could ensue from planned strikes, but also for plausible less-than-best-case scenarios. And they should specify the broader strategic objectives they want military plans to achieve. One former high-ranking Indian official who participated in decision-making during military crises and the Kargil conflict laughed in a 2014 interview when presented with the notion that air strikes on terrorist infrastructure in Kashmir could teach Pakistan a lesson with little risk. 'So, I take out five camps; do it perfectly. Then he takes out the Srinagar airfield, saying to the world that India started it. Then what do we do?'[32] A retired Indian Air Marshal offered a similar reflection. 'I used to be a hawk,' this veteran said, 'but from a mature point of view, escalation dominance is only a theoretical proposition. It is an illusion. Can you control intensity of conflict, ratchet up and down? Remember, this would be in a contested airspace.'[33]

Part of the analytic challenge here is the inherent difficulty of predicting how an adversary will interpret one's military action. Indian decision makers may believe certain reprisals are restrained, but Pakistani leaders could actually perceive them very differently, as acts of war. The differences in perception reflect what experimental psychologists and neuro-scientists call 'prediction errors'. Nicholas Wright summarizes the problematic dynamic that can ensue:

When we make an action, we largely know when, where and how we will make the action. But the adversary does not have such insider knowledge. So, to the adversary the action is more unexpected, has a larger associated prediction error and so has a stronger psychological impact than we understand ourselves. As this occurs with the actions of both sides, it can lead to a spiral of inadvertent escalation.[34]

In an ideal world, Indian decision makers undertaking what they intend to be limited, precise reprisal strikes on Pakistan could rely on the supposition that Pakistani leaders would perceive an attack just as India intended it to be perceived: limited, justified, and meant to end the conflict. But, given the uncertain psychological processes involved, and the history of Indo-Pakistani relations and conflicts, caution is called for.

In this regard, war games and simulations can help elucidate how competitors may act in various conflict scenarios, albeit with understandable caveats about generalizing from the outcomes of these scripted exercises. A March 2013 simulation involving teams of former senior Indian and Pakistani Army and Naval officers and academic specialists is useful to consider at some length here.[35] The game participants were tasked to respond to a crisis that was imagined to begin in November 2018 with a terrorist attack on a cricket match in Jaipur that killed the Indian defence minister and hundreds of spectators. After a brief and unsuccessful diplomatic interlude, the Indian team imposed a 'Maritime Exclusion Zone' of the Makran coast and began air, artillery, and special forces strikes against Pakistani infrastructure and military targets along the LoC in Kashmir. Targets included alleged terrorist training camps, bridges, and brigade headquarters.

Although the Pakistani team 'had expected India to retaliate', it anticipated reprisals against the terrorist source of the Jaipur attack. The Pakistanis felt that the Indian team 'went too far by striking against Pakistani soldiers, who had nothing to do with the Jaipur incident'.[36] For its part, the Indian team felt that evidence 'that elements of the Pakistani government had knowledge of the impending attack in Jaipur' provided justification for attacking the Army brigade headquarters in Kashmir. Furthermore, and realistically, the Indian team argued that it was difficult to identify and target specific LeT operatives and facilities, and that even if such targets could be hit, they would not decisively affect the organization. Nor, in the Indian view, would attacking LeT targets alone 'deter the Pakistan government from supporting terrorist organizations in the future'. 'In short, the India team argued that the Jaipur attack was a Pakistani act of war, whereas the Pakistan team portrayed India's disproportionate aggression...as an act of war.'[37] Thus, 'what began as a limited war escalated quickly to a full-scale war'.[38] The simulation ended as the Pakistani team authorized the release of nuclear weapons to the Strategic Forces Command with associated signalling of missile tests and other public statements.

Reviewing the events, the simulation's authors concluded, among other things, 'that a conflict might remain limited if Indian aggression is restricted to one-off airstrikes against terrorist targets situated in the disputed territory of Jammu and Kashmir'.[39] Indeed, our interviews with former high-ranking Pakistani military officers suggest a similar conclusion. However, this merely restates the problem that India confronts: the military action it could take against Pakistan with the least risk of escalation would likely not be sufficient to compel Pakistani authorities to decisively demobilize the most effective anti-India terrorist organizations. Limited air strikes against terrorist targets across the LoC could demonstrate India's willingness to act militarily and punish Pakistan, but the confined nature and objective of the action would at the same time suggest an inability and/or lack of resolve to compel Pakistani decision makers to change their policies.

Assessing Capabilities

For any of the scenarios considered above, India would need a suite
of intelligence, surveillance, and reconnaissance (ISR) capabilities
and airborne weaponry. Here we briefly describe, based on open
sources, the availability of such capabilities today and over the
next ten years. This analysis can be nowhere near as detailed
as that which would fully inform Indian officials or even what
independent analysts could provide if they were tasked to do so.
Indeed, the Naresh Chandra Task Force on National Security in
2012 urged that the government require preparation of an annual
classified report on military readiness to be provided to the
Cabinet Committee on Security for this purpose: to inject more
realism into national security policymaking and to improve force
planning and acquisition. Clear-eyed assessments of current and
forthcoming capabilities to conduct limited, precise air strikes
on targets which would be prioritized under a counter-terrorism
strategy should be conducted *before* Indian officials and media
trumpet them as viable means to change Pakistan's behaviour.

As noted earlier, conducting precise strikes on terrorist-related
targets requires extensive, reliable, and timely '24/7' intelligence.
If individuals are the target, then one needs accurate intelligence
to identify, locate, and track them, recognizing that they will
often move. If facilities—camps, depots, command buildings,
or apartments—are the target, they need to be identified and
monitored in order to ascertain who and what is within them.
Hitting empty or misidentified facilities or ones with women and
children in them can backfire in multiple ways.

The acquisition of such intelligence can come from multiple
sources. These include communications signals; imagery and
other information provided by satellites or unmanned aerial
vehicles (UAVs); and human intelligence, which can be especially
vital in avoiding mistakes and collateral damage in targeting
individuals. For all its vaunted technology, Israel's capacity to
target individual enemies has depended heavily on extensive
arrays of human sources.[40] Similarly, US targeting of individuals

in Iraq and Afghanistan also has depended frequently on human sources and extremely sophisticated signals-intelligence fused with rapid-action forces.

Much of India's capacity in these types of intelligence is publicly unknowable. However, interviews and experience suggest that there is vast room for improvement. A recently retired high-ranking IAF officer acknowledged this after speaking longingly of Israel's capabilities:

To be effective your intelligence has to be top flight. ISR has to be much better. How long will it take until we can do this? We still have a long way to go to get to the point where we can react quickly with precision. We are not in a position to react quickly now. You need constant intelligence with high accuracy, which we don't have.

India needs eight modern satellites for ISR, this man added, and now only has four. The acquisition process, he complained, 'is exceedingly slow'. The Mumbai attacks and other more recent events suggest that India does possess significant capabilities to intercept cell phone and radio communications from Pakistan. In the area of human intelligence in Pakistan, recently retired Indian officials intimated in interviews a serious inadequacy, as discussed more in Chapter 4.[41]

India's operational UAV inventory, and the capabilities of platforms with on-board detection systems, is difficult to assess from open sources. India has procured the Israeli Heron system, which is an earlier-generation surveillance drone that on paper features a 350-kilometre range and 52-hour endurance. In September 2015, Indian media indicated the government would proceed with a $400 million procurement from Israel of an upgraded version, the Heron TP, which would provide it with the option for 'covert cross-border strikes'.[42] Other reports indicate India is also seeking to purchase armed Predator drones from the United States.[43] India's DRDO has several domestic surveillance and tactical UAV programmes under development, but it appears that these programmes are unlikely to bear fruit at least for another five years and probably more.[44] In any case, using

UAVs for intelligence gathering or conducting strikes in Pakistan would have to contend with Pakistani air defences.

Perhaps the most significant challenge India faces in mounting air strikes in Pakistan is in what one might term 'information fusion'. For time-sensitive intelligence to prove useful, communications systems and procedures must be available to move it in a timely manner from intelligence assets to analysts to decision makers to operators of weapons who would strike a chosen target. Airborne information-control platforms are essential for this task. India's DRDO has been developing an indigenous airborne early-warning and control system, which it has mounted on an Embraer-145 jet, but this system is not yet in service with the IAF. India reportedly has also purchased two modules of the Israeli-made Phalcon early-warning and control system, which is mounted on the larger but slower Il-76 aircraft.[45] Thus, for the time being, India appears to lack adequate capabilities in this area, particularly if the task involved precision targeting that requires real-time intelligence.

The late Air Commodore Jasjit Singh assessed in 2011 that

since the retirement of the MiG-25, the IAF does not possess strategic intelligence capability and RISTA (reconnaissance, intelligence, surveillance, and target acquisition) system for employment of precision-guided munitions. This will partly be taken care of with AESA (Active Electronically-Scanned Array) radar of combat aircraft [being developed by DRDO] and suitable weapon suit [sic] duly integrated to the aircraft. But IAF badly needs integral air intelligence capabilities possibly from near earth satellites and high-altitude long endurance UAVs.[46]

Unlike ISR, much more is known about the status of India's kinetic capabilities, for these tend to be written about more frequently and authoritatively by Indian analysts. A survey of this literature indicates that India currently maintains several squadrons of fighter and attack aircraft—the most capable being the MiG-29, Su-30, and Mirage 2000—which it is seeking to improve through a number of major (albeit delayed) procurement programmes. But Indian efforts to transition the IAF to more modern systems have been painful, and reliability remains a serious challenge. For example, the entire Su-30 fleet was grounded, for the third time, for nearly a month in the fall of 2014. According to one critical Indian analyst, the

Combat aircraft fleet is substantially depleted, its transport fleet is inadequate to meet strategic airlift requirements and the helicopter force is barely capable of achieving all its tasks. The IAF needs more Flight Refuelling Aircraft (FRA) and airborne early warning systems to cover all contingencies. The basic trainer aircraft fleet is grounded and advanced training is severely hampered by the absence of a modern trainer aircraft in sufficient numbers. The airfield infrastructure needs to be modernized to operate new acquisitions.[47]

It is apparently a similar story regarding precision-guided munitions and other ordnance that India might use in a strike on Pakistan. India has numerous Russian-origin air-delivered weapons, some with stand-off capability and dual guidance systems for beyond-visual range targeting.[48] The DRDO is also reportedly developing laser-guided bombs and other precision-guided munitions, but the organization's disappointing track record suggests that combat-ready capabilities are not on the near horizon.[49] Interoperability with India's varied squadrons of fighter aircraft, some of which are in the midst of upgrade programmes, is an apparent problem.

In the next decade, on paper at least, India will upgrade its fighter capabilities through procurement of 36 new medium, multi-role combat aircraft, the French-supplied Rafale. If this purchase actually is completed, and the planes are delivered, they may resolve some of the reliability problems plaguing current weapons platforms. Yet, unless and until India addresses the numerous integration challenges of its air platforms and delivery systems, it seems likely the country will not possesses the kind of penetration capabilities that would facilitate successful strikes in Pakistan. In the words of one Indian analyst,

Like in Kargil, the Indian Air Force will be able to carry out limited precision strikes from heavily protected airspace, but will not be able to do so from inside Pakistani air space owing to heightened vulnerability and susceptibility to being intercepted...Should the current trajectory persist...the IAF will not be in a position to be a fully functioning force by 2030.... Consequently, India appears, not at least until 2030, to be able to conduct the kind of warfare it seeks to carry out—emulating Western offensives, coercion, or dissuasion that are largely air-based.[50]

It is worth noting that the IAF has not fought a full-scale war since 1971, when the information-management and force-integration challenges inherent in twenty-first century warfare did not pertain. Two generations of technological change have since occurred in fighter-bomber aircraft. But beyond the limited and largely uncontested experience in Kargil, Indian air forces have had little practice with modern systems in conducting operations like those that would be prescribed in a land–air war with Pakistan. In the Kargil conflict, as detailed by the RAND Corporation's Benjamin Lambeth and numerous Indian accounts, the Indian Army and Air Force experienced a 'near-total lack of transparency and open communications'.[51] Operationally, on 27 May 1999, two days after the air force was ordered into action, engine failure downed a Mig-21 and a Pakistani surface-to-air missile shot down a Mig-27. Pakistan captured the pilot of the first plane; the second pilot was killed. A day later, a Pakistani Stinger missile struck down a Mi-17 helicopter. A surveillance plane also was hit but made it back to base safely. The IAF quickly adapted and ended up playing a vital role in helping to win the conflict, but Kargil revealed numerous problems that many observers still believe have not been adequately redressed.

Finally, as discussed above, the strategic and operational value of highly synergistic air and land forces is indisputable. Overall, India's current readiness to conduct effective operations synergizing the Army and Air Force is questionable.[52] In an excellent analysis of the conventional military balance, Walter Ladwig reports that the Indian Air Force has not embraced the mission of providing close air support to the Army, and that 'based on recent experience there are good reasons to believe that the ability of aircraft to target defenders in well-prepared fighting positions, even with precision guided munitions (PGMs) is limited'.[53]

The problems extend from the lack of interoperable communications systems and air defences to unreconciled doctrinal preferences and actual combat experience. Much of India's air arsenal entails incompatible systems procured from multiple sources with varying degrees of quality. Military exercises are no substitute for actual combat practice with suboptimal systems. Even at the level of exercises, the Indian Army and Air Force have not inspired each other's confidence in their capacity to conduct effective combined operations in realistic warfare conditions.

★   ★   ★

In a world where the US and Israel are the models of forceful trans-border military action to strike terrorists and related infrastructure, it is natural that Indian analysts and officials long to emulate them. India faces terrorist threats emanating from Pakistan that are at least as severe as those faced by the US and Israel. Yet—however one evaluates the long-term strategic benefits and costs of US airborne attacks on terrorists in Iraq, Afghanistan, Yemen, and other places, and of Israeli air campaigns in Gaza and Lebanon—India for the foreseeable future lacks the various air power capabilities deployed by Israel and the US. As importantly, India confronts in Pakistan an adversary that has nuclear weapons and other offensive and defensive capabilities that complicate India's options in ways that US and Israeli adversaries do not limit theirs.

Yet, India's armed forces and intelligence agencies, as well as other responsible organs of the state, necessarily will continue to search for ways to apply military instruments and tactics to the challenge of blunting and punishing potential terrorists and motivating Pakistani authorities to do the same. Precise, airborne strikes are, broadly, a serious option.

This chapter has explored some of the considerations that would inform the development of capabilities, plans, and decision-making about whether, when, and how to exercise this form of kinetic power. Our analysis, which we offer for debate and improvement by Indians and others, suggests that the surface attraction of limited, precise airborne strikes is offset significantly, if not equally, by risks and inadequacies. Many of the experienced Indians whom we interviewed recognize these points. Beyond the relatively easy-to-obtain objective of visibly inflicting damage on targets in Pakistan, which could have important domestic political value, the attainment of larger strategic goals through such strikes would be unlikely.

Notes and References

1. Ladwig, 'A Cold Start for Hot Wars?', 158–90; Joshi, 'India's Military Instrument'.

2. Manmohan Bahadur, 'Air Power: An Evaluation of the Threats and Challenges before the IAF', *FORCE*, August 2013. Available at: http://www.forceindia.net/AirPower.aspx.

3. Maj. Gen. (ret.) G.D. Bakshi, *Limited Wars in South Asia: Need for an Indian Doctrine* (New Delhi: Knowledge Books, 2010), 59.

4. Bakshi, *Limited Wars in South Asia*, devotes an entire chapter to lessons India can draw from Israel. See also N.C. Bipindra and Natalie Obiko Pearson, 'Modi Revives India-Israel Ties as Terrorism Threat Grows', *Bloomberg*, 20 November 2014.

5. Air Commodore Arjun Subramaniam, 'Air Power & Irregular Warfare in the Indian Context', *Indian Defence Review* 24, no. 1 (January–March 2009). Available at: http://www.indiandefencereview.com/interviews/air-power-irregular-warfare-in-the-indian-context/.

6. Regarding the 2006 Lebanon war, for instance, see Yogil Henkin, 'And What If We Did Not Deter Hizbollah?' *Military and Strategic Affairs* 6, no. 3 (December 2014): 123–49.

7. Interview with former senior official, New Delhi, 23 April 2014.

8. Michael Morell with Bill Harlow, *The Great War of Our Time* (New York: Twelve, 2015), 22.

9. Interview with former Indian intelligence officer in New Delhi, 24 April 2014.

10. Interview with BJP foreign policy advisor, New Delhi, 23 April 2014.

11. Amir Mir, 'India May Target Muridke to Avenge Attacks', *The News International*, 2 December 2008. Available at: http://www.thenews.com.pk/TodaysPrintDetail.aspx?ID=18732&Cat=13&dt=12/2/2008.

12. The literature on strategic bombing is generally supportive of the conclusion that targeting populations is an ineffective strategy for achieving political objectives. Michael Horowitz and Dan Reiter, 'When Does Aerial Bombing Work?', *Journal of Conflict Resolution*

45, no. 2 (April 2001): 155. For more discussion on strategic bombing, see: Ronald Schaffer, *Wings of Judgment: American Bombing in World War II* (Oxford University Press: 1985); Matthew Adam Kocher, Thomas B. Pepinsky, and Stathis N. Kalyvas, 'Aerial Bombing and Counterinsurgency in the Vietnam War', *American Journal of Political Science* 55, no. 2 (April 2011): 201–18; and Robert Pape, *Bombing to Win: Air Power and Coercion in War* (Ithaca, NY: Cornell University Press, 1996).

13. Interview with former ISI director general, Rawalpindi, 22 October 2013.

14. Dean Nelson and Rob Crilly, 'Pakistani Charity Is a Terror Front Which Attacked Indian Consulate, Says US', *The Telegraph*, 26 June 2014. Available at: http://www.telegraph.co.uk/news/worldnews/asia/pakistan/10928363/Pakistani-charity-is-a-terror-front-which-attacked-Indian-consulate-says-US.html.

15. Daniel Byman, in his major book on Israel's counterterrorism experience, notes the view of a close advisor to Yasir Arafat and writes that 'killing cell leaders often leads to revenge and becomes [sic] harder for moderates to champion a political, nonviolent alternative without looking like collaborators'. Daniel Byman, *A High Price: The Triumphs and Failures of Israeli Counterterrorism* (Washington, DC: Brookings Institution, 2011), 317.

16. Interview with former senior intelligence official, New Delhi, 24 April 2014.

17. Scott Shane, 'Dead Reckoning', *The New York Times Magazine*, 30 August 2015, 58. The list includes, among others, Mohammod Youssuf Abdulazeez, who killed four Marines and a sailor in Chattanooga, Tennessee, in 2015; two men who fired gunshots into a Prophet Muhammad cartoon contest in Garland, Texas, in 2015; and the Tsarnaev brothers, who bombed the Boston Marathon in 2013.

18. Shane, 'Dead Reckoning', 62.

19. The scholarly literature on the strategic effects of killing leadership figures suggests that the results are mixed at best. As one recent review of the leading studies of this subject concludes, there is no basis yet 'for making general pronouncements on whether targeted killing is or is not an effective counter-terrorism tactic'. Stephanie Carvin, 'The Trouble With Targeted Killing', *Security Studies* 21, no. 3 (Fall 2012): 529. See also Steven R. David, 'Fatal Choices: Israel's Policy of Targeted Killing', *Mideast Security and Policy Studies*, no. 51 (2002).

Available at: http://www.biu.ac.il/Besa/david.pdf; Bryan C. Price, 'Targeting Top Terrorists: How Leadership Decapitation Contributes to Counterterrorism', *International Security* 6, no. 4 (Spring 2012): 9–46; Audrey X. Cronin, *How Terrorism Ends: Understanding the Decline and Demise of Terrorist Campaigns* (Princeton: Princeton University Press, 2009); and David Ignatius, 'Killing Top Terrorists Is Not Enough', *Washington Post*, 5 March 2015.

20. It remains uncertain whether this order represented a strategic judgment about minimizing escalation or was a consequence of two Indian MiG aircraft being downed in the first two days of Air Force action in Kargil.

21. 'Pakistan Upgrades Air Defenses on Afghan Border,' *Express Tribune*, 9 December 2011. Available at: http://tribune.com.pk/story/304098/ pakistan-upgrades-air-defences-on-afghan-border/.

22. Captain B. Menon, 'Fifth Generation Fighter Aircraft for the Indian Air Force', *Indian Defence Review* 28, no. 2 (April–June 2013). Available at: http://www.indiandefencereview.com/news/ fifth-generation-fighter-aircraft-for-the-indian-air-force/.

23. Dilip Kumar Mekala, 'Good Times Ahead', *FORCE*, August 2013. Available at: http://www.forceindia.net/GoodTimesAhead.aspx.

24. Bakshi, *Limited Wars in South Asia*, 59.

25. Interview with former senior military officer, Rawalpindi, 25 October 2013.

26. Interview with former ISI director general, Rawalpindi, 22 October 2013. In 2011, NATO forces in Afghanistan conducted a cross-border raid on the checkpoint at Salala that killed 24 Pakistani soldiers and injured thirteen others. Pakistani officials strongly condemned the attack and briefly closed key supply routes to NATO forces in Afghanistan. Nick Childs, 'Pakistan Outrage After "Nato Attack Kills Soldiers"', BBC News, 26 November 2011. Available at: http:// www.bbc.co.uk/news/world-asia-15901363.

27. Interview with former senior Air Force officer, New Delhi, 24 April 2014.

28. Interview with senior official, New Delhi, 25 April 2014.

29. Bakshi, *Limited Wars in South Asia*, 150.

30. Bakshi, *Limited Wars in South Asia*, 151.

31. Bakshi, *Limited Wars in South Asia*, 59. The issue of escalation dominance is explored further in Chapter 5.

32. Interview with former senior official, Gurgaon, 23 April 2014.

33. Interview with former Indian Air Marshal, New Delhi, 12 November 2014.

34. Wright, 'Knowing How Your Adversary Thinks'; and Nicholas D. Wright, 'Neural Prediction Error is Central to Diplomatic and Military Signaling', in Diane DiEuliis, William Casebeer, Jim Giordano, Nicholas D. Wright, and Hriar Cabayan (eds), *White Paper on Leveraging Neuroscientific and Neurotechnological (NeuroS&T) Developments with Focus on Influence and Deterrence in a Networked World*, US Department of Defense Joint Staff, 2014.

35. Khan and French, 'South Asian Stability Workshop'.

36. A key conclusion of the simulation was that actions considered limited by one side have a significant potential to escalate. No matter how limited India perceives its response to be, Pakistan may perceive Indian actions as 'disproportionate and maximal' given India's significant military advantage. And, even if India were able to effectively signal the limited nature of its attack, it is unlikely that Pakistan would trust these claims. Khan and French, 'South Asian Stability Workshop', 14.

37. Khan and French, 'South Asian Stability Workshop', 14.

38. Khan and French, 'South Asian Stability Workshop', 1.

39. Khan and French, 'South Asian Stability Workshop', 2.

40. Byman, *A High Price*; Noam Ophir, 'Back to Ground Rules: Some Limitations of Airpower in the Fighting in Lebanon', *Strategic Assessment* 9, no. 2 (August 2006): 30–2.

41. Interviews with a former senior Air Force officer and a former senior defence official, New Delhi, 24 and 26 April 2014.

42. Sanjeev Miglani, 'India Turns to Israel for Armed Drones as Pakistan, China Build Fleet', *Reuters*, 22 September 2015.

43. N.C. Bipindra and Tom Lasseter, 'India Seeks Armed Drones from U.S. in Challenge to Pakistan', *Bloomberg*, 9 November 2015.

44. Regarding a DRDO UAV development programme, one assessment finds that 'given the DRDO's history of delays, a realistic estimate would be to assume that it will enter into service only by 2019–2020.' 'The Rise of Drones', *FORCE*, September 2014. Available at: http://www.forceindia.net/TheRiseofDrones.aspx. After a series of crashes of the DRDO-developed Nishant UAV, the Indian Army announced it would not induct any more of these drones into service. 'After Crashes, Army Set to Junk Nishant UAVs', *Times of India*, 20 November 2015.

45. Atul Chandra, 'Tough Task: Developing a Home-Grown AEW&C Platform is Going to be Time Consuming', *FORCE*, February 2013. Available at: http://www.forceindia.net/AeroIndia2013_ToughTask.aspx.

46. Air Cmde Jasjit Singh, 'Poised for Precision', *FORCE*, February 2011. Available at: http://forceindia.net/Forcemay/OctAirforcepdfs/Poised%20for%20Precision.pdf.

47. K.B. Menon, 'Modernization of India's Military Aviation', *Indian Defence Review* 26, no. 1 (January–March 2011). Available at: http://www.indiandefencereview.com/news/modernisation-of-indias-military-aviation/.

48. See for example articles on AS-11 (2014), Kh-29 (2014), Kh-59M (2014), and Kh-31 (2014), all in *Jane's Weapons: Air-Launched*, IHS Jane's.

49. DRDO chief Avinash Chander was fired in January 2015 after two reports slamming the agency were released by the Comptroller and Auditor Gen. (CAG) and Parliament's Standing Committee on Defence. The agency was found to have a poor track record of bringing projects to completion and also for keeping in mind the requirements of the end user. For example, of the forty-three major projects initiated by DRDO as part of its 11th Five Year Plan, not one has reached completion. Dilip Kumar Mekala, 'Off Target', *FORCE*, February 2015. Available at: http://www.forceindia.net/OffTarget_Feb 2015.aspx; 'ER-PGM (Enhanced Range Precision-Guided Munition)', *Jane's Weapons: Air-Launched*, IHS Jane's, 16 January 2015.

50. Abhijit Iyer-Mitra, *Flying Blind: Limitations on Innovation in the Indian Air Force* (Washington, DC: Carnegie Endowment for International Peace, forthcoming).

51. Lambeth, *Airpower at 18,000'*, 2. Indeed, the Chief of the IAF at the time, Air Chief Marshal A.Y. Tipnis recounted 'a total lack of army-air force staff work'. For his part, the then vice chief of the Army derided Tipnis and the Air Force for a series of alleged judgments and actions. See Lambeth, *Airpower at 18,000'*, 12–13.

52. B.S. Pawar, 'A Case for Jointness', *FORCE*, October 2013. Available at: http://www.forceindia.net/ACaseforJointness.aspx; Manmohan Bahadur, 'Separated at Birth', *FORCE*, September 2013. Available at: http://www.forceindia.net/SeparatedatBirth.aspx.

53. Ladwig, 'Indian Military Modernization and Conventional Deterrence in South Asia', 24.

4

COVERT OPERATIONS

Chapters 2 and 3 conveyed some of the considerable escalatory risks that conventional military operations could pose to India and Pakistan. These risks would obtain even after India overcame the deficits in military and intelligence capabilities that make an army-centric military campaign and/or precision air strikes inadvisable today. Recognizing these challenges, some current and former officials with relevant expertise suggest that India would be wiser to apply more subtle forms of coercion to punish Pakistan for not doing more to prevent terrorism against India. Covert action—targeting terrorists directly, or harming Pakistani state interests in order to motivate authorities to demobilize anti-India terrorists—conceivably could influence Pakistan with lower costs and risks of escalation than more conventional military alternatives.

One former Indian external intelligence officer summarized the case for covert operations this way: 'A strike on big camps or big installations can turn into conflagration. Lots can go wrong in terms of direct effects, mistaken targets, and in terms of Pakistan's reactions. Our riposte should be deniable. We should do things with deniability.'[1] In a February 2014 lecture three months prior to his appointment as national security advisor, Ajit Doval proffered a similar idea more colourfully. He suggested that Pakistan should be made to understand: 'You can do one Mumbai and you may lose Balochistan.'[2] Narendra Modi himself, in an April 2014 campaign speech, alluded to the possibility of India's targeting Dawood Ibrahim, the infamous alleged mastermind of the 1993 bombings of civilian targets in Mumbai, who is believed to be hiding now under Pakistani protection.[3]

In May 2015, India's Defence Minister Manohar Parrikar brought the issue of covert operations to the foreground of Indian debate and Indo-Pak relations. In a public meeting he stated, 'If any country, [say] Pakistan, is planning something against my country, I will take proactive steps. Of course, not in the public domain. But I have to do, I will do it. Whether it is diplomatic, whether it is pressure tactics or whether it is using the...*kaante se kaanta nikaalna* (using a thorn to extract a thorn).' To make his meaning clear, he reportedly went on: 'We have to use terrorists to neutralize terrorists.'[4]

Parrikar's remark came days after Pakistan's Prime Minister and Army Chief of Staff had met to discuss allegations that India's external intelligence agency, RAW, had intensified operations in Pakistan. This confluence of events highlighted the salience of covert operations in the two countries' relationship and perhaps suggested a potential symmetry that India had long denied. National Security Advisor Ajit Doval quickly sought to tamp the issue: 'Interpreting "kaante se kaanta nikalna" as [doing] covert operations...is not necessarily the correct interpretation', Doval said. 'It is a question of balancing the response to the threat. That is, your response capability and response plans must be compatible with the quantum and gravity of the threat so as to build up a deterrent.'[5]

The Parrikar and Doval remarks, and the Pakistani reaction to them, present some of the key attractions and challenges of covert operations. These are clandestine actions that states take to undermine the interests of opponents in lieu of normal diplomatic or military action. Covert operations may or may not involve the use of force. They are a form of coercion and interference in another state's internal affairs that the perpetrator will deny having conducted. Covert operations are attractive as an alternative to 'doing nothing' to deter or retaliate against an adversary and 'doing too much'.

The world is replete with examples of covert actions meant to threaten adversaries' interests enough to make them change their behaviour. The scale of such operations varies widely, reflecting degrees of coercive intent and calculations of risks and benefits that particular decision makers apply. States routinely recruit spies in other countries and produce and promulgate propaganda—truthful or otherwise—to advance their interests in adversary states. Some states clandestinely fund political and/or religious groups that may advance their interests abroad. States with advanced cyber capabilities can use them to manipulate communications systems without loss of life, or to cause other forms of economic and psychological disruption. Some states covertly provide arms or other instruments to actors who challenge the interests of adversaries, again with varying degrees of intensity and potential destructive effect. Further up the ladder of intensity, states have covertly sabotaged economic resources— gas pipelines, automated control systems, agriculture. More violently, states have covertly assassinated terrorists, political leaders, and others. And, of course, more than a few states have orchestrated clandestine coups, incursions, and other violent campaigns against foes.

In recent years, some states have employed uniformed military special forces for what are intended to be covert operations. These forces' operations are covert in the sense that they rely on stealth and secrecy and tend to involve relatively small units that enter and depart from foreign territory quickly. The United States' use of special forces in Afghanistan, Iraq, and elsewhere follows this pattern. In situations when deniability is especially important and the Laws of Armed Conflict may not be strictly followed, these American forces conduct operations under the mantle of the CIA. Recent conflicts in the Middle East, South Asia, and Ukraine further blur distinctions between armed conflict and clandestine operations. Russia, in its 'hybrid' invasion of Crimea and intervention in Eastern Ukraine, deployed military commandos without identifying insignia on their uniforms and equipment, denying that these forces are in fact Russian. The 9 June 2015 raid by Indian commandos against Indian rebels located on the Myanmar side of the border is yet a different example of a covert military operation, insofar as India reportedly notified Myanmar's government and was targeting Indian nationals, not those of Myanmar.

Operations are conducted covertly because their perpetrator does not want to be publicly identified. Secrecy is tactically necessary to enable the penetration of the adversary's domain to conduct operations. Often, covertness is sought because the action transgresses international law and/or is an exception made to normal national law, for example prohibitions on assassination. Covertness also can serve the strategic purpose of enabling the adversary to save face if 'he' changes behaviour in response to the signal sent by the attacking state. It may be easier for leaders to change current or planned behaviour in the face of covert threats than to be seen backing down from overt ones. The political–legal shadiness of covert operations should make law-respecting states seek a legal basis for conducting them even if this basis is discussed only in government councils and not publicly. A sense of legal correctness (albeit domestic) can buttress the morale of personnel carrying out such operations and can be indispensable in bilateral and multilateral diplomacy, even if India would still deny conducting such operations.

In the case of operations targeting terrorists in Pakistan or intending to motivate Pakistani authorities to demobilize such actors, Indian leaders could argue internally that Pakistan has proved either unwilling or unable to uphold its legal responsibility under UN Security Council Resolution 1373. Pakistan's failure to prevent terrorists from operating on its territory could then arguably, justify India acting in self-defence on Pakistani territory to pursue objectives that the Pakistani state is otherwise obligated to pursue. Of course, making such arguments publicly would invite cantering and negate the intended benefits of covertness.

For purposes of analysing the desirability and feasibility of Indian covert operations against Pakistan, we focus primarily on actions for which India would want to deny responsibility, and which India would not intend as acts of war justifying Pakistani military responses. Such actions would fall into the 'classic' category of covert operations. We focus on this category because Indian leaders generally recognize that Pakistan's security establishment would treat interventions by Indian military special forces on Pakistani territory as actions that would have to be retaliated against, with attendant risks of escalation. One of the attractions of non-military covert operations, by distinction, is that their deniability creates ambiguities that leave space for opponents not to retaliate, or to retaliate symmetrically without escalation. These characteristics help explain, for example, why knowledgeable Indian commentators recognized that the commando raid in Myanmar was not a model to be applied against Pakistan.[6]

Covert operations present a number of inherent risks and tensions. Mistakes can be made—wrong targets may be hit, correct targets may be missed, operations may achieve less damage or more damage than intended. Covert operations may be exposed and responsibility attributed to the perpetrator.

Clearly, tensions inhere between the political desire to demonstrate resolute strength by inflicting punishment on the adversary, and the strategic interest in deniability. While covert operations—by virtue of their secrecy and limited scale—may give the adversary political space to change its behaviour without appearing to give in to the state that is conducting them, this logic, again, limits the domestic political utility of covert operations. Moreover, the process of signalling via covert operations is difficult to calibrate with confidence.

Recognizing these risks and tensions (or not), India conceivably could seek to pursue many sorts of covert operations against Pakistan (much as Pakistan has against India, and the US, Russia, Israel, Iran, and others have against their adversaries). Such actions could be conducted in lieu of kinetic military operations such as air strikes and ground incursions of various scope, or they could be undertaken in tandem with, for example, largely symbolic air strikes on targets in Kashmir, as discussed in the prior chapter. Visible, symbolic air strikes could satisfy a domestic political imperative to demonstrate resolve, while covert operations could be intended to more directly threaten the interests of the Pakistani security establishment and thereby motivate it to demobilize anti-Indian groups.

Of course, as with options such as Cold Start or precision air strikes, major questions about Indian capabilities would need to be addressed. The intelligence officer quoted earlier in the chapter ruefully acknowledged, 'I don't think we have the capability' to conduct covert operations that would compel Pakistani authorities to demobilize anti-Indian terrorist groups.[7] Yet, before considering what sorts of capabilities India would need to develop, difficult strategic questions need to be answered. Beyond the immediate tactical effects of potential covert operations, it is important to consider the sequence of actions and reactions they may trigger. Assessment of the risks and benefits of possible action-reaction cycles can only be meaningful if the state's larger foreign policy objectives are clear and invoked in the analysis.

Evolution of Covert Operations in South Asia

To provide context for analysing future covert action policies that India might consider, it is useful to survey the history of India's and Pakistan's experiences with covert operations against each other. This discussion is not meant to be comprehensive; it is necessarily thin because covert operations are by definition secret and little reliable public information exists about them.

Pakistan has long undertaken covert actions to challenge India.[8] In the first conflict, in 1947, Pakistani authorities mobilized non-uniformed, 'irregular' forces to fight in Kashmir. In the 1980s, the ISI recruited, equipped, and trained Indian Sikhs who were part of the Khalistan movement that was waging a violent, terroristic campaign to create an independent country on the territory of Indian Punjab.[9]

Following rigged elections in the Indian state of Jammu and Kashmir in 1987, the Pakistani security establishment intensified covert operations in Kashmir. When Indian Muslims protested the election results, the ISI sought to mobilize disaffected Kashmiri groups. Pakistani political parties competed over who was most dedicated to helping Kashmiri Muslims. Benazir Bhutto's government was dismissed in 1990 and replaced by a coalition led by Nawaz Sharif, whose members had become especially vocal about liberating Kashmir. Coincidentally, the Soviet occupation of Afghanistan was winding down, leaving large numbers of battle-hardened mujahideen and their ISI handlers free to be redeployed eastward to Kashmir. With the new dispensation in Islamabad, the ISI moved boldly to mobilize and control the Kashmir insurgency, and to infuse foreign freedom fighters into the mix who were less independent-minded than native Kashmiris.[10] The Kashmir struggle flamed throughout the 1990s.

In 1993, Pakistan's intelligence service widened its reach and modus operandi in India. This move was prompted by a Hindu-extremist mob's demolition of the Babri Masjid in Ayodhya, India, on 6 December 1992. This mosque had been built in the sixteenth century to commemorate the Mughal invader Babur who had taken suzerainty over much of northern India. Many Hindus believe that this site marked the birthplace of the god Ram, and that a temple commemorating Ram had existed there and been torn down by the Muslims who built the Babri Masjid in its place. With so much historical and religious meaning invested in this one site, it was long the object of communal tensions. Bharatiya Janata Party leader L.K. Advani had elevated the demand to destroy the mosque into a central campaign objective during the 1989 national elections. Indian intelligence officials warned the government that demolition of this cherished structure would trigger communal violence in India and perhaps unleash a sequence of unwelcome events. For whatever reasons, the Indian authorities did not prevent the demolition on 6 December. Communal riots ensued. Three months later, on 12 March 1993, a series of 12 well-orchestrated explosions ripped through Mumbai, killing 235 innocent civilians. The attack caught the Indian intelligence and security apparatus completely off guard.[11] This was the first incident of mass casualty terrorism on Indian territory, and also the first directed against significant economic targets. Indian officials subsequently concluded that the ISI had instigated and supported the attack. The direct perpetrators were led by an Indian Muslim mafia boss, Dawood Ibrahim, who was then living in Dubai, and subsequently was said to be living intermittently in Pakistan and Afghanistan.

The 1993 Mumbai attack signalled several portentous developments. Since 1947, according to B. Raman, a long-time senior RAW official, Pakistan had been unable 'to instigate the Muslim youth of India outside J&K [Jammu and Kashmir] to take to jihad to assert the rights of the Muslim community and to protect themselves from the Hindus and what was perceived as the pro-Hindu police'.[12] Neither had Indian Muslims been lured to Pakistan to join the jihad against the Soviet occupation in Afghanistan. After the demolition of the Babri Masjid, however, Muslim youth outside of Kashmir became more susceptible to radicalization and recruitment into militancy. This changed environment helped embolden and enable the ISI to undertake, through proxies, terrorist violence in the Indian heartland.

In 1999, Pakistan returned to the covert form of intervention that it had undertaken in Kashmir in 1947. Pakistani forces, dressed as indigenous insurgents, infiltrated the Kargil area of Kashmir and captured a number of outposts, precipitating the Kargil conflict. Two years later, in 2001, terrorists allegedly with ties to Pakistan attacked the Parliament in New Delhi. In November 2008, operatives of the LeT attacked civilian targets in Mumbai, directed in real time by controllers in Karachi.

Throughout recent decades, Indian intelligence veterans add, Pakistani agents have distributed counterfeit currency, small arms, and drugs into India as part of their effort to undermine it.[13]

We recount these episodes to introduce the broad category of 'covert operations' and to sketch how the Pakistani security establishment has relied on them to exacerbate communal tensions, to divert India's military, intelligence, and internal security resources, and, in theory, to coerce it to be more forthcoming in accommodating Pakistani interests regarding Kashmir and other issues. Pakistani officials often have accused India of undertaking similar actions, but the publicly available evidence is not plentiful. This could be because India has in fact done much less than Pakistani officials assert, or because Indian officials have maintained effective secrecy. Knowledgeable Indians with high-level governmental service assert that India has conducted 'hardly any' violent covert action in Pakistan. Yet, to be true to the purposes of covertness, such knowledgeable people are expected to say this, whether it is true or not.[14] In any case, looking forward in an era when covert or 'hybrid' warfare seems to be more practical than overt conventional warfare, Indian policymakers will be tempted to invest more energy and resources into covert operations than their predecessors did.[15]

India established its foreign intelligence apparatus in 1968 with the creation of the RAW. Its primary mission was and is to collect and analyse intelligence on external threats. Like other such intelligence services, the RAW also developed an operational arm. This arm was first extensively used in 1971, as unrest mounted in East Pakistan after politicians and the Army in West Pakistan refused to heed the demands for autonomy made by the Bengali political party that had won a majority in the December 1970 Pakistani elections. When the Pakistan Army moved to crush the Awami League in East Pakistan, civil conflict erupted. Massive streams of refugees—the vast majority of them Hindus who were being targeted for killing—flowed into India. Indian leaders began to prepare to intervene, both to remove the cause of the human inflow and to defeat the Pakistan Army. The RAW operatives undertook covert operations to support, train, and arm the Bengali resistance and to prepare the ground for the subsequent intervention by Indian armed forces that created the independent country of Bangladesh. During this period, India is also thought to have supported insurgent groups in Balochistan and Afghanistan. According to Praveen Swami, following the major victory over Pakistan in 1971, 'India withdrew support for Baloch guerrillas fighting the Pakistan army, and slashed its involvement with anti-Islamabad forces in Afghanistan.'[16]

The RAW's next major covert campaign occurred in the 1980s to contest Pakistan's covert support of the Khalistan movement among Sikhs in India's Punjab. The RAW reportedly learned through its contacts with Afghanistan's intelligence service that the ISI was hosting training sites for Sikh militants in tribal areas of the then Northwest Frontier Province (known as Khyber-Pakhtunkhwa today), and providing arms and ammunition from Army stocks. Prime Minister Rajiv Gandhi ordered the RAW to counter the Khalistan movement and ISI's support for it. According to an Indian media report, 'RAW set up two covert groups of its own...the first targeting Pakistan in general and the second directed specifically at the Khalistani groups. The two groups were responsible for carrying out insurgency inside Pakistan! A low-grade but steady campaign of bombings in major Pakistani cities, notably Karachi and Lahore were carried out.'[17]

The RAW's covert counter-campaign of violence in Pakistan created a logic for both countries to negotiate reciprocal disengagement from violence in each other's territory, though it remains murky whether officials acted on this logic.[18] In any case, the perception took hold in Pakistan and India that the Indian covert operations in Pakistan helped motivate the ISI to stop interfering in Indian Punjab.[19] Former Indian officials add that the ISI's diminished involvement in Punjab corresponded with its mobilization of the violent insurgency in Kashmir.

Pakistani authorities from the 1980s through the mid-1990s also accused India of covertly fomenting challenges by disaffected elements in Sindh against the Punjab-dominated central government. Indian sources generally deny this, arguing that the problems in Sindh were of the ISI's own making.

In 1997, Inder Gujral became Prime Minister of India at the head of a coalition government. As foreign minister in the preceding years, and then as prime minister, he developed and sought to implement what became known as the 'Gujral Doctrine'. In his own words, this was

a doctrine of good neighbourliness. In South Asia, India is the largest country and the largest economy. All the countries of the neighbourhood put together cannot match India. Therefore, it is my doctrine, that in the post-Cold War era, all the neighbours must look up to India as a friendly neighbour. For doing so, if concessions have to be given, they should. But these concessions do not include two things: no transfer of sovereignty of any part of India, including Kashmir; and second, we will not compromise on our basic secular, democratic polity. Minus these two factors, we are willing to give concessions as long as it does not hurt our defence.[20]

As part of his peace offensive, Gujral ordered the RAW to cease covert actions in Pakistan and to demobilize the assets that had been developed to pursue them. The RAW was now to confine its activities in Pakistan to collecting intelligence. In Raman's words, 'What Gujral ordered to be closed accounted for only about 15 per cent of the R&AW's operations in Pakistan. He encouraged the remaining 85 per cent to continue,'[21] which was focused on collecting and analysing intelligence.

Gujral's decision had long-term implications. As Raman reported, 'Many intelligence officers met Gujral and tried to explain that building a covert action capability took a long time. If one day the Government felt the need for resuming covert actions, there would be no trained and experienced assets on the ground.' It takes years to identify, recruit, and cultivate reliable human agents in an environment where opposing intelligence and security services are doing all they can to root out such spies or turn them into double agents. According to Raman, Gujral 'could not be convinced'.[22]

Gujral's tenure ended in 1998, when the BJP returned to power under the prime ministership of Atal Behari Vajpayee. (In 1996, Vajpayee and the BJP headed the government for 13 days before losing a vote of confidence in the parliament.) Given the new government's hawkish predilections, many in the intelligence community hoped that Vajpayee would reverse Gujral's decision and authorize resumed covert actions in Pakistan. To their surprise, Vajpayee declined. Raman's account of his own attempt to persuade the leadership to change course is illuminating. 'Some serving officers, who felt disappointed by the reluctance of Vajpayee to resume covert actions, arranged a meeting for me with Brajesh Mishra, the then National Security

Adviser,' Raman wrote. 'I met him in his office in New Delhi, and explained to him the importance of resuming our covert action operations in Pakistan. He gave me a patient hearing and said: "I am already convinced. You don't have to convince me. But the Prime Minister (Vajpayee) thinks otherwise. We have to carry out his wishes."'[23]

Critics still blame Inder Gujral for the diminution of India's willingness and capability to conduct covert operations in Pakistan; the fact that the revered Vajpayee concurred in this judgment deserves more attention. As the journalist Praveen Swami reflected on the eve of Narendra Modi's ascension to national leadership in 2014,

Vajpayee's silence [on covert action], like that of his predecessors, wasn't cowardice. The use of covert action inside Pakistan will, almost certainly, invite retaliation—ending, thus, in more violence, at least in the short run. It can cause large-scale civilian fatalities, with damaging international consequences. It can end in the arrest of Indian assets, damaging the country's credibility. It can succeed in its aims, as Israel, the US, and the United Kingdom have sometimes proved—or, as those very countries have learned, just as easily fail.

It is difficult to know whether Vajpayee and his immediate successor, Manmohan Singh, continued to eschew covert operations in and against Pakistan. When reminded that a number of reports say that since the late 1990s India had eschewed covert operations against Pakistan, a senior official in the second Manmohan Singh government said, 'There are a lot of urban myths.'[24] (As we discuss later in the chapter, beginning in 2010 a unit in military intelligence reportedly was tasked to conduct covert operations in Jammu and Kashmir and Pakistan.)

Pakistani authorities have long charged India with supporting insurgents in Balochistan, including by funding and facilitating actors who operate out of Afghanistan. Pakistani officials in 2009 presented allegations to this effect to India's Foreign Secretary and then to Prime Minister Singh during a bilateral meeting in Sharm el-Sheikh, Egypt. The joint statement released after the meeting noted that the issue had been raised, without saying that India admitted playing a role in Balochistan.[25] In the ensuing press conference, Prime Minister Singh said he would look into the matter. Pakistani and Indian commentators made much out of Singh's statement, but in the ensuing years little public follow up occurred.[26] Whatever role Indian agents have played in Balochistan, objective analysts in Pakistan and elsewhere note that the causes of the insurgency in Balochistan are long-standing and not the product of Indian intervention, but rather a result of intra-Pakistan dynamics. Indeed, it is most likely that the causes of discord in Balochistan are internal and that Indian agents have merely helped sustain Baloch opponents of the Pakistan Army.

The American scholar, Christine Fair, reported that in 2009 she visited the Indian mission in Zahedan, Iran, and concluded that it was an element of a broader covert action programme against Pakistan.

I can assure you they are not issuing visas as the main activity! Moreover, India has run operations from its mission in Mazar [-i-Sharif] (through which it supported the Northern Alliance) and is likely doing so from the other consulates it has reopened in Jalalabad and Qandahar along the border. Indian officials have told me privately that they are pumping money into Baluchistan.[27]

Reports and allegations of Indian covert involvement in Balochistan and elsewhere invite distinctions to be made and debated. India, like other states and sympathetic outsiders, could draw a line between providing funds, logistical support, and political encouragement to dissident groups in Pakistan and, alternatively, providing equipment, training, and operational support for violent action. Pakistan naturally would oppose both categories of interference. Yet, in moral, political, and physical terms the two categories may be meaningfully distinct. We have not been able to learn whether Indian decision makers think about covert operations with these distinctions, either explicitly or implicitly. Reports of Indian practice over the past decades suggest that covert violence has been rare, but covert funding for political agitation less so.

In Karachi it is likely that India has provided funds to some leaders of the Muttahida Quami Movement (MQM).[28] This party represents the interests of Pakistanis whose families emigrated from India during Partition and typically favours less bellicose policies toward India than do Punjab-based political parties. Like other major regional and global powers, India could perceive an interest in covertly funding relatively friendly political movements and parties in another country. The MQM in Karachi has provided an opportunity to do so.

In May 2010, one month after becoming India's Army Chief of Staff, Gen. V.K. Singh, according to numerous media reports, mobilized a covert operations cell within a Military Intelligence unit based in Delhi.[29] Singh, the first commando to ascend to the Army's top position, mobilized the 'Technical Support Division' (TSD) to 'enable the military intelligence directorate to provide a quick response to any act of state-sponsored terrorism with a high degree of deniability', according to a document quoted by the *Hindustan Times*.[30] Singh was determined to develop a capability to respond quickly, secretly, and more-or-less symmetrically to another Mumbai-like attack. The unit reportedly was authorized by the Defence Minister, the National Security Advisor, and other top MoD officials.[31] A knowledgeable former official denies that this authorization occurred, but this denial itself is difficult to interpret.[32] A 2015 article in the *Indian Express* reports that a 1 March 2015 letter from a leader of the TSD to Defence Minister Manohar Parrikar states that the TSD was established on 'deniability, that is covert operations.... TSD as a unit was formally never set up because of the clause of deniability'.[33] According to various reports, the unit conducted at least three operations in Kashmir and one in Pakistan, including 'eight low-intensity bomb blasts in a neighbouring country', presumably Pakistan.[34] (If this unit conducted covert actions in Pakistan as reports suggest, then it could validate the earlier-quoted statement that it is an 'urban myth' that India conducted no covert operations in Pakistan after Gujral banned them in 1997.)

The TSD was short-lived, however, thanks to political controversy that erupted when allegations were leaked to the press that the body had interfered in Indian domestic politics and misused funds.[35] The scandal was heightened by Gen. Singh's involvement in politics upon his retirement from the military. The resultant legal case continued in 2015 to wind through the Indian military and superior courts, even as Singh was elected as a BJP member to the Lok Sabha and became Minister of State for External Affairs in the Modi government.

Afghanistan has been the scene of unrelenting competition among Afghan, Pakistani, and Indian intelligence services. The Afghan KhAD (Khadamat-e Aetela'-e-Dawlati, also known as the National Directorate of Security) and the ISI each has collaborators among Pashtun fighting groups, and each has motives to inflict harm on the other's state. The RAW's historic ties to the KhAD make it highly plausible that the two services could cooperate in operations against Pakistani interests. A former high-level Pakistani ISI officer grinned wryly during an interview in 2014 as he recounted a recent story:

Not long ago, the US captured the number two man in the TTP, Latifullah Mesud, driving from Kabul to Khost. He was in a convoy of 16 SUVs. They caught him with $6 million in cash. While in Kabul, he had been a guest of Afghan intelligence. He met with the Indian ambassador in Kabul. Has the US said anything to India about this? So, Indians don't have to train operators in India. They can do it in Afghanistan.[36]

From this brief survey, it is safe to say that India has not been purely abstemious in the use of covert agents and actions against Pakistan. This is especially evident when Afghanistan is included along with Pakistani territory as the area of operations for Indian agents. But Indian authorities have been very careful to preserve their reputational advantage over Pakistan in this domain of statecraft. Since the 1990s, prime ministers have been morally, politically, and strategically averse to fomenting and supporting violent operations on anything like the scale of, say, Pakistan's Kargil incursion or the 1993 and 2008 Mumbai attacks. The relative improvements of India's economic and political conditions, and its international reputation as a victim rather than a perpetrator of cross-border violence and subversion, suggest that this caution has not been unwise.

Future Options

Covert operations may be attractive if the alternative choices are to do nothing or to conduct major conventional military operations on the ground, in the air, and/or at sea. The attractiveness of covert action of course would depend on the existence of requisite capabilities. Yet, before exploring the capabilities India might need, it is sensible first to consider possible benefits and risks of various types of operations. Ideally, benefits and risks would be assessed both in the short and the long terms, tactically and strategically. What are the likelihoods of operational success and failure, and how would adversaries most probably react in the ensuing months? Longer term, how would covert operations change the Pakistani security establishment's policies toward India?

India could consider covert operations to pursue two reasonable objectives in Pakistan: first, to deter and/or disrupt Pakistani terrorist groups from conducting major attacks on India and to diminish recruitment of new terrorists; and second, to create incentives for the Pakistani security establishment to act decisively to prevent future terrorist attacks against India. The first objective could be achieved by killing, intimidating, or discrediting leaders of anti-Indian groups and impeding their capacity to conduct attacks on India. The second, in theory, could be accomplished if Indian operations caused enough internal discord and disruption in Pakistan to make Pakistani authorities conclude that they lose more from allowing anti-Indian groups to operate in Pakistan than they gain from the potential harm these groups do to India. In theory, India could devise covert operations that would seek simultaneously to directly deter actors in Pakistan from acting violently against India and to compel Pakistani authorities to demobilize the actors who most threaten India. However, it is difficult to describe feasible operations that would plausibly achieve both objectives.

Directly Targeting Terrorists

Directly seeking to capture or, more likely, kill leaders and key members of terrorist groups and to weaken their capacity to act against India would be the most proportionate and least escalatory policy for India to pursue. Terrorists—if correctly identified—are belligerents. They and the populations in which they live expect them to be targeted, much as soldiers in battle expect to be targets.

Yet, targeting individuals for attack raises complicated and portentous legal, political, and strategic issues, beyond the physical challenges of identifying, tracking, and striking the intended target. In India (as in the US and other countries) it is illegal to kill individuals on other states' territories during peacetime. Beyond other implications, this means that anyone who would conduct such a killing could be liable to criminal prosecution. Politically, especially in democracies, the state's conduct of assassinations can be expected to produce heated political and legal debate. Strategically, the killing of individuals in other states may invite reciprocation from the state in which the killing occurred and/or from other states and sympathizers. Such killings are also known to stimulate recruitment of new personnel into terrorist ranks.

The US' struggle to settle the legal, political, and strategic controversies over the killings it has conducted in the aftermath of the 11 September 2001 terrorist attacks on New York and Washington point to some of the difficulties India would confront. A relatively strong legal argument can be made that targeting an individual who is an active member of an organization that has engaged in violent conflict with one's own state is an act of self-defence permissible under Article 51 of the UN Charter. This is especially plausible if it can be demonstrated that the individual needed to be targeted because the state in which he is residing is unwilling or unable to prevent that person from carrying out attacks on one's own state. The legal arguments for taking such action would be stronger if it could be shown that the targeted individual was preparing to conduct an attack and therefore posed an imminent threat. In short, to the extent that a target for attack can be fairly defined as a legitimate military target, rather than a non-violent person, legal cover may be obtained.

But achieving this identification—for legal and tactical purposes—can be very challenging. Terrorists do not wear uniforms and they often locate themselves and their infrastructures in the midst of non-combatants. Locating particular individuals and facilities and establishing their involvement in terrorism with confidence is difficult.[37] Decision makers of the attacking state, in this case India, must establish criteria for the level of confidence they require in the identification of a potential target, and the amount of collateral damage in lives and property that they deem appropriate to risk inflicting in order to strike a target. Each of these calculations may become subject to intense national and international scrutiny, especially if something goes wrong. If the intended target is proved to be absent or not struck, and/or significant damage is done to innocents, the attacking state can be put on the defensive in relation to the state whose territory was encroached upon and in the eyes of the broader international community. Attacks that kill innocents are especially likely to prompt family members of victims to join terrorist groups to seek revenge.[38] More obviously, decision makers must calculate how much risk they are willing to take that the agents conducting the intended attack will be captured or killed.

These targeting challenges obtain whether attacks are to be carried out via precision air strikes, as discussed in the previous chapter, or agents on the ground. The risks of the former depend heavily on whether ordnance is to be delivered by piloted aircraft, UAVs, or missiles, and the quality of defences that are arrayed against them. Leaders may take more chances if they believe their operatives are at low risk of being captured or killed. With on-the-ground operations the risks to one's own agents may be felt more acutely, depending on the relationships of the agents to the attacking state. States tend to be more careful when they deploy their own nationals than when they deploy volunteers recruited from the society in which the attack is occurring.[39] Risks are greatest when national military commandos are involved, both in terms of how one's own public and media would react to their death or capture and how the adversary would. Concerns about agents being captured, interrogated, and used in propaganda raise the importance of being confident that the targeted individuals have been precisely identified and are indeed of great enough value to warrant the associated risks.

The June 2015 Indian commando raid against insurgents in Myanmar reflected some of these challenges. According to a senior military intelligence official, the insurgents' camps struck in Onzia and Ponyo did not contain perpetrators of the earlier, 4 June ambush that killed 18 Army personnel and motivated New Delhi to strike. 'These camps were chosen for reasons of tactical viability, rather than specific retaliatory intent,' the official reportedly said.[40] One leader of the insurgent group and a number of cadres had left the camp before the strike. Military sources told the reporters that the more lethal of the Army's strikes was against a camp whose inhabitants were not part of the two groups that had claimed responsibility for the earlier attack on Indian forces. In comparison, the challenges of accurately identifying and striking individuals in a populated area of Pakistan, with civilians nearby, would be much greater than the challenges of the Myanmar operation, as would be the political and strategic risks of not hitting high-value targets.

Timing also presents major challenges. As we discussed in the previous chapter, it is easier to locate and hit individuals when they are not expecting it, just as training camps and other supporting facilities are more likely to contain valuable assets when the terrorists who use them have not already dispersed. In the hours and days after another major terrorist attack on India, the perpetrators and their supporters in Pakistan probably would make themselves much harder to target. Yet, if India sought the element of surprise by striking individuals and support facilities before another major attack on India, Pakistanis and the wider world would be more likely to see India as an aggressor. To avoid being labelled as such, India would need to provide unmistakable evidence that the targeted individuals were responsible for earlier attacks and/or planning new attacks, and that Pakistani authorities were unable or unwilling to arrest them and try them or transfer them to India. Targeting alleged terrorists is hardest to achieve in the windows of time in which it is strategically, politically, and legally least risky to do so—directly following or preceding a major terrorist attack. Moreover, the domestic political benefits of harming terrorists would be greatest immediately after India had suffered an attack. Retribution meted years afterward might engender public enthusiasm, but such delayed action would not relieve the political pressure leaders would feel in the immediate aftermath of an attack.

Perhaps the best option would be to create the impression that India has the means to target individuals and disrupt operations, but will not employ them unless and until India is attacked again. This is the logic of deterrence. However, making deterrence credible is much easier said than done. India would need the capacity to identify and track leaders and operatives, and then to signal this—either directly to the terrorists, or indirectly through Pakistani authorities who could then deliver the message. Assuming India acquired the capabilities to do this, which do not appear to exist today, how could this capacity be communicated to terrorists and/or Pakistani authorities for purposes of deterrence without at the same time revealing methods that could enable the adversaries to adapt and make themselves more difficult to track?

Again, the June 2015 Indian commando attack in Myanmar demonstrates some of the challenges of predicting the signalling effects of covert operations. This action was not covert insofar as India notified Myanmar and then announced it publicly. But whether or not Indian decision makers intended also to send a message of resolve to Pakistan militants, and security officials in Pakistan no doubt noticed it. The question then arises how they interpreted the signal. Jingoistic commentators and politicians in India wanted adversaries in Pakistan to take it as a warning that should inspire caution. However, the strategic effect could be the opposite of what was intended. By running a commando operation in a non-hostile country, Myanmar, against Indian nationals, facing no significant defence, and targeting camps selected on the basis of ease of access rather than importance, the Indian government may have invited Pakistanis to conclude that India would not risk conducting a similar operation against Pakistani nationals on Pakistani territory which would invite Pakistani retaliation. Such an interpretation could reassure Pakistani leaders; Indian leaders were merely seeking domestic propaganda benefits. That reassurance could quiet impulses for Pakistan to demonstrate its own resolve not to be intimidated. On the other hand, Pakistani leaders and/or militants could interpret the operation as a sign of Indian weakness and therefore be emboldened to undertake provocations to demonstrate that India will not retaliate.

These uncertainties highlight the strategically vital question: Would targeting anti-India terrorists on Pakistani territory motivate Pakistani authorities to change policies? This effect could be produced directly in the minds of Pakistani decision makers, or indirectly by mobilizing public opinion to press the state to act more decisively to demobilize terrorists that threaten India. One variable is whether Pakistani authorities and/or influential segments of society view anti-India terrorists as expendable. If so, then India's targeting of terrorists would not likely augment Pakistan's resolve to demobilize these groups. Many in Pakistan could say, 'good riddance', and leave the burden of removing anti-India terrorists to India rather than to the Pakistani state itself. More positively for India, if Pakistanis regard anti-India terrorists as expendable, then the targeting of such terrorists would be less likely to prompt Pakistani retaliation and attendant risks of escalation, as long as ambiguity existed about India's responsibility for the operation.[41] Conversely, if the Pakistani security establishment and/or influential segments of the population really cared about the individuals and groups that were targeted, such operations would run a risk of retaliation and escalation.

Israelis have learned the risks as well as the benefits of targeting terrorists through trial and more than a few errors. One illuminating example occurred following the January 1996 assassination of the famous Hamas bomb maker, Yehya Ayyash, who had created devices used in suicide attacks that killed dozens of Israelis. As Raviv and Melman write, with prodigious effort and skill, Israeli agents had tracked 'The Engineer' to Gaza and managed to recruit one of his close associates.[42] Israeli technicians deployed miniaturized high explosives in a cell phone that their new Palestinian agent then gave to Ayyash. Shortly thereafter, the phone rang, Ayyash answered it, and the bomb detonated.

Leaving aside the real gaps between Israel's and India's capabilities to penetrate so close to its adversaries' leaders and accomplish such an operation, the strategic effects deserve analysis. Hamas struck back in the ensuing weeks and months. It sent a series of suicide bombers into Israel. In one week in late March 1996, 57 Israelis were killed. These reprisals in turn caused public support of the prime minister, Shimon Peres, to fall, and the popularity of his opponent, Binyamin Netanyahu to rise. Feeling pressed to demonstrate strength, Peres in April authorized a military incursion into Lebanon to target Hezbollah and Palestinian forces there. In the Lebanon campaign, Israeli artillery inadvertently hit a UN refugee camp in southern Lebanon, killing more than 100 civilians. Netanyahu won the May election.

Israel is not alone in experiencing covert missions that either failed at the tactical level or had unwelcome strategic consequences. The US has successfully used drone strikes to kill many violent militants in Pakistan, but the overall effect of these operations on US influence and on Pakistani society and decision makers is unclear.[43] For the foreseeable future, India will be much less capable than Israel and the US to conduct dramatic targeted killings of adversaries and much more vulnerable than Israel and the US to reprisals. This is one reason why M.K. Narayanan, drawing on decades of intelligence and national security policymaking experience, warned Indians to 'understand the inherent dangers in following a US–Israel analogy'.[44]

Coercing the Pakistani State

Instead of targeting individuals and groups directly involved in threatening violence against India, or in addition to such operations, India could consider covert operations that would cause enough trouble for Pakistani leaders to motivate them to change policies in ways that India seeks. Such an approach would mirror the strategy behind Pakistan's use of sub-conventional campaigns to compel India to accommodate Pakistani demands regarding Kashmir. (Indians themselves are the best judges of whether or not Pakistan's strategy has worked.)

India presumably would not seek to overthrow the government of Pakistan. Such a wholesale political objective would be infeasible for Indian covert operatives to imagine achieving. Moreover, the putative benefits of instigating regime change would depend on the nature and purposes of the government that followed, which could not be predictable either in the near or long term. Indeed, it is difficult to find cases where an outside power clandestinely helped bring down a foreign government and then derived lasting benefits from the effort.[45]

More practical would be actions that could make power centres in Pakistan conclude that changing policies towards India is in their interest. In theory, India could consider a strategy of offering positive inducements to make Pakistani leaders change their behaviour, such as accommodations on Kashmir, or India could undertake a strategy of coercion. Since the Kargil conflict in 1999, discourse in the Indian policy community has tended to focus on coercion, as we noted earlier in explaining this book's focus on coercive options. This may reflect a judgement that Pakistani leaders will be more responsive to pain than to positive inducements, and/or a preference of Indian leaders and voters to inflict costs rather than offer rewards to change Pakistani calculations.

The repertoire of potential covert operations is nearly boundless. We discuss several possible types of action that other states have employed. This is for analytical purposes to invite thinking about whether India would have the capabilities or the interests to pursue them.

India could secretly finance political parties that challenge the security establishment's position in Pakistan. In theory this could be done via layers of agents so that the ultimate recipients would not know that the funds originated from India. Indian agents also could find Pakistani politicians who would wittingly receive gifts from India. Whatever the possible methods and their feasibility, Indian efforts to manipulate politics in Pakistan would carry significant risks. If Pakistani counter-intelligence or anyone else found evidence of Indian funding, the recipients could be severely tarnished (or worse). A backlash could be predicted, not only in Pakistan but also in India and other countries. The spring 2015 initiative by the Pakistani security services and competing political parties to crush the MQM Party in Karachi included charges that the Party and its leaders have been funded by India. There are reasons to conclude that these charges are valid and, moreover, that the ISI knew about Indian funding for years but chose not to publicize it.[46] When the security establishment's assessment of the MQM's role in Karachi and national politics changed, the funding story became part of the campaign to undermine the party.

Another covert tactic that states often use is to plant disinformation that could threaten the reputation and standing of leaders of a target—in this case Pakistan. Yet, Pakistanis are very good at undermining their leaders without foreign assistance. The Pakistani press is relatively open and disposed to political conflict, albeit within limits set by the ISI, which is known to use physical threats and money to prevent coverage that challenges its interests—either through direct payments or by channelling advertising business to or away from particular media outlets. Overall, the marginal value of mobilizing informational and political challenges to particular leaders or parties in Pakistan would seem slight compared with the risks of exposure that would make such covert action counterproductive.

India could dedicate human and technical resources to penetrate Pakistani information and communications systems to obtain compromising information about leaders and institutions. For example, Indian agents could obtain data about hidden bank accounts or property holdings of Pakistani military leaders, revealing major corruption. Or, they could uncover information about the ISI's interference in domestic politics. However, in order to make acquired information credible, Indian agencies could risk revealing how they obtained it. Intelligence agencies are loath to do this for fear of compromising the methods they use. Edward Snowden's release of purloined files from the US National Security Agency offers a powerful recent example of the double-edged nature of information operations. Snowden revealed a number of tools and kinds of operations that US officials have found important for gathering intelligence and influencing other states. At the same time, the exposure of these tools and activities created powerful waves of internal and external challenges to US policymakers.

More aggressively, Indian decision makers could seek to facilitate occasional, small-scale violent attacks by insurgent groups on the Pakistan Army and ISI. For example, Indian agents, perhaps operating from Afghanistan, could arm insurgents with improvised explosive devices (IEDs) that could be planted near roadways to be detonated against military convoys. Such attacks could, in theory, demoralize Pakistani forces and society and motivate the leadership to consider changing policies so as to obtain commitments to make such attacks cease. (However, as a long-time Indian official not known for sympathy toward Pakistan exclaimed, this form of violence is 'against the Indian ethos'.[47]) This policy objective could only be achieved if it were clear with whom Pakistan should negotiate and what is to be negotiated. Yet, when it became clear that Indian interests were to be addressed in return for a cessation of IED attacks, Pakistan could accuse India of threatening aggression in its territory. The prospects of mutual accommodation then would become quite dim. More likely,

Pakistan would seek to encourage and equip sympathetic actors in India to conduct reprisals against Indian armed forces. As a veteran BJP foreign policy advisor noted in an interview, 'We've not had car bombs in India. Nothing like the frequency and scale of violence in Iraq. If by causing trouble in Pakistan we gave them the motivation to do more in India, that would be a big loss for India.'[48]

Indeed, the mobilization of violence against Pakistani state institutions—as distinct from violence meted directly against terrorists—would cross a threshold that would raise risks of escalation and damage India's regional and international standing. Such uses of force would invite reprisal by the ISI and its collaborators in India. While competition in covert violence could be less damaging and escalatory than conventional military action, this is an analytic and policy question that would need to be addressed rigorously.

Other states that engage in covert conflict have found economic sabotage to be less risky than violence against persons. Interrupting supply of electricity can harm economic interests and perhaps motivate businesses and citizens to question the competence and priorities of their leadership. Electricity supplies could be sabotaged by several means, including malware. Yet, Pakistan already suffers enormously from electricity shortages of its own making. Such shortages have mobilized powerful economic players and average voters to seek political change. In the 2014 national elections, Nawaz Sharif's party gained a large mandate in part by promising improvement in energy supplies. This reflected a broader popular desire for Pakistan's authorities to concentrate more on the country's internal well-being. Were India to be accused with credible evidence of sabotaging Pakistan's electricity system, it could relieve rather than intensify pressures on the Pakistani state to devote more attention and resources to internal problems. This would be contrary to India's larger interest.

If Indian agents could identify economic enterprises that enrich Pakistani military leaders (directly or through family ties) and then harm their business operations or profitability, this could register. Presumably, Pakistani military leaders would be quick to conclude that Indian hands were behind the 'attack'. The question then would be whether the harmed individuals would motivate the state to do more to reassure India that Pakistan was doing all it can to prevent terrorism against India. Or, instead, would the Pakistani fraternity of military leaders seek revenge of some sort against Indian interests—economic or otherwise?

A more dramatic form of economic sabotage would be a covert cyberattack that disrupted the Karachi stock exchange or another vital economic node. Indian cyber experts presumably would make it extremely difficult to attribute such an attack confidently to India. Yet, such an attack would produce grave concern in all states with major stock exchanges, not only Pakistan. Authorities in the US, the United Kingdom, China, and elsewhere would react with alarm, fearing the precedent. Intelligence agencies and private consultants in states that fear cyberattacks on their own financial institutions would seek to identify the source of the cyberattack, and India would be a likely suspect. This would be especially true if the cyber disruption closely followed a terrorist attack against India, which is precisely the time when India would be most likely to entertain the idea. Given the importance of India's own stock exchange, and the country's interest in gaining international confidence as an economic hub, covert operations against Pakistan's financial sector would be excessively risky.

Finally, India could provide financial and logistical support to Pakistani groups that challenge the state in multifaceted ways. A number of such groups operate within and around Balochistan, using a variety of tactics ranging from political protests to economic sabotage to violence against the Pakistan Army. Some of these groups retain legitimacy within the Baloch population and under the Pakistani Constitution, while others have given up political struggle and concentrate more on violence. Indian agents, including those operating in Afghanistan, could select groups to support according to multiple criteria and using various means, including money, logistical assistance, and weaponry. Depending on the character and tactics of the groups that India would support and the type of assistance India would give them, India could place itself closer to or further from violating international laws and norms regarding support for terrorists.

Pakistan has long accused India of fomenting the Baloch insurgency. Yet, Pakistani authorities have not presented evidence publicly that is specific and damning enough to persuade many Pakistanis and outside observers that the troubles in Balochistan stem significantly from Indian intervention and not from intra-Pakistan dynamics.[49] As long as India could obscure its role in Balochistan, it could retain opportunities to undermine the Pakistani security establishment's interests there and create leverage to press for Pakistani cooperation in demobilizing anti-India terrorist groups.

But there are limits to how hard and far India could push this lever without harming its own interests. If credible evidence were produced and widely promulgated that India was facilitating terrorist activities against Pakistani civilians, for example, India's political standing on the terrorism issue would suffer in the international community and, perhaps, within Indian politics. In theory, India could seek to confine the violence committed by actors it supported to military targets and avoid being implicated in attacks on non-combatants. But India still would be interfering violently in the internal affairs of Pakistan. And, if the violence in Balochistan (or elsewhere) escalated to the point where the writ of the Pakistani state no longer could be enforced there, India could face the alarming prospect of greater mayhem in the territory to its west with no other state capable of controlling it. As a former high-ranking Indian intelligence official put it, 'The minute any one says Pakistan might break up, that scares the shit out of me.'[50] More broadly, this man registered doubts about the need for more robust Indian covert actions in Pakistan: 'There is nothing more deadly and harmful that India could do, as compared to what Pakistan as a state can do, and is doing, to itself.'

This somewhat cursory discussion of possible covert operations highlights a number of risks and dilemmas for India. (The prospects of such operations also create risks and dilemmas for Pakistan, of course.) Perhaps the most important dilemmas for India relate to covertness and to India's identity as a state that has been a victim of sub-conventional violence rather than a perpetrator. The two dilemmas are related.

A former top-level Indian policymaker explained the problem of covertness in a November 2014 interview.

You need political credit at home to be seen doing something. But to be effective, what you do should not be visible.... The jihadis and their supporters seem to respond to covert messages. But such actions are so closely held we don't get political benefit from them.... So the two imperatives work in opposite directions: the need for visible use of force, versus the effectiveness of covert force. If you want them to change what they are doing, you have to act secretly so they can save face when they change policy.[51]

This latter point is extremely important. To be strategically effective, an action should do more than satisfy an impulse for revenge and retribution. It also should have a prospect of improving one's situation overtime, in this case by changing the behaviours of potential terrorists in Pakistan and/or the authorities who could reduce the threat posed by terrorists. Pakistan's security establishment, like most others, displays a determination not to be cowed or deterred by competitors. To be coerced into changing one's behaviour is seen as a sign of weakness that is intrinsically humiliating and instrumentally dangerous insofar as it may embolden domestic opponents to challenge individual leaders or institutions. It is less risky for authorities to change behaviour if they are perceived to do so voluntarily or, at least, reciprocally, not in retreat from the exertion of an adversary. This is one of the potential values of covert operations, but maintaining the requisite covertness is very difficult.

The second risk of covertness—or, more accurately, covertness that is exposed—has less to do with the effect on the opponent than on the implications for one's own reputation and standing in the international system. As an exceptionally experienced counsellor to several Indian prime ministers cautioned in an interview, 'It is not in our interest to have people think we are little different from the ISI. We are different. But if Pakistanis assert we are just like them, it is bad for us. Then the international community will say that "they both do it", and the pressure falls off Pakistan and the Pakistanis can justify what they do.'[52]

This point is not lost on Pakistani leaders. When asked how a reinvigorated programme of Indian covert actions would affect Pakistan, a former high-ranking ISI officer smiled:

Indian covert ops—if they did that in a bigger way, at least it will expose that there is an interaction, that they do it too. We have been painted black. The Indians have painted themselves as Angels. We don't mind if the Indians do covert operations, because then at least we will be on the same plane for everyone to see. Let them do it.[53]

Discounting for bravado, the former ISI officer's comment foreshadowed a Pakistani political–diplomatic counteroffensive that appeared months after our interview. On 5 May 2015, the Corps Commanders issued a rare statement explicitly accusing the RAW of 'whipping up terrorism in Pakistan'. Pakistani authorities have long accused India of nefarious activities within Pakistan, but it was unusual for the Army's top leadership to formally and pointedly accuse the Indian intelligence service of fanning terrorism. The Corps Commanders' statement came days after two MQM workers were arrested in Karachi for allegedly inciting violence at the behest of the RAW.[54] The Army's charge was soon echoed by the Prime Minister's Adviser on National Security and Foreign Affairs, Sartaj Aziz, and by Foreign Secretary Aizaz Ahmad Chaudhry, who emphasized that RAW should not be allowed to operate from Afghanistan against Pakistan. Nawaz Sharif then met with Army Chief of Staff, Gen. Raheel Sharif, and the two reportedly addressed the threat from RAW.[55] Again, the allegations were neither specific nor new; the important signal was that the Pakistani leadership had decided to wage a political–diplomatic campaign to establish symmetry between India's and Pakistan's reputations for using black arts against each other.

When Indian Defence Minister Manohar Parrikar volunteered days later in response to a question that India will do what it has to, including using 'terrorists to neutralise terrorists', he, wittingly or not, endorsed the extension of symmetry and proportionality into the domain of sub-conventional operations. We discuss opportunities that may arise from such a strategy in the conclusion of this chapter.

Capabilities

In assessing the capabilities India currently possesses or could strive to develop in order to conduct effective covert operations against Pakistan, it is useful to distinguish between actions to capture or kill individual terrorists and destroy their infrastructure, and actions intended to coerce adversary leaders to change their behaviour.

In environments like Pakistan, where potential targets of India are likely to be highly vigilant, it is extremely difficult to get close enough to individuals or their places of work to confirm their identity and destroy them, and then to exfiltrate the attackers before they can be captured or killed. Such operations are not impossible. The US raid on Osama bin Laden's compound in Abbotabad, and assassinations by others of Pakistani ministers and Taliban leaders demonstrate the possibility of targeted killing. Still, outside of Kashmir where Indian operatives have been able to turn militants against their former brethren, there are no indications that India has been able to recruit insiders from LeT and similar groups who would then be willing to kill or to help other Indian agents kill prime targets. Nor are there publicly known examples of India's own operatives penetrating the key echelons of anti-India terrorist groups in Pakistan, so that they could learn the locations and patterns of movement necessary to be able to capture or kill high-value targets. In the absence of reliable on-the-ground sources, India presumably would rely on signals intelligence and overhead reconnaissance to locate and then, with luck, track potential targets. As discussed in greater detail in Chapter 3, available information suggests that Indian reconnaissance and intelligence fusion capabilities are not yet sufficiently developed to be able to execute this type of operation with confidence.

Identifying and tracking targets is only one step; the next steps are to emplace human assets and their equipment in sufficient numbers and proximity to capture or kill the target, and then to remove these assets so that they cannot be taken (dead or alive) and used in a media contest. Here, again, we are aware of no examples where Indian agents have conducted such operations in Pakistani cities. There are reports of rather random bombings attributed to Indian agents. However, leaving a bomb on a street side or in a building and then detonating it after the agent has left is a very different challenge than getting close enough to a high-value individual to fire a weapon or detonate a bomb at the precise moment they are within range, and then departing without being captured or killed.

A *Times of India* story in 2012 revealed the unresolved state of India's preparedness. 'Most officers who have served in Pakistan say that India has the capability to hit [LeT] in Pakistan, but the government doesn't allow such covert actions,' the story began. 'We don't do covert operations like the CIA, MI6 and Mossad,' said a former officer quoted in the story.[56] 'This doesn't mean that we don't have the capability. Given a chance, we could prove equal to all these agencies.' According to the reporters, a senior RAW official said, 'Our charter does not include the job of getting (or assassinating) people from other countries.'

Then the reporting turned from self-serving bravado to analysis. The reporters recounted Prime Minister Inder Gujral's decision to dismantle covert operations in Pakistan 'purely on moral grounds', according to their intelligence source. This source explained that the Indian 'political class' had not restored a 'structure' for covert operations because this class 'believes that covert operations could spoil bilateral relations'. According to this report, RAW 'now conducts operations primarily by paying money to local operatives in Pakistan instead of its own agents. But such groups can't hit out at ISI-protected figures like Hafiz Saeed and Dawood Ibrahim'. Another intelligence officer was quoted saying, 'It takes a great deal of money and time to cultivate sources in foreign soil. We don't have either in plenty, unlike countries in the West. Pakistan's ISI is better off in this as the state sponsors terrorism.' The article continued, in an understatement, that 'most intelligence officers believe that they need better equipment for surveillance as well as the go-ahead for covert tactics'.[57]

In a 2014 interview, a veteran RAW expert on Pakistan reinforced doubts about Indian capabilities. 'Elements among non-state actors and the ISI have a larger than life sense of our capabilities,' this man said.[58]

They perpetrate myths of our capabilities. This helps us. But the reality is that our capacity to act covertly has atrophied over the years. So it needs to be built up so that it's there for immediate response, immediate use, if there's another attack like Mumbai. We need to build up the capacity to hit LeT, Jaish, or others. We would have to do this through mercenaries: Afghans, others. And we would have to use other territory to prepare, again, Afghanistan or maybe Iran or the UAE. This capacity would have to be built up.

The challenge of recruiting potential agents from Afghanistan is complicated by the ISI's penetration of many of the groups from which India might wish to draw. Indeed, reading the history of the US' CIA, one is struck by how many of the foreign national agents that the US thought it had recruited were actually double agents of the Soviet Union, Cuba, Iran, and other target countries.

Assuming India could identify and recruit agents who would penetrate into Pakistan and work reliably for India, intelligence professionals say it takes more than a few years to train an effective clandestine operative. 'There is not an on/off switch,' an exceptionally knowledgeable former Indian official mused. 'If you lose these capabilities it takes time to build them back. Especially human intelligence and resources. But,' the man continued, 'it's extremely difficult for India to do human intelligence. It's also extremely difficult for the US. We have courts, habeas corpus, reviews. These limitations have to be appreciated. We have a free society, media, courts with judicial review. It's much easier for the ISI to do mischief in India.'[59]

It is reasonable to say that today India is far from having the technical and human reconnaissance capabilities and the on-the-ground clandestine operatives necessary to effectively target key terrorists in Pakistan.

Other forms of covert operations could be much more within India's capabilities. Providing financial and material support to Baloch and other disaffected groups is operationally simpler and less risky than emplacing agents to attack individuals in Pakistani cities. Similarly, offering funds to political parties, whose priorities are more congenial to India's interests than the priorities of the Pakistani security establishment, is not hard to do, even if the benefits are not obvious. Compared to attacking well-guarded LeT leaders, infiltrating operatives to blow up natural gas pipelines or electricity transmission infrastructure is simple. And, if Indian officials wish to dramatically enhance their capacities both to gather intelligence and potentially to coerce Pakistan, they could deploy major financial and human resources into the cyber field. However, there would be a risk that the acquisition of capabilities would outpace the political leadership's definition of objectives and policies.

★ ★ ★

Discussions on the benefits and risks of covert operations tend to focus on the operations themselves. Was the intended target killed or captured without collateral damage to innocents, and without one's own agents being captured and turned into hostages? Was information (or disinformation) successfully implanted into debates in the target country? Was valuable economic infrastructure sabotaged, inflicting significant costs? Depending on the nature of the operation, success may not be publicly disclosed. Failure, on the other hand, is more likely to become public, not least because the targeted state finds advantage in embarrassing the perpetrator.

Fixating on the risks of operational failure or the satisfaction of success is natural, but experience suggests that more attention should be paid to examining and debating the longer-term strategic effects particular covert operations could be expected to have. Such things are inherently uncertain, of course, so probabilistic estimates informed by historical analogies may be useful. The records of states that have relied heavily on covert actions—the

US, Israel, and Pakistan among them—offer clear warnings that even tactical successes often do not yield strategic gains. This record indicates further that the people who authorize and conduct covert actions have focused on short-term effects and not enough on how various forms of covert action support longer-term strategies to shape future relations with the states they are targeting.[60]

'Going back to the history of CIA covert operations,' the former Director of US National Intelligence, Admiral (ret.) Dennis Blair, concluded, 'I think you can make the argument that if we had done none of them we would probably be better off, and certainly no worse off than we are today.'[61] Another distinguished veteran of US intelligence, former CIA deputy director John McMahon, reflected ruefully: 'In covert action, you always have to think of the endgame before you start it. And we don't always do that.'[62] The strategic value of covert operations, as distinct from their tactical effects, cannot be separated from broader foreign policies. As Hank Crumpton, a former CIA counterterrorism leader put it, 'Absent a foreign policy, covert action isn't going to work.'[63]

Pakistan's experience in this domain is telling too. Even tactically successful operations such as the Kargil incursion in 1999, the Parliament attack in 2001, and the Mumbai attack in 2008 resulted in serious harm to Pakistan's international standing and, arguably, to its population's sense of well-being. In conversations, well-educated and widely travelled Pakistani officials have told us that RAW was behind the Mumbai attack. When we expressed incredulity, they explained that 'India won'. The world saw the attack on television and had sympathy for India and saw Pakistan as a bunch of terrorists. As one young Pakistani officer put it, 'Terrorism emanating from Pakistan does not pay. If India can make Pakistan appear to be the source of terror, Pakistan is the laughing stock, the one the world condemns. This is a better result for India than they would get from a war!'[64]

Notwithstanding the cautionary lessons to be learned from other countries' experiences, India could conclude that covert actions in response to another major terrorist attack could entail fewer risks of escalation than conventional military responses, and could therefore be relatively attractive. In contemplating this course, Indian leaders will be mindful that their country is highly susceptible to retaliation by individuals and groups emanating from Pakistan and/or by Indian citizens that could be recruited by these Pakistani groups. The US has conducted most of its covert operations far from its territory—in Central America, Southeast Asia, the Middle East, Afghanistan, and Pakistan. Israel is close to its adversaries, so it has protected itself from blow back by building a wall in the West Bank and Jerusalem and deploying the Iron Dome missile defence. India has neither the good fortune of distance nor the smallness of territory to be defended. Nor does it have the wealth and widespread prosperity that allow its elected leaders to conclude that their constituents will support spending vast sums of money on developing high-quality capabilities and defences against blow back. India continues to invest in fencing and other barriers along the LoC and the international boundary with Pakistan, but achieving physical immunity from Pakistan-backed terrorism remains an unlikely prospect. For these and other reasons, Indian leaders as different as Inder Gujral and Atal Behari Vajpayee generally have been risk-averse in the covert operations domain.

Whatever covert operations Indian leaders might choose to pursue will serve the country's overall interests only if they are incorporated into a broader strategy for motivating Pakistani authorities to end their reliance on violent proxies to inflict harm on India. In other words, the development of capabilities and the threat to use covert operations must be part of a bargaining strategy. The logic would be: if Pakistani authorities, especially the military command, act to curtail the operations of individuals and groups that target India, Indian leaders will desist from undertaking covert operations against Pakistan's interests. If Pakistani leaders reject this course, then India is prepared to raise the costs for them. This is the logic of deterrence and compellence.

For purposes of managing escalation dynamics, proportionality is more credible than posturing to respond to sub-conventional aggression with conventional force. It is intuitively 'fair' to take an eye for an eye (though it can lead to mutual blindness). Pakistan has long engaged in sub-conventional operations against India, and India generally has not matched them, but instead has sought to deter such operations through unconvincing asymmetric threats of conventional response. The proposition in the future would be either symmetry, in which the interests of both countries may suffer, or instead mutual rejection of offensive operations of any type against each other.

In a conversation in Rawalpindi in October 2013, a high-level Pakistani security official recognized the implications of a roughly symmetrical balance between India and Pakistan at the sub-conventional, conventional, and nuclear levels. 'There is a realization on our side that these games have to stop,' this man said. 'But they have to stop mutually.'[65] He stated as fact that India was stoking violence and insurgency in Balochistan and Karachi. When asked if there had been an inflection—a point at which the Indian instigation had increased significantly—he said, 'in the last five years', meaning since 2008, the year of the Mumbai attack. Like other knowledgeable members of the Pakistani security establishment, he noted that there had not been another major terrorist attack on India since then. When asked whether he believed that if Pakistan-based groups were to attack India, India would stoke fires that threaten to burn Pakistan from within, he said, 'The focus now should be on making peace.' Six months later, Nawaz Sharif came to power through a campaign that highlighted Pakistan's interest in normalizing relations with India.

In 2015, when Pakistani authorities mounted a concerted effort to publicize that India, too, engaged in covert subversive activities, and the Indian defence minister then spoke of 'using a thorn to extract a thorn', the two states (consciously or not) created a new opportunity for bargaining. Previously, as long as Pakistan was perceived as the sole perpetrator of terrorism, India could demand that Pakistan cease as a precondition for substantial diplomacy, without India having to offer anything comparable in return. In Pakistani politics, this amounted to a requirement for unilateral concession, which is difficult for leaders in any polity to undertake. If a sense of symmetry is created—however artificial or debatable—then neither party needs to make unilateral concessions to begin negotiations. Both can save face by saying that the object of negotiations will be reciprocal, symmetrical action to prevent further violent interference in each other's internal affairs.

The creation of the perception of symmetrical competition and a rough balance of threats at the sub-conventional (covert), conventional, and nuclear levels is only half of a bargaining strategy, however. The other half would entail diplomacy—negotiation—to resolve the central disputes between the two states. This speaks to the lessons proffered by the veterans of US covert operations quoted above: forceful coercion, in any form, will only achieve meaningful results if it is embedded in a foreign policy. Mutual threats of symmetric competition at the covert level could calm the Indo-Pak competition for a while, but without progress on the diplomatic front, the equilibrium would be difficult to sustain. Without a sense that mutual restraint is leading to a mutually tolerable resolution of fundamental issues, populations and leaders will be unable to deflect the shockwaves of assaults that militant forces may conduct to reignite conflict.[66]

Positive bargaining is probably too much to expect in the near-term, though. Without unambiguous and substantial signals from Pakistan's security establishment, Indian foreign policy leaders are likely to remain sceptical that more forthcoming positions on their part will lead to meaningful, durable pacification of the two states' relationship. Still, even if there were deep doubts that Pakistan would enact an agreement for both countries to eschew violent interference in each other's internal affairs, India could gain political and diplomatic leverage on the Pakistani security establishment by making such a proposal as part of diplomacy to resolve issues related to Jammu and Kashmir. If Pakistan rejected, or failed to take privately-agreed measures to implement such an agreement, India's capacity to rally international action against Pakistan would grow. We return to this strategic approach in Chapter 6.

Notes and References

1. Interview with former Indian intelligence officer, New Delhi, 24 April 2014.

2. Ajit Doval, speech at Sastra University, 21 February 2014. Video available at: https://www.youtube.com/watch?v=N7ESR5RU3X4.

3. Shubham Ghosh, 'Narendra Modi Breaks Silence on Dawood Ibrahim in Interview', *One India*, 26 April 2014. Available at: http://www.oneindia.com/new-delhi/narendra-modi-breaks-silence-on-dawood-ibrahim-in-interview-lse-1436789.html.

4. 'wohuskoboltehainna Marathi meinkaante se kaantanikaaltehain... Hindi meinbhirahega... you have to neutralise terrorist through terrorist only.' See Pranav Kulkarni, '"You have to neutralize terrorist through terrorist only," says Defence Minister Manohar Parrikar', *Indian Express*, 22 May 2015. Available at: http://indianexpress.com/article/india/india-others/kill-terrorist-with-terrorist-defence-minister-manohar-parrikars-idea-2/#sthash.rUWMDnXt.dpuf. Parrikar's statement echoed closely one by then-National Security Advisor M.K. Narayanan who, following the July 2008 bombing of the Indian embassy in Kabul, said: 'I think we need to pay back in the same coin...Talk-talk is better than fight-fight, but it hasn't worked so far.' Quoted in Praveen Swami, 'Fighting Pakistan's "Informal War,"' *Hindu*, 15 July 2008. Available at: http://www.thehindu.com/todays-paper/t-opinion/fighting-pakistans-informal-war/article1296668.ece?

5. 'Pakistan Expresses Concern over Parrikar's "Terror-for-Terror" Comment,' *The Wire*, 24 May 2015. Available at: http://thewire.in/2015/05/24/pakistan-expresses-concern-over-parrikars-terror-for-terror-comment/.

6. 'It is important to underline the fact that the action India undertook in the aftermath of the Manipur ambush may not be replicable in the other theatres of terror, like Jammu and Kashmir or other states bordering Pakistan.' Wasbir Hussain, 'What India's "Hot Pursuit" Strategy Is and Is Not', *The Wire*, 11 June 2015. Available at: http://thewire.in/2015/06/11/what-indias-hot-pursuit-strategy-is-and-is-not/. Myanmar is not hostile to India or capable of retaliating, as Pakistan is. Former head of RAW, Vikram Sood, wrote a damning critique of the publicity the media (and government) gave to this operation, with a warning that such operations in other places could be much

more challenging: 'Border Op Big Stick Needs Soft Talk', *The Wire*, 10 June 2015. Available at: http://thewire.in/2015/06/10/border-op-big-stick-needs-soft-talk/. Former National Security Advisor, M.K. Narayanan wrote, 'What is disconcerting are the outpourings of "triumphalism" with even official spokesmen—ministers not excluded—indulging in verbal excesses. Whether all this signals a change in India's counter terrorism strategy or not, it certainly creates the impression that a new and aggressive phase in the battle against terrorism has begun....If such statements were only intended to convey a new "machismo image" of India, then those who make these statements need to understand that this could prove to be counterproductive.' M.K. Narayanan, 'Muscle-flexing that May Backfire', *Hindu*, 22 June 2015. Available at: http://www. thehindu.com/opinion/lead/muscleflexing-that-may-backfire/ article7339493.ece.

7. Interview with former Indian intelligence officer, New Delhi, 24 April 2014.

8. Pakistan also has long used proxies in Afghanistan.

9. See Haqqani, *Pakistan: Between Mosque and Military*, 270–2. The US State Department, in *Patterns of Global Terrorism: 1991*, reported that 'There were continuing credible reports throughout 1991 of official Pakistani support for Kashmiri militant groups engaged in terrorism in Indian-controlled Kashmir, as well as support to Sikh militant groups engaged in terrorism in Indian Punjab. This support allegedly includes provision of weapons and training.' Given that the US government had been working so closely with the ISI in Afghanistan at that time, and prior to 1990 soft-pedalled problematic Pakistani behaviour, it is reasonable to posit that the 1991 report was something of an understatement.

10. Haqqani, *Pakistan*, 287–90.

11. B. Raman, *The Kaoboys of R&AW* (New Delhi: Lancer, 2013), 268.

12. Raman, *The Kaoboys of R&AW*.

13. Author email correspondence with K.C. Verma, 15 July 2015.

14. Interview with former senior official, Washington, 14 July 2015.

15. There is no one accepted definition of 'hybrid warfare', but common phenomena associated with 'it' are: ambiguity of attribution, in large part to make retaliation difficult to justify and direct; involvement of military and non-military personnel and targeting of civilian as well as military targets; use of psychological operations, disinformation,

and propaganda; and violence on a lesser scale and intensity than normally associated with military units.

16. Praveen Swami, 'Fighting Pakistan's "Informal War"', *Hindu*, 15 July 2008. Available at: http://www.thehindu.com/todays-paper/ tp-opinion/fighting-pakistans-informal-war/article1296668.ece.

17. Wilmerdon, 'Why RAW Succeeds and ISI Fails?' *Medium*, 7 May 2014. Available at: https://medium.com/@wilmerdon/what-isi-can-learn-from-raw-274e67674f48.

18. Varied accounts by former Indian intelligence officials, especially A.K. Verma and B. Raman, suggest that the then-leaders of India and Pakistan, Rajiv Gandhi and Zia ul-Haq, tasked their intelligence chiefs—Verma and Hamid Gul—to secretly explore ways to temper the two states' competition. It remains unclear from this literature whether these talks resulted in a reciprocal arrangement to desist from violent covert operations in the two countries' heartlands. See, A.K. Verma, 'When Hamid Gul Offered India Peace', *Hindu*, 28 August 2015. Available at: http://www. thehindu.com/opinion/op-ed/comment-article-on-indiapakistan-bilateral-ties-when-hamid-gul-offered-india-peace/article7587371. ece?homepage=true; Raman, *Kaoboys of R&AW*, 161, confirmed by Verma in 'When Hamid Gul Offered India Peace'; 'Bhutto Accuses Rajiv of Not Keeping "Promise" in 1988,' Khalistan.net, 21 December 2007. Available at: http://www.khalistan.net/?p=931. See also, Neena Gopal, '"I Kept My Word, Rajiv Didn't"', *Outlook*, 31 December 2007. Available at: http://www.outlookindia.com/ article/i-kept-my-word-rajiv-didnt/236386.

19. Swami, 'Fighting Pakistan's "Informal War"'.

20. I.K. Gujral, 'The Rediff Interview', Rediff.com, 20 October 1998. Available at: http://www.rediff.com/news/1998/oct/20guj1.htm.

21. B. Raman, 'RAW Operations in Pakistan', *Indian Defence Review*, 27 February 2013. Available at: http://www.indiandefencereview.com/ news/raw-operations-in-pakistan/.

22. Raman, 'RAW Operations in Pakistan'.

23. Raman, 'RAW Operations in Pakistan'.

24. Interview with senior official, New Delhi, 10 November 2014.

25. A source with direct knowledge of Indian deliberations at Sharm el-Sheikh says that Prime Minister Singh allowed mention of Balochistan because India was not involved in violence there. Interview with former senior official, Washington, 14 July 2015.

26. The Pakistani journalist Hamid Mir reported that Pakistani sources said their government had arrested three Indian nationals who had been working out of India's Kandahar consulate in Afghanistan to support the Balochistan Liberation Army, and that the Indian side agreed in Sharm El Sheikh to formally reference the issue in return for Pakistan's not publicly parading the arrested Indian nationals. Hamid Mir, 'Pakistan has Proof of "3 Indian Kasabs" in Baluchistan', Rediff.com, 28 July 2009. Available at: http://www.rediff.com/news/special/hamid-mir-on-the-real-reason-why-india-agreed-to-discuss-baluchistan/20090728.htm. However, a knowledgeable Indian denied this. Moreover, even if Mir's report was accurate, it did not allege that the Indian consular official was directly facilitating violence in Balochistan.

27. Christine Fair, 'What's the Problem with Pakistan?', ForeignAffairs.com, 31 March 2009. Available at: https://www.foreignaffairs.com/discussions/roundtables/whats-the-problem-with-pakistan. This discussion was taken offline, but Fair also cites this URL in her book, *Fighting to the End.*

28. Interviews with knowledgeable Pakistani sources in Karachi, January 2012, and Washington DC, September 2013.

29. Sandeep Unnithan and Asit Jolly, 'Dirty Tricks', *India Today*, 7 October 2013. Available at: http://search.proquest.com/docview/1438039944?accountid=40995. Another source told us that the Technical Support Division existed previously and that Gen. Singh repurposed it.

30. Harinder Baweja, 'Army Spook Unit Carried Out Covert Ops in Pakistan', *Hindustan Times*, 21 September 2013. Available at: http://www.hindustantimes.com/india-news/newdelhi/army-spook-unit-carried-out-covert-ops-in-pakistan/article1-1125008.aspx.

31. Yatish Yadav and N.C. Bipindra, 'The Great Betrayal', *Indian Express*, 6 October 2013. Available at: www.newindianexpress.com/magazine/The-great-betrayal/2013/10/06/article1816098.ece.

32. Interview with former senior official, Washington, 14 July 2015.

33. Ritu Sarin, 'Don't Give Info, Cover will be Blown, Former Head of Army Covert Unit Writes to Manohar Parrikar', *Indian Express*, 4 April 2015. Available at: http://indianexpress.com/article/india/india-others/dont-give-info-cover-will-be-blown-former-head-of-army-covert-unit-writes-to-parrikar/2/.

34. Unnithan and Jolly, 'Dirty Tricks'.

35. Dhananjay Mahapatra, 'Gen VK Singh Loses Battle for Age, Tries to Save Some Honour', *Times of India*, 11 February 2012; Yadav and Bipindra, 'The Great Betrayal'.

36. Interview with former ISI officer, Rawalpindi, 17 November 2014.

37. The US' conduct of 'signature' strikes is especially problematic insofar as the people targeted are not identified as particular, named individuals, but rather are deemed 'guilty' due to patterns of activities, attributes, and locations that lead US officials to conclude that they are terrorists.

38. See, for example, Mia Bloom, 'Mother. Daughter. Sister. Bomber', *Bulletin of the Atomic Scientists* 61, no. 6 (November/December 2005): 54–62; Riaz Hassan, 'What Motivates Suicide Bombers?', Yale Global Online, 3 September 2009. Available at: http://yaleglobal.yale.edu/content/what-motivates-suicide-bombers-0.

39. For multiple examples of cavalier CIA treatment of local-national volunteers for covert operations, see Tim Weiner, *Legacy of Ashes* (New York: Anchor Books, paperback edition, 2008).

40. Pranav Kulkarni, Praveen Swami, and Vijaita Singh, 'Myanmar Strike: Seven Dead Bodies Recovered, Less than a Dozen Injured, Say Official Sources', *Indian Express*, 12 June 2015. Available at: http://indianexpress.com/article/india/india-others/myanmar-cross-border-strike-7-bodies-less-than-a-dozen-injured/? utm.

41. The commando attack in Myanmar may be instructive. The government and presumably the citizenry of Myanmar had no affinity for the Indian nationals that were targeted in the strike, and did not protest on those grounds. But, when the Indian strike became public, thanks to Indian government statements, the government in Myanmar became embarrassed and had to protest that its sovereignty had been violated. Thus, the Indian National Security Advisor, Ajit Doval, felt compelled to travel to Myanmar on 16 June to limit damage. It is doubtful that Pakistani authorities would be so accommodating after a similar Indian operation on Pakistani territory, which Indian leaders no doubt comprehend.

42. Dan Raviv and Yossi Melman, *Spies Against Armageddon: Inside Israel's Secret Wars* (Sea Cliff, NY: Levant Books, 2012), 264.

43. For a relatively positive view of drone strikes, see Christine Fair, 'Drone Wars', *Foreign Policy*, 28 May 2010. Available at: http://foreignpolicy.com/2010/05/28/drone-wars-2/; for a more critical

view, see Steve Coll, 'The Unblinking Stare', *The New Yorker*, 24 November 2014. Available at: http://www.newyorker.com/magazine/2014/11/24/unblinking-stare.

44. M.K. Narayanan, 'Muscle-Flexing that May Backfire'.

45. US experiences in Chile, Greece, Guatemala, Iraq, Iran, Vietnam, and elsewhere typify regime-change initiatives that were more costly than beneficial to US interests.

46. Interview with Pakistani politician, Washington, 12 September 2013. This source explained that Pakistan's security establishment did not want information about Indian funding of the MQM to exacerbate violent strife in Karachi.

47. Interview with former senior official, Washington, 14 July 2015.

48. Interview with BJP foreign policy advisor, New Delhi, 23 April 2014.

49. Cyril Almeida, 'One Country, Three Policies', *Dawn*, 4 October 2015. Available at: http://www.dawn.com/news/1210729.

50. Interview with former Indian intelligence official, New Delhi, 26 April 2014.

51. Interview with former senior Indian policymaker, New Delhi, 10 November 2014.

52. Interview with former senior Indian official, New Delhi, 11 November 2014.

53. Interview with former high-ranking ISI officer, Rawalpindi, 17 November 2014.

54. Kamran Yousaf, 'Out in the Open: Army Accuses RAW of Fuelling Terror', *The Express Tribune*, 6 May 2015.

55. 'PM, Army Chief Discuss National Security, RAW Involvement', *News*, 18 May 2015. Available at: http://www.thenews.com.pk/article-185202-PM-Army-Chief-discuss-national-security-RAW-involvement.

56. Manimugdha S. Sharma and Deeptimaan Tiwary, 'Why Indian Intelligence Doesn't Work Too Well in Pakistan', *Times of India*, 8 April 2012. Available at: http://timesofindia.indiatimes.com/home/sunday-times/deep-focus/Why-Indian-intelligence-doesnt-work-too-well-in-Pakistan/articleshow/12577068.cms.

57. Sharma and Tiwary, 'Why Indian Intelligence Doesn't Work Too Well in Pakistan'.

58. Interview with former senior intelligence officer, New Delhi, 24 April 2014.

59. Interview with former senior Indian official, New Delhi, 11 November 2014.

60. At the time of writing it is too early to say what the strategic effects of the Indian commando operation in Myanmar were. 'The attack was a tactical success,' Ajai Sahni of the Institute of Conflict Management said, 'but by itself, its strategic value is exactly zero.' Kulkarni, Swami, and Singh, 'Myanmar Strike'.

61. Mark Mazetti, *The Way of the Knife* (New York: Penguin, 2013), 60.

62. Weiner, *Legacy of Ashes*, 385.

63. Mazetti, *The Way of the Knife*, 143.

64. Chatham House Rule seminar at Institute for Strategic Studies, Islamabad, 24 October 2013.

65. Interview with Pakistani security official, Rawalpindi, 25 October 2013.

66. The difficulty of preventing outbreaks of major violence in the absence of serious diplomatic efforts to redress underlying disputes can be seen not only in the subcontinent and Afghanistan, but also in the Israeli-Palestinian contest and, increasingly, in the Iran-Saudi competition in the Levant and the Gulf. These are circular problems of course. Violence makes diplomacy more difficult to conduct and sustain. But when violence does subside and diplomatic progress is not then pursued, a return to violence should be expected, and should be attributed at least to some degree to the failure of political leaders to use calmer periods to achieve diplomatic progress, however politically risky that may be.

5

NUCLEAR CAPABILITIES

The preceding chapters analysed potential risks and benefits of options involving conventional military force and/or covert operations that India could develop and deploy to motivate Pakistani authorities to prevent further terrorist attacks on India. India would seek both to deter terrorists and Pakistani authorities from conducting or permitting such attacks, and to compel authorities to demobilize actors who seek to conduct them. Much of our analysis focused on the challenge of deterring Pakistan from escalating conflict if and when India retaliated forcefully to another major terrorist attack.

Tensions clearly emerged in this analysis. Modest ground and/or air strikes against targets in Pakistan-administered Kashmir, and the most plausible types of covert operations, could leave Pakistani authorities political and strategic 'room' not to escalate the conflict, thus bolstering the deterrent value of these options. But these largely symbolic punitive actions would be less likely to compel Pakistani authorities to clamp down on anti-India terrorists than, conceivably, would more robust ground and/or air operations against the Pakistan Army and targets in the Pakistani heartland. But robust conventional and/or covert operations that would be more likely to compel Pakistani leaders also would be more likely to prompt Pakistani conventional and sub-conventional retaliation against India. In this case, Indian and Pakistani leaders would confront the uncertain dangers of managing escalatory warfare. Were India to succeed in imposing defeats on Pakistani forces, especially in the heartland, the prospect of Pakistan's using nuclear weapons against attacking Indian forces would become real. Indian leaders then would face portentous decisions about whether and when to use their nuclear weapons.

This possibility informs sober analysis of the options India could and should consider pursuing to achieve its security objectives toward Pakistan, as we have discussed in the prior chapters. In this chapter we focus on the nuclear dimension. We examine questions of doctrine and capabilities that Indian leaders could pursue to enhance their capacity to manage risks of escalation up to and including the use of nuclear weapons. We do not suggest that nuclear weapons are a substitute for conventional military capabilities or covert operations. Rather, they can be seen as a complement to India's conventional military instruments in scenarios with escalatory potential. We do not imagine that Pakistan or India would seek to conduct bolt-from-the-blue nuclear attacks on each other, or that Pakistan would risk initiating major conventional war against India. A myriad of national interests backed by mutual second-strike nuclear deterrence render these threats unrealistic in South Asia. The focus here is on the role of nuclear weapons in an escalatory competition that would begin with a major terrorist attack on India emanating from Pakistan.

This analysis draws primarily on Indian debates and sources. Where the literature and experiences of non-South Asian sources may illuminate the dilemmas Indian officials and analysts confront, we refer to them. As noted in the introduction, no other nuclear-armed competitors have faced challenges as complex as those that Indians and Pakistanis now face. This largely has to do with the potential role of terrorism as the trigger for escalation up the ladder from sub-conventional to conventional to nuclear conflict.

India faces an additional challenge—China—which we do not address in this chapter. China's strategic capabilities may be the benchmark against which India measures its ultimate requirements for nuclear weapons, delivery systems, reconnaissance, and command and control. Indian nuclear doctrine must apply in whole or in part to China. Yet, as long as one assumes, as we do, that China would not initiate use of nuclear weapons against India in order to retaliate for Indian use of nuclear weapons against Pakistan, India's nuclear challenge from Pakistan can be treated separately. We base this assessment on two considerations: first, that the scenario of conflict begins with sub-conventional violence emanating from Pakistan; and second, that India's use of nuclear weapons would be in response to Pakistan's first use of such weapons, which itself would be contrary to China's own no-first-use doctrine. To be sure, China has assisted Pakistan's nuclear and missile programmes, which is a factor in India's overall threat calculus. But the difficulties and dilemmas that we examine here in India's nuclear relationship with Pakistan would not be resolved if China ended such assistance. Finally, whether or not China is involved in India's calculations of how to manage nuclear deterrence with Pakistan, Indian leaders and experts must still wrestle with each of the challenges discussed in the following pages.

Evolving Nuclear Landscape

The shadow of nuclear deterrence has loomed over the security landscape in South Asia since well before May 1998, when India and Pakistan both conducted nuclear weapons test explosions. Scientists and strategists in both countries began writing about the atomic bomb in the 1950s in parallel to the development of their nuclear science and energy programmes.[1] Global developments—in particular India's defeat in a border conflict with China in 1962, China's first nuclear weapons test in 1964, and the perceived intrusion of the United States and the Soviet Union on India's autonomy during the 1971 war with Pakistan—were among the factors that drove India to conduct a 'peaceful' nuclear test in 1974. Despite this test and the resulting denial of trade and assistance to India's nuclear energy programme, India's leaders took few steps to weaponize the fissile material it produced. India did not build a nuclear arsenal or even seek to exercise nuclear deterrence against its neighbours until the mid-1980s.[2] Instead, Indian leaders chose to emphasize quite different nuclear-related policies, including challenging the discriminatory nature of the Treaty on the Non-Proliferation of Nuclear Weapons (NPT) and the dangers of arms racing by the Cold War superpowers, and offering proposals to jumpstart a nuclear disarmament process. The unusually slow pace of nuclear weapons development, coupled with the importance given to disarmament and non-proliferation in India's foreign policy, speaks to the Indian elite's enduring view of nuclear weapons as political rather than military tools.[3]

Pakistan's nuclear weapons programme, meanwhile, was initiated following the ignominious loss of the eastern half of the country in the 1971 war with India.[4] The sense of existential threat and insecurity that followed the bifurcation of the country clearly motivated the origins of the Pakistani bomb. For Pakistani politicians and military officers, nuclear weapons became a way to deter future conventional war with India that might threaten further territorial losses or even the survival of the state. Pakistan opted to pursue its nuclear weapons efforts quietly, drawing on clandestine procurement of foreign technologies and equipment, and aided on several occasions by China. Importantly, Gen. Zia ul Haq's 1977 coup d'état, which ushered in a lengthy period of military rule in Pakistan, placed the responsibility and control of nuclear weapons development in the military's hands, an arrangement unchanged until today despite periods of democratic rule. As a result, the roles and requirements for nuclear weapons in Pakistan's national security policy have been defined by the military. Consequently, and in stark contrast to India, most Pakistani officials and experts view nuclear weapons largely in terms of military capabilities.

Although the public record does not clearly indicate precise dates by which India and Pakistan possessed deliverable nuclear weapons, indirect deterrence signalling between the two began to emerge first in the later stages of the 1987 Brasstacks crisis.[5] The Kashmir crisis in 1990 saw more direct, albeit ambiguous, nuclear signalling, with references to the mutual possession of nuclear weapons made by senior military officers in both countries. These signals, and the potential that the crisis might turn confrontational and escalate to nuclear use, spurred intervention by the United States to lower the temperature.

These early experiences with nuclear-shadowed crises appear to have reinforced the very different views held by the policy elite in each country about the utility and practice of nuclear deterrence. In India, the crises underscored that nuclear weapons were not primary instruments of India's defence policy, and that the possession of nuclear weapons by both states made potential escalation very dangerous. In Pakistan, on the other hand, these crises affirmed that nuclear threats had 'catalytic' value—as a means for attracting the attention of outside powers, namely the US, who would then intercede to calm tensions and, Pakistani strategists believed, validate the legitimacy of Pakistan's grievances against India.[6] Pakistani strategists may have concluded after the 1990 Kashmir crisis that possession of nuclear weapons would allow Pakistan to give more direct support to proxy groups such as LeT that attack India, insofar as the risk of escalation could dissuade India from retaliating. These attitudes persist today, despite the maturation of nuclear technologies and gradual stockpiling of nuclear weapons by each state.

The 1998 nuclear tests not only brought the nuclear situation in South Asia more into the open, they also forced both states to grapple with the need to formulate and enunciate policies on nuclear deterrence that would reassure the international community that India and Pakistan would be responsible stewards of nuclear weapons and materials. Both states faced enormous international pressure following the tests, including through UN Security Council Resolution 1172 which urged India and Pakistan 'to exercise maximum restraint', to 'resume dialogue on all outstanding issues', and 'to stop their nuclear weapon development programmes'.[7] Although this resolution was roundly criticized in both countries, international concerns did seem to factor into their decision-making.

Indeed, for a time it seemed that nuclear weapons would stabilize the subcontinent. The then prime ministers, Nawaz

Sharif of Pakistan and Atal Bihari Vajpayee of India, met first in New York in September 1998 and then in Lahore in February 1999 and announced a series of nuclear-related confidence-building measures. This progress was quickly halted, however, by the Kargil conflict in spring 1999. Notably, the overt possession of nuclear weapons by both sides did not deter Pakistan from undertaking the Kargil operation, or India from responding and escalating the level of violence with the use of airpower. However, it is clear from New Delhi's policy deliberations at the time that concerns about the potential for nuclear escalation and India's desire to be seen as a responsible nuclear power did constrain India's response.[8]

Following the Kargil conflict, as Indian officials and experts contemplated developing a nuclear doctrine, an overriding concern was to 'establish India's role as a responsible nuclear-armed state that is willing to pursue confidence-building measures in its region'.[9] Accordingly, in August of 1999 when the Indian government released a report prepared by the National Security Advisory Board (NSAB) on the parameters for India's nuclear policy, it prefaced doctrinal pronouncements with a reiteration of prior Indian positions on the NPT, disarmament and non-proliferation. The NSAB report stressed 'India's primary objective...to achieve economic, political, social, scientific and technological development within a peaceful and democratic framework'.[10] The report then described three major pillars of Indian nuclear policy: credible minimum deterrence; no first use (NFU) of nuclear weapons; and 'punitive' retaliation to inflict 'unacceptable damage' in response to a nuclear attack on India. The report clarified that 'the fundamental purpose of Indian nuclear weapons is to deter the use and threat of use of nuclear weapons by any State or entity against India and its forces'. It further indicated that India would develop a triad of nuclear forces, and would organize these forces and command and control systems 'for very high survivability against surprise attacks and for rapid punitive response'. The 'unofficial' status of this document—a report from a group of civilian expert advisors to the government—obscured whether it reflected India's official policy, but the ideas contained within the report were closely aligned with those stated by government officials on several occasions.[11]

In January 2003, just three months after the conclusion of the 2001–2 crisis, the Indian Cabinet Committee on Security released a short statement that made India's doctrine official. It reiterated most of the major points of the 1999 draft doctrine, but altered two of the pillars in important ways. First, the NFU policy was caveated, so that India might retaliate not just to a nuclear attack on Indian territory, but also 'on Indian forces anywhere'. Second, 'punitive retaliation' was reconfigured as 'massive retaliation'.[12] These changes leave much to interpretation; their significance and how they figure in the current Indian discourse will be addressed later in this chapter.[13]

Since India's doctrine established that nuclear weapons would be used only to deter a nuclear attack, Indian strategists were forced to search for non-nuclear options to deter, dissuade, or compel Pakistan to cease supporting or harbouring groups that attack India. Operation Parakram, in which India massed half a million troops on the International Border in late 2001, was in some ways effective in forcing Pakistani leaders to agree to outlaw LeT and cease supporting militant infiltration in Kashmir. But this slow, massive mobilization came at a very heavy price and frustrated Indian military leaders and security analysts who felt that the eschewal of punitive military action weakened India's deterrence and compellence of Pakistan.

The putative Cold Start doctrine described in Chapter 2 offered a visible example of the Indian Army's search for more effective means to coerce Pakistan, drawing on the lessons of Operation Parakram. But the essential problem in India's effort to develop military options—to put conventional rungs on the escalation ladder below the nuclear threshold—is that Pakistan's nuclear strategy and capabilities are intended to deter exactly such options. The more apparent it seems that India is contemplating robust and timely conventional military operations, the more Pakistani military leaders seek to raise the salience of first use of nuclear weapons to deter such operations.

While India was wrestling with, and ultimately opting not to execute, a doctrine like Cold Start from 2002 through the 2008 Mumbai crisis, Pakistan was developing nuclear-capable ballistic and cruise missiles whose purpose was clearly enunciated when Pakistani officials began to talk in 2011 of exercising 'full-spectrum' deterrence.[14]

Some Indian analysts doubt Pakistan's technical capabilities to conduct 'full-spectrum' nuclear operations and dismiss the threat to do so as a bluff to generate alarm, confound a slow-moving Indian policy process, and catalyse outside intervention.[15] Of course, India, too, has also played up the 'flashpoint' fear. For instance, during the 2001–2 crisis, veteran Indian strategic affairs journalist C. Raja Mohan observed that India was 'subtly using the threat of nuclear war to get the international community to pressure Pakistan to end terrorism'.[16]

Looking back at the period of crisis and conflict since 1990, many analysts conclude that Pakistan's nuclear posture has effectively deterred India from undertaking conventional military responses or otherwise escalating militarized crises. Vipin Narang finds, for instance, that 'Pakistan has been able to uniquely and directly achieve deterrent success against India'.[17] This is quite a strong conclusion and probably overstates the specific role of Pakistan's nuclear posture in deterrence, while undervaluing the cautious approach of India's civilian leaders, who have tended to eschew risks of escalation that might threaten other governing priorities, particularly economic growth.

However, Indians recognize that nuclear weapons will not deter Pakistan and terrorists from perpetrating small-scale violence against India.

The late P.R. Chari, one of India's eminent thinkers on nuclear strategy, asserted that

nuclear weapons cannot provide any defense against the subconventional threats to India's national security from extremist elements within its own territory, or, especially, against those who receive moral and material assistance from across the border.... Nuclear deterrence can only provide security against the use of nuclear weapons or major conventional attack. In other words, nuclear deterrence cannot accomplish any vital national security goals other than preventing an adversary from using nuclear weapons.[18]

Indian foreign policy experts and officials tend to share the view that the sole purpose of India's nuclear weapons should be to deter nuclear aggression. But for others, including many military officers, Pakistan's current nuclear posture amounts to 'nuclear blackmail', and thus India's nuclear weapons ought to be postured to counter it. One central figure in the former Manmohan Singh government summed up the situation this way in an interview:

The new debate over nuclear policy has started because tactical nuclear weapons are being developed and deployed in Pakistan, so how do we respond? Pakistan is turning to Cold War tenets that were proved untenable before. Why should we follow them? The mainstream view here has been remarkably consistent. The military may want more options and symmetry—the usual macho sentiment—but this can be swiftly put aside.[19]

As this view makes clear, the debate about India's doctrine is in many ways a larger contest about foreign policy and nuclear strategy. For 40 years, India's nuclear weapons have served primarily domestic and foreign policy objectives of projecting India as a major technological power. Deterrence has been more an abstract concept and secondary objective, rather than a military tool, especially insofar as military officers and planners have been deliberately excluded from decisions about nuclear policy, doctrine, and force posture. It is therefore not a coincidence that many of the more strident voices in India's nuclear debate are retired military officers. They contend that much is wrong with India's nuclear policy and argue that corrections to doctrine, posture, and capabilities can provide India greater leverage to change Pakistan's calculus.

Current Nuclear Debates

Many of the issues currently discussed by Indian experts continue debates begun well before the nuclear tests in 1998 and the release of the NSAB doctrine report in 1999. But this issue gained political prominence during the 2014 Indian general election for several reasons. India's civilian and military leaders had not found feasible military options to punish Pakistan following the 2008 attacks by LeT in Mumbai. India appeared to be falling behind Pakistan in both quantity and quality of nuclear weapons and delivery vehicles, as Pakistan introduced the short-range Nasr missile and announced its posture of 'full-spectrum' deterrence. Indian military officers expressed frustration at the slow pace and lack of prioritization accorded management and control of Indian nuclear forces. These factors had led former Foreign Minister Jaswant Singh, for example, to assert in 2011 that the nuclear policy he had helped put in place after the 1998 tests was 'very greatly in need of revision because the situation that warranted the enunciation of the policy of "no-first-use" or "non-use against non-nuclear weapons", "credible deterrence with minimum force", etc. has long been overtaken by events. You cannot continue to sit in yesterday's policy. We need to re-address it.'[20] Picking up this argument, the drafters of the 2014 BJP election manifesto charged that the 'strategic gains acquired by India during the Atal Bihari Vajpayee regime on the nuclear program have been frittered away by Congress'.[21]

The factors noted above, with impetus added by the BJP election manifesto, have spurred thinking about how changes in Indian nuclear doctrine and capabilities might better motivate the Pakistani security establishment to demobilize militant groups that attack India. Interest in altering India's nuclear policy comes generally from a perception that, in the pointed words of retired Indian Air Marshal Brijesh Jayal, the nuclear doctrine is 'good in theory, but not credible in practice'.[22] Responding to this sense of inadequacy, Indian National Security Advisor Ajit Doval affirmed in an October 2014 speech in Munich 'that India is shifting its posture from credible minimum deterrence to credible deterrence'.[23]

Yet, this is clearly not a boundless debate. There are limits to what even those who argue for more options are willing to entertain. As one former Indian Strategic Forces Commander indicated in an interview, speaking of the US effort to develop limited nuclear options, 'Nowhere has it worked. McNamara repudiated it. There is no realistic model for it. It has arms race potential'.[24] Thus, the room for potential changes in Indian nuclear policy seems relatively narrow at this juncture. But in order to weigh potential future options, it is necessary to consider arguments about India's current policy. The three streams of argument that are most pertinent have to do with India's NFU policy, massive retaliation, and nuclear inferiority.

No First Use

Consistent with the 'moral politik' that drove India's nuclear-related foreign policy from the 1960s, as well as the conviction that nuclear weapons are political tools not intended to be used in a military conflict, no first use of nuclear weapons has been an enduring feature of India's nuclear strategy.[25] Both the 1999 and 2003 doctrinal statements reiterate the NFU policy, though both also introduced caveats. Fealty to NFU remains strong among Indian politicians. Then-candidate Narendra Modi for example declared it a 'reflection of our cultural inheritance'.[26] Still, long-standing reservations also exist about the credibility and relevance of India's NFU policy to its strategic environment.

One scenario in particular seems to concern Indian strategists: If Pakistani leaders opted to cross the nuclear threshold and use nuclear weapons against Indian armoured forces entering Pakistani territory, Pakistani leaders would know that this use might spark an Indian nuclear response. This possibility might encourage Pakistani leaders to then seek to limit damage from a possible Indian retaliatory nuclear attack by launching simultaneously a large strike against India's nuclear arsenal, thereby degrading India's capability to retaliate 'massively'. According to this scenario, India's NFU policy could give Pakistani leaders confidence that they could deter or defeat a conventional military campaign by India in retaliation to a terrorist attack. The possibility that India would face significant devastation on its own territory, without the capability to respond in ways that threaten 'unacceptable damage', would degrade the credibility of Indian deterrence.

This seems to be a major concern, for example, of former Indian strategic forces commander Lt. Gen. B.S. Nagal (ret.), who asserts, 'NFU implies probable large scale destruction in own country'. He extends the logic further:

NFU policy cannot conduct a first strike on the adversary's counterforce targets, thus allowing the adversary full capability to attrite [India's] capability. In the current environment of mobile systems on land and SSBNs at sea, the probability of destruction of the adversary strategic assets will be extremely low or negligible in a second strike, this therefore limits [India's] retaliatory nuclear strikes to counter value targets, once again a moral dilemma.[27]

Conceivably, India could address this issue by introducing additional ambiguity into its declaratory policy, beyond the existing caveat that permits use of nuclear weapons in retaliation for an attack 'on Indian forces anywhere'. If Pakistani leaders had reason to doubt that India would be bound to NFU (which some of them already are inclined to doubt), they would be less certain that India would not try to pre-empt or disarm Pakistan before it could launch a large counter-capability nuclear strike. This would enhance the perceived credibility of India's deterrence against a first strike, while also reducing the possibility that a large portion of India's nuclear assets might be destroyed in a major counter-force attack. For these reasons, Chari concluded that 'adoption of a deliberately vague policy in regard to nuclear retaliation, instead of the certitude of a no-first-use declaration, might have better served India's overall strategic ends'.[28]

Massive Retaliation

It is not clear what drove Indian officials to change terminology from 'punitive' to 'massive' retaliation between the 1999 and 2003 doctrinal statements. The timing of the 2003 statement, coming on the heels of the 2001–2 crisis, may indicate frustration and simply a desire for tough public posturing.[29] Whereas 'punitive' suggests proportionality and flexibility in the scale of a nuclear counter-attack, 'massive' is far less nuanced and intended to leave no doubt that any nuclear attack will invite widespread and perhaps total destruction. As one participant in a November 2014 policy seminar in New Delhi averred, 'If you say proportionate response, that invites war-fighting. Massive retaliation is better; they will be deterred.'[30]

One justification for the massive retaliation policy, offered by former foreign secretary Shyam Saran, rests on the conviction that there is no distinction between strategic and tactical nuclear use. 'Any nuclear exchange, once initiated, would swiftly and inexorably escalate to the strategic level'.[31] Because the sole purpose of India's nuclear weapons posture is to deter use of nuclear weapons against India, as opposed to lesser contingencies, India can treat all nuclear threats equally. This should deter Pakistani first use even if it is against Indian troops on Pakistani territory. As another participant in the aforementioned Delhi seminar put it, 'We have no doubt they can do residual damage to India, but the possibility that we would hit them massively will deter them.'[32] For proponents of this policy, massive retaliation is an important bulwark against sliding into contemplation of limited nuclear war or even war-fighting. It is a necessary condition for preserving the political nature of India's deterrence. But just as there are potential issues of credibility with NFU, massive retaliation also invites scepticism.

Retired Admiral Raja Menon, for instance, asserts that 'the ideational systems that will ensure the "massive" retaliation promised in the doctrine are being increasingly questioned by scholars and analysts worldwide'.[33] Chari similarly found massive retaliation 'an unrealistic certitude because, ethically, punishing large numbers of noncombatants contravenes the laws of war. Besides, threatening massive retaliation against any level of nuclear attack, which would inevitably trigger assured nuclear annihilation in a binary adversarial situation, is hardly a credible option'.[34] Manoj Joshi adds that some in India do not 'believe that if Pakistan uses a singular nuclear detonation for signaling purposes, a massive retaliatory response is likely or, indeed, in India's security interest'.[35] If the choice before Indian decision makers is all or nothing, the threshold for an order to execute massive retaliation will be quite high, intensifying dilemmas in responding, for example, to a demonstration nuclear blast by Pakistan or confined detonations on the battlefield in Pakistan. Graduated responses would in theory lower the political threshold for ordering nuclear retaliation, and could—if escalation could be managed—prevent major damage that would result from a large nuclear exchange.

Were Pakistan to use nuclear weapons first in a limited way, the resolve required of India's civilian and political leaders to follow through on the commitment to massive retaliation would be harshly tested. It is not surprising, therefore, that the political credibility of massive retaliation invites scepticism, as well as worry. Manpreet Sethi argues, for instance, that India should

focus on enhancing the credibility of its nuclear deterrence. Pakistan does not doubt India's capability, but its political will in mounting retaliation.... The doubt in the mind of the adversary appears to be whether India with a strategic culture of military restraint would find it prudent, and more importantly, morally acceptable to inflict damage (and risk more on itself) in response to a threat that is not itself mortal.[36]

Nagal also described the political commitment problem that currently exists for India: 'It is absolutely certain, resolved, definite, unambiguous and assured that the political leadership will take correct decisions in the face of nuclear attacks.'[37] It is not clear whether he was seeking to reassure himself that India's political leadership would follow through with massive retaliation or, more subtly, that he was highlighting the improbability that India's leaders would make such a decision. Given these doubts about massive retaliation, it is not surprising that many Indian experts, former officials, and retired military officers urge shifting to an assured retaliation posture that doesn't depend on such a high political threshold—for example, a return to the prior formulation of a 'punitive' response guaranteeing unacceptable damage contained in the 1999 NSAB report.

Nuclear Inferiority

Pakistan's development of the Nasr short-range ballistic missile and the Ra'ad and Babur cruise missiles provides it with several 'full-spectrum' deterrence delivery options—assuming it has also invested in enabling capabilities, command and control, and operational concepts that could permit their use in counter-force roles. In recent years Pakistan has quadrupled its plutonium production capability, adding to the facilities it possesses to enrich uranium for nuclear weapons. Estimates of Indian and Pakistani fissile material production capability suggest that Pakistan may now be able to make four or more nuclear weapons for each one that India can make, provided India does not also expand its fissile material production capacity.[38]

Recently, awareness has grown in India that it has fallen behind Pakistan in nuclear capability. For instance, in a 2011 speech before the Lok Sabha, Jaswant Singh warned, 'Pakistan is already in possession of about 100–110 nuclear warheads that are deliverable whereas I know that India has 50 to 60. I do not know why we are keeping these facts as hidden. Why are we not having an open debate about this matter?'[39] If India remains primarily concerned about the 'minimum' in its policy of credible minimum deterrence, then whether or not Pakistan has twice as many nuclear weapons as India need not matter. But if it is more concerned with the 'credibility' aspect of this policy, then relative capabilities are important.

Since 1998, and really since the 1980s, India has been content to build its nuclear arsenal slowly.[40] In 1999, the NSAB report indicated that India would pursue a triad of delivery vehicles. Air delivered bombs were the first option India possessed. Since then it has inducted several nuclear-capable ballistic missiles into its arsenal. The sea-leg of its triad has been slowest to mature. In late 2014, India initiated sea trials of its first nuclear-powered submarine, the INS Arihant which was declared ready for service in 2016. India plans to construct two additional boats in this class before building a larger submarine more suited for lengthy deterrence patrols and capable of carrying missiles with longer ranges.[41] India also has been developing a sea-launched ballistic missile, the Sagarika, whose current range of 750 kilometres provides some capability against Pakistan but very limited range against China. Thus, India remains years away from a sea-leg of the triad that could provide the desired assured second-strike capability.[42]

Two other issues have exacerbated the concerns that emerge from the combination of Pakistan's evolving nuclear superiority and the rather torpid development of India's nuclear arsenal. Some quarters in India are sceptical that the thermonuclear device reportedly tested in May 1998 actually performed as claimed by the scientists who conducted the test. Weapons with high yield are meant to provide the backbone of India's massive retaliation posture. Controversy erupted in September 2009 when K. Santhanam, a senior scientist from the DRDO in charge of instrumentation during the 1998 nuclear tests, claimed that the thermonuclear test 'fizzled'.[43] Government agencies and a number of other scientists involved in the tests rebutted Santhanam's claims, but apparently there was sufficient concern that the Prime Minister's Office ordered a secret committee to investigate.[44] Further questioning the viability of this design, Santhanam asserted

that even after 11 years the TN device has not been weaponised by [the Bhabha Atomic Research Centre] while the 25 kiloton fission device has been fully weaponised and operationally deployed on multiple weapon platforms. It would be farcical to use a 3500-kilometres range Agni-3 missile with a 25 kiloton fission warhead as the core of our CMD. Only a 150 – 350 kiloton if not megaton TN bomb can do so which we do not have.[45]

While yields at the lower end of Santhanam's postulated range could be achieved by boosted-fission weapons as distinct from thermonuclear ones, concerns about the political credibility of India's nuclear doctrine are now matched by doubts about the technical credibility of India's nuclear weapons.[46]

The second issue is the consistent lacklustre performance of India's DRDO, which has a documented record of over-promising and under-delivering on the development of major weapons systems. In a review of India's military modernization, for example, Stephen Cohen and Sunil Dasgupta concluded in 2010 that 'DRDO has not delivered a single major weapon system to the armed forces in five decades of existence...'[47] Press releases from DRDO following missile test launches always claim perfect performance, but there has been no public independent audit of the organization to examine whether these claims are true. Scepticism abounds, particularly amongst military officers. Gaurav Kampani notes that the military and DRDO 'have clashed over whether the testing of components and subsystems in test facilities is a robust proxy for complete system tests under realistic launch conditions. Only recently has the Strategic Forces Command, the Indian military agency responsible for nuclear operations, begun the process of randomly selecting missiles from the existing inventory and test-firing them independently.'[48] It seems reasonable to wonder whether an agency that lacks the trust of its military customers will be able to deliver on the high-technology systems needed for a nuclear posture more demanding than massive retaliation.[49]

Not only is India behind in the quantity of nuclear weapons, but it also appears to be qualitatively behind Pakistan when it comes to nuclear missiles. There are doubts that India's nuclear scientific enterprise is capable of producing more advanced and accurate nuclear weapons without a major overhaul. As Indian strategists consider ways to strengthen deterrence with Pakistan, clearly the credibility of nuclear capabilities must be foremost amongst the issues to address.

The Appeal of Escalation Dominance

Behind the issues discussed above lies a deceptively tricky question: how can India make its nuclear doctrine and posture more credible in ways that would buttress India's overall deterrence of Pakistani sub-conventional violence? If the basic issue is, as Narang asserts, divergent nuclear postures—that Pakistan's asymmetric escalation posture provides dominant deterrence compared to India's assured retaliation posture[50]—then one way India could enhance deterrence is by making its nuclear posture more like Pakistan's.

As noted briefly in the Introduction of this book, Western strategic literature uses an arcane term for the challenge that derives from deterrence: escalation dominance. Simply defined, escalation dominance is 'a condition in which a combatant has the ability to escalate a conflict in ways that will be disadvantageous or costly to the adversary, while the adversary cannot do the same in return, either because it has no escalation option or because the available options would not improve the adversary's position'.[51] This terminology gained prominence during the 1960s as American nuclear strategists contemplated fighting a war against the Soviet Union under conditions of relative nuclear parity. It is a useful concept for weighing the conditions that might contribute to deterrence. The simplistic view is that 'success through escalation dominance depended on a favorable asymmetry of capabilities'.[52] But as with many theories of nuclear strategy, the concept does not permit absolute conclusions and instead defaults to uncertain psychology on critical points. After developing a highly detailed typology of 44 rungs on an escalation ladder in his treatise *On Escalation*, for instance, Herman Kahn admitted that an important variable affecting escalation dominance 'is each side's relative fear of eruption [of violence]. That side which has least to lose by eruption, or fears eruption the least, will automatically have an element of escalation dominance'.[53] Recent psychological research also demonstrates the exceeding difficulty of accurately predicting how opponents perceive each other's relative stakes in a given escalation scenario.[54]

Reviewing the record of conflicts and crises in South Asia since 1990 through a prism of escalation dominance indicates that the threat of any conflict becoming nuclear has had a dampening effect on Indian strategy and decision-making.[55] This possibility drove India to limit the geographic scope of its air strikes during the 1999 Kargil crisis. It was also a major element of the decision calculus that led India to mobilize forces but not cross the border in the 2001–2 crisis, and to limit responses to economic and diplomatic means following the attacks in Mumbai in 2008. None of the military options at India's disposal in these confrontations could have been used in ways that would clearly avoid further escalation and thereby ensure that India would prevent unacceptable harm to its overall strategic interests. By threatening use of nuclear weapons in response to effective Indian conventional military operations, and by accepting greater risk of escalation accordingly, it appears that Pakistan has prevented India from dominating the escalation ladder in South Asia.

Pakistan's acquisition of short-range nuclear weapons that it asserts can be used on the battlefield has compounded India's dilemmas. These Pakistani capabilities further frustrate India's efforts to put conventional rungs on the escalation ladder below the nuclear threshold. Now, any potent kinetic option India evaluates must contend with the possibility that it could result in escalation to nuclear use by Pakistan at a relatively low threshold. Many Indian and Pakistani strategists believe that India's current nuclear deterrence capabilities and doctrine are ineffective in this situation.

If Indian policymakers were to accept this framing of the problem—that they need to find means to address Pakistan's capacity to deny India's escalation dominance—then one obvious answer is to build more flexibility and symmetry into India's nuclear force posture. Indian deterrence could be strengthened by developing operational concepts and capabilities to add *nuclear* rungs to the escalation ladder, rather than continuing to pursue only *conventional* escalation options that risk triggering Pakistani nuclear retaliation. As Ali Ahmed writes in favour of this proposition, 'Being able to respond at an equally low escalatory rung has the advantage of permitting early conflict termination; retaining the moral high ground, important for political point scoring; and maintaining dominance at the same level of conflict. Escalation dominance in favor of India will encourage rationality in any Pakistani counter.'[56]

During the 1950s and 1960s, American strategists confronted a similar dilemma as India in perceiving that the all-or-nothing nature of massive retaliation was no longer credible in deterring lower-order threats. The US and its North Atlantic Treaty Organization (NATO) allies spent much of the 1960s and 1970s considering a range of nuclear strategies to deter Soviet aggression. From this deliberation emerged 'flexible response', the guiding principle of which was to acquire multiple options, both conventional and nuclear, to respond to the range of contingencies that might arise. (However, flexible response was not operationalized insofar as NATO did not undertake the posited build-up of conventional forces that was called for to raise the nuclear threshold.) In 1974, the Nixon Administration evolved a policy of limited nuclear options to 'enable the United States to conduct selected nuclear operations, in concert with conventional forces, which protect vital US interests and limit enemy capabilities to continue aggression. In addition, these options should enable the United States to communicate to the enemy a determination to resist aggression, coupled with a desire to exercise restraint.'[57] Each of these concepts faced major challenges, and the debate about the correct approach to deterrence continued through the end of the Cold War and still persists today.[58]

Some American scholars advocate that India adopt the logic of limited nuclear options in order to change the deterrence equation with Pakistan and assert escalation dominance. Here, too, the purpose would be to avoid dilemmas India currently faces, while communicating resolve to Pakistan that India can more credibly respond to nuclear threats on the battlefield. For example, Evan Montgomery and Eric Edelman, a former US undersecretary of defence, argue that India should follow Pakistan's lead and acquire limited nuclear capabilities that would allow it to target Pakistani military assets. This

could potentially deter nuclear use in the event of a limited conventional conflict. That is, by holding out the threat of a symmetrical and proportional response, [India] would avoid the 'all or nothing' nuclear retaliation dilemma it now seems to face.... Confronting an opponent with its own battlefield nuclear weapons, Islamabad could not reasonably conclude that limited nuclear strikes against invading ground forces would stop an invasion without triggering a nuclear reprisal.[59]

Were India to adopt this approach and build the capabilities to execute it, the deterrence balance between the two states would shift. Pakistan, according to this argument, would lose confidence that it could dominate India in the escalatory process between conventional war and nuclear use. India's threat to retaliate in kind against limited Pakistani nuclear use on the battlefield would be more credible than massive retaliation, meaning that Pakistan would have greater concern that its own nuclear first use would result in a nuclear reprisal. This would in effect force Pakistan to raise its nuclear threshold. Thus, according to this logic, the adoption of limited nuclear options could re-open space for Indian conventional military operations against Pakistan.

If this logic operated in practice, limited nuclear options could seemingly give India greater leverage to deter Pakistan's tolerance or embrace of proxy groups that attack India. Montgomery and Edelman explain:

As a result [of developing limited nuclear counter-force options], the threat of an Indian conventional assault in response to a major terrorist attack would become far more credible, and Pakistan would no longer be able to justify its support for militant proxies as a low-risk method of imposing costs on India....Under these conditions, it is even possible that Pakistan might be compelled to rein in militant groups rather than simply cut ties with them....Should India achieve escalation dominance by posing credible conventional and nuclear retaliatory threats, therefore, Pakistan might actively seek to prevent militant groups from launching attacks on their own to avoid being held hostage by their actions.[60]

This logic is theoretically persuasive insofar as it has the potential to break Pakistan's linkage of sub-conventional warfare with nuclear deterrence. Symmetry of nuclear force posture and counter-force capabilities could allow India to punish Pakistan for future terror attacks in ways that are currently infeasible. Given that Pakistani leaders would have to worry about Indian reprisal for attacks that were not necessarily sponsored or desired by the Pakistani state, Islamabad would have greater incentive to demobilize groups that threaten to conduct such attacks.

In practice, there are a host of challenges, as Indian officials and commentators recognize. No one has real-world experience in conducting battlefield nuclear warfare and controlling escalation. (Proponents would say that this historical fact validates the effectiveness of this form of nuclear deterrence.) India would face heavy financial, technological, and perhaps political–ideological burdens in developing the requisite nuclear warheads and precision delivery systems, as well as the suite of enabling capabilities required for counter-capability targeting, beyond those required for massive retaliation.

Indian decision makers would contemplate these challenges prior to adopting or asserting a policy of limited nuclear options. In doing so, they would be wise to give special attention to the potential risks of declaring new policies before the capabilities exist to field the nuclear forces required to implement them. To announce a policy not backed up by credible capability would invite Pakistani countermoves that would be self-defeating for India or, worse, disastrous in the case of miscalculation in a future crisis. On the other hand, it would also be risky to develop some capability to employ limited nuclear options without working through the strategic and tactical implications in a formal way. We now explore the implications of pursuing escalation dominance through limited nuclear options.

No Data: What Happens After a Nuclear Strike?

It is worth reiterating that most literature on nuclear strategy is based on assumptions about human behaviour that may or may not hold if a nuclear weapon were actually used during conflict. Many of these assumptions—such as rational decision-making by unitary actors, consistent preferences, and perfect information and communications—derive from the game-theoretic modelling conducted by western strategists during the Cold War. But there is no empirical evidence about how states, and leaders of states, would actually behave during such a conflict to prove the validity of these assumptions. Indeed, much of what has been learned about the neuroscience and psychology of decision-making since the classics of nuclear theory were published should induce considerable caution about these assumptions.[61] Experience from the US–Soviet context, including the Cuban Missile Crisis and subsequent efforts at deterrence signalling, indicates that neat theories often are not supported by real-world evidence. Thus, any answer to the question of whether nuclear conflict can remain limited ultimately comes down to belief. Robert Jervis, whose work on the psychology of deterrence remains the standard in the field, assesses that no scholar has made a persuasive argument that nuclear war would be kept limited.[62]

Consider the options available to India if it suffers a small-scale nuclear first strike by Pakistan, such as during a Cold Start-style operation, and had developed its own tactical nuclear weapons. In addition to the options to back down or retaliate massively with nuclear weapons, it could press a conventional assault, relying on the possibility that it might conduct nuclear strikes on Pakistani military assets to deter further nuclear attack. Or it could opt for a proportionate nuclear strike against Pakistani targets on the battlefield or against military targets further from the battle zone, such as supply lines, storage depots, or airfields. Exercising either of these options most likely would result in casualties—including Indian—much greater than those suffered in the initial triggering terrorist event. But would the mere possession of these options be sufficient to compel Pakistan to end its tolerance of militants that attack India? The answer depends again on belief; in this instance, what one believes about how Pakistani leaders would respond if they believed India would choose either option.

In case India was to press ahead with a conventional advance, would Pakistan's military leaders capitulate and seek to terminate the conflict after having already used nuclear weapons once without effect? Or would they double down and escalate further in the belief that India's leaders are more risk averse and have more to lose? Given that Pakistanis tend to think of nuclear weapons in military terms, one suspects that if a first nuclear use intended for signalling failed to deter India, Pakistan would worry that its deterrent had been eroded.[63] Pakistani military leaders, having propounded a narrative that nuclear weapons would prevent war and deter existential threats, would face very strong pressures to escalate further in order to demonstrate resolve and restore credibility of deterrent threats, regardless of whether India possessed tactical nuclear weapons or not.

If India chose to respond with nuclear weapons on the battlefield, it is entirely possible that Pakistani military leaders might misinterpret a 'limited' Indian nuclear attack on Pakistani territory as the first salvo in a total war seeking elimination of the Pakistani state and/or the Army. (Of course, Indian strategists who argue that massive retaliation is credible against Pakistan make a similar assumption in reverse: that Pakistani leaders will perceive that even their own limited use of nuclear weapons could be interpreted in India as an all-out attack, thereby triggering massive retaliation by India. Thus, the Indian argument goes, Pakistani leaders will not actually implement their first-use threat.) Given that Pakistan's nuclear weapons could be integrated with its regular Army corps on the battlefield, or deployed at air bases that also have conventional assets, an Indian attack on those facilities could be interpreted by Pakistan as nuclear pre-emption. In that case, might Pakistan face a 'use or lose' situation and opt to escalate with nuclear strikes on targets in India to limit further nuclear damage? What would India do at that point, assuming it retained second-strike nuclear forces? If conflict terminated at any of these points, would India be better off or more politically satisfied than it was prior to the escalation?

The 'what happens next' question is at the heart of most Indian critical scholarship on limited nuclear conflict, and has been an effective defence for Indian civilian leaders who push back against the urging of some military officers and hawkish analysts for the development of limited nuclear options. Shyam Saran, for example, argues that India should 'reject the notion that a nuclear war could be fought and won or that a limited nuclear war is at all credible'.[64] Some former military leaders appear to share this thinking. Admiral Verghese Koithara (ret.)

warns that 'whatever weight India might choose for its retaliatory strike it should think carefully what that strike must seek to achieve. Revenge seeking and venting rage can have no place in this decision matrix. The primary objective at that point should be to stop nuclear strikes immediately.'[65] But others prefer the possible deterrence gains that might come from limited options. Ali Ahmed, for one, argues that 'A nuclear-weapons employment strategy of commensurate response, at least for early, lower order nuclear first use, is preferable. This would deter first use since such a response is guaranteed by self-deterrence caused by the fear of receiving unacceptable damage...'[66] Some Indian hawks prefer to go further, to the logical end of war fighting. Bharat Karnad, for instance, argues:

While deterrence is a mind-game, to nevertheless believe that New Delhi will be so psychologically bridled by the prospect of the loss of a few Indian cities as to not seek the logical end-state, full-fledged nuclear retaliation, is to discount the internal political dynamic that will emerge once a nuclear first strike is absorbed and, in any case, is too big a risk for Pakistani strategists to court.[67]

These calculations are complicated by the role that China might play if a conflict were to turn nuclear, and how Indian decision makers perceive it. As one former senior Indian civilian official queried in an interview, 'How will a nuclear exchange, often posited between India and Pakistan, impact on China and would India be prudent not to factor that into its nuclear deterrence calculations?' More specifically, would China come to Pakistan's defence in an escalating crisis, either by opening a second front to a conventional war or threatening nuclear attack if India retaliated with nuclear weapons against Pakistan? Our own view is that China is unlikely to intervene with its own nuclear forces, especially if India had not initiated the use of nuclear weapons in the conflict. However, as China pursues major infrastructure projects in Pakistan, and thousands of Chinese nationals reside there, Beijing's stakes in a potential Indo-Pak nuclear conflict will grow significantly. 'It is because of this complexity,' the former official concluded, 'that notions of flexible response and counter-force targeting, which appeared to have a certain logic in a binary US–Soviet context, lose their relevance in the multi-dimensional threat scenario which prevails in our region'.[68]

Would the Pakistani Military Rather Lose Than Use?

If one believes that proportionate or graduated nuclear responses permit nuclear conflicts to remain limited, it implies that states have an ability to control or manage escalation. Escalation control cannot be determined by a single state. It requires all parties to a conflict to deliberately restrain their employment of military capabilities. In his classic work *Strategy and the Missile Age*, the American strategist Bernard Brodie concluded, 'It takes only one to start a total war, but it takes two to keep a war limited.... The major question is: How large can a war get and still remain limited?.... It is obvious that the larger the conflict, the more pressure there must be for abandoning limitations.'[69]

With the exception of the 1971 war, which is anomalous in many ways, none of the wars fought between India and Pakistan have escalated significantly in scale and time. In each of the conflicts and crises since partition, the two antagonists have observed important limits. Of the 1965 and 1971 wars, for instance, Chari observed that both sides sought to control escalation by 'excluding population centers as targets for air attack [which] was largely informed by an awareness of their mutual vulnerabilities. Neither India nor Pakistan could have defended their cities and retained the "war wastage reserves" needed to prosecute the war. These circumstances have not changed, nor have the perceptions of the two military leaderships altered.'[70] Other self-imposed limitations are similarly notable. For example, during none of the confrontations has India abrogated the Indus Waters Treaty, which governs water sharing between India and Pakistan, and disrupted Pakistan's main source of water. Even the regular shelling along the LoC in Kashmir has a typical pattern of exchange that avoids upward pressures to escalate violence, although the Modi government has changed this pattern by conducting disproportionate responses and advertising it. Only twice in the last 20 years has India escalated a confrontation in important ways that surprised Pakistan: utilizing airpower to target Pakistani positions in Kargil in 1999; and expanding the scale and geographical scope of cross-border shelling along the working boundary in Kashmir in fall 2014. Yet, neither of these escalations provoked a Pakistani conventional counter-escalation, suggesting that both sides desired to keep the conflict at certain levels of violence and contained in Kashmir, rather than spilling onto the plains in Punjab.

How might the mutual restraint necessary to contain a conflict work if both parties are postured to employ limited nuclear options? Would historical limits on locations or scope of conflict continue to be observed, especially when India faces considerable uncertainty about Pakistan's nuclear redlines? In most respects, these questions are unanswerable. Brodie's observation in 1959 still holds true: 'When we describe limited war today as requiring deliberate non-use of a gigantically powerful military instrument, one that remains ready at hand to be used, we are differentiating modern limited war from anything that has happened in the past.'[71] Chari similarly concluded that in South Asia, 'There is no definite reply to these questions, which perplexes the strategic community and governments alike.'[72] Thus, the certainty of mutual restraint to stay below the nuclear threshold is essentially an untested assumption about escalation dominance.

The gains and losses experienced in the conduct of conflict itself can change opponents' willingness to expand the means they use, as well as their objectives. Regular exchange of artillery across the LoC is an example of mutual limits on means of warfare. But take a different example, such as an Indian Cold Start operation with the objective of gaining and holding Pakistani territory—here there are no explicit limits on the means India might undertake to achieve this territorial objective if Pakistan successfully stymied India's initial thrusts. Even if Indian leaders knew their objectives were limited to a certain geographical depth, Pakistan's leaders might not perceive this, and in any case, their objective would be to deter and/or deny India this territory. Once launched, India would face great domestic pressure to achieve this objective; terminating conflict short of it would be considered a defeat. Alternatively, if India easily achieved its initial objective, its leaders might also be tempted to expand its aims to seek greater bargaining leverage.

Meanwhile, if Pakistan's conventional military means were insufficient to deny victory to India, the military leadership would suffer great reputational damage for this failure. According to Lt. Gen. (ret.) V.R. Raghavan, former Indian Director General of Military Operations, the problem is, 'How deep would be enough for India to obtain its objectives; and how deep would be too much for Pakistan, is unclear and will always remain so.'[73]

Neil Joeck, a veteran US government analyst of South Asia, notes that 'A country, like a man, cannot be hanged twice. Therefore, threatening Pakistani leaders with nuclear devastation when they already think they are facing the same outcome via conventional means might not deter Pakistan from using its tactical nuclear weapons.'[74] Thus, India's possession of limited nuclear options seems unlikely to deter Pakistan from using nuclear weapons first in circumstances that Pakistani leaders would perceive as existential defeat for the Pakistani military, even if India's objectives were in fact limited. It is not obvious how Indian pursuit of escalation dominance through limited nuclear options would avoid this problem, especially insofar as asymmetry in first-use provisions of each side's doctrines precludes agreement between the parties on mutual nuclear restraint. Responding to this dilemma, one former senior Indian official concluded, 'There is an air of unreality in thinking about limited nuclear war, which is why it is dangerous to think that this is feasible. You can't make escalation rational—it requires perfect knowledge, perfect communications, etc.'[75]

Fortunately, there has yet to be a confrontation in South Asia that has seriously tested the mutual restraint that has facilitated escalation control. As discussed in Chapter 3, crisis simulations involving Indian and Pakistani military officials demonstrate the significant escalatory pressures that could arise in a conflict. The conveners of a March 2013 simulation, for instance, found that what began as a limited war escalated quickly to a full-scale war...[as] military necessity on both sides led to extensive mobilizations and horizontal escalation. By the end of the third move, Pakistan was preparing to release warheads to its Strategic Forces Commands, readying nuclear missile launchers for possible battlefield deployment, and conducting nuclear signaling through missile tests and public statements. The exercise concluded at this point when neither side was able to terminate the war on its terms.[76]

Indian strategists acknowledge the concerns about escalation and war termination brought out in these simulated crises. Adm. Vijay Shankar (ret.), former commander of Indian strategic forces, asserts, 'the distinct absence of escalatory control negates any notional gains that limited nuclear options bestow'.[77] Koithara similarly concludes, 'the possibility of deterrence failure can never be wholly discounted.... The logic of escalation, which makes each country want to shift the context to a more advantageous plane, could eventually push the contestants over the nuclear brink. This is the reason why a nuclear strategy must necessarily deal with the issues of war termination and post-war management.'[78]

Capabilities to Fight a Nuclear War

In order for limited nuclear options to be credible the strategy must be paired with an operationalized nuclear force that has the capability to carry out strikes against military targets. A theoretical possibility of Indian limited nuclear options, absent real military capability, is not sufficient to deter Pakistan and gain escalation dominance.

A central tenet of nuclear war-fighting is damage limitation. Damage limitation takes two forms: defensive capabilities and actions to reduce the damage the opponent can inflict through nuclear attacks, and offensive capabilities and actions to destroy the opponent's nuclear capabilities before they can be used. The defensive component of damage limitation includes capabilities such as anti-ballistic missile systems, but also much broader civil defences. Bomb shelters, hardening of critical infrastructure, and 'duck and cover' exercises are manifestations of such defences designed to enhance survivability in the face of nuclear attack. India possesses a significant land mass, large population, distributed resources, and multiple centres of commerce. In theory, and probably in reality, it could survive a nuclear attack. But even if India could limit damage on its own territory, the prevailing winds for much of the year would carry radioactive contamination from nuclear detonations in Pakistan over large swaths of India including its agricultural belt and major population centres.[79] Furthermore, building up civil defences sufficient to reconstitute governance after a nuclear attack is, needless to say, an exceedingly expensive proposition. Attempting to prepare a population for the possibility of nuclear attack is also a major political challenge, especially in a democracy. In a large, economically developing, geographically diverse, politically fractious country such as India, the probability that a government could prioritize civil defence over other requirements is quite low. As Nagal admitted, 'In India, there is not an iota of work on public awareness or construction of nuclear defense shelters for the public, no education of civil servants or bureaucrats, and our disaster management is knee jerk and extremely limited in scope.'[80]

Another important component of a defensive damage limitation strategy is ballistic missile defence (BMD) to intercept incoming enemy nuclear missiles. If a decision to threaten or even to launch limited nuclear options is girded by the confidence of a missile defence capability, then the defence must work as advertised. The DRDO has been developing a missile defence system based on the Prithvi missile with an advertised capability to intercept missiles with a 2,000 kilometre range. DRDO officials indicate that the first phase of testing of this system is nearing completion and it could be deployed—either to protect cities or Indian command and control—in the near future.[81] Astoundingly, prior to a test failure in 2015, DRDO claimed a 99.8 per cent probability of hitting incoming missiles.[82] But there is considerable scepticism in India's strategic community that DRDO can deliver on its BMD promise. Sawhney and Wahab, for example, conclude that

'DRDO is woefully inadequate in all BMD subsystems as well as interceptors with acceptable assurance.'[83] Given DRDO's track record and the scepticism of Indian analysts, it is fair to assume that unless India receives considerable external assistance, it probably is a decade or more away from being able to field a limited missile defence system. Simply put, India is in no position today, and will not be for the foreseeable future, to implement a comprehensive defensive damage limitation strategy.

The offensive form of damage limitation is the ability to target the adversary's nuclear assets as a way to reduce the number of nuclear weapons that might be detonated on one's own territory. Currently, India's nuclear arsenal and its NFU policy limit contemplation of nuclear counter-force targeting under most circumstances. It is conceivable that India might use conventionally armed ballistic or cruise missiles, or other air-delivered ordnance, to target Pakistani missile launchers. However, the operational challenges in the face of Pakistani air defences and the dispersal and protection of its nuclear forces make this an enormous technological and operational challenge.[84] Of course, Pakistani strategists have thought through this possibility. One retired senior Pakistani military officer with considerable experience in nuclear matters gave this assessment in an interview:

An Indian Air Force attack on Nasr is a hypothetical that won't happen. Nasr would not be exposed early, before land operations began. So the idea that they could do pre-emptive or early air strike against it is just wrong. The Indians won't have a chance to do counter-force air strikes before the war is on...I am confident that they can't take out more than 15–20 percent of our land and air force nuclear capabilities. There will be a balance of at least 50% to hit back at them.[85]

Tellingly, this officer had clearly thought through what counter-force options are present for Pakistan. 'India is a flat country,' he offered. 'There are a few mountains in the middle of the country, but it is basically flat. A flat country has difficulty hiding weapons. We have a lot of mountains.' What he did not add is that Pakistan also has a diversity of nuclear delivery systems and an expanding nuclear arsenal that permits, at least, contemplation of a nuclear counter-force strike, with sufficient reserves for an assured second strike capability.

If India were to develop limited nuclear options with a view toward a counter-force capability, it would need to make major adjustments to at least two facets of its current nuclear practice. One change would involve the militarization of India's nuclear strategy and decision-making. Recalling the discussion of the decision-making context in Chapter 1, this would be a revolutionary change in how India plans and executes its national security policy. The second change, discussed further below, would be the procurement of a suite of military hardware and software upgrades that would provide it with the capabilities to carry out precise, time-sensitive nuclear strikes on Pakistani mobile missiles.

As noted above, India's gradual development of its nuclear arsenal has left it facing what may be an emerging gap in nuclear capabilities vis-à-vis Pakistan. If India chose to redress this gap and to develop credible limited nuclear options for counter-force targeting, the Indian leadership would need to direct considerable attention both to the bureaucratic problems that have plagued India's military modernization, and to the fragmented complex that produces various components of India's nuclear weapon systems. First and foremost, this would require instilling a new culture of performance and coordination, rather than the policy paralysis, secrecy, and compartmentalization that has characterized India's weaponization efforts since the 1980s.[86] Some organizational changes—the formation of a Strategic Forces Command and an interagency nuclear planning advisory group in the prime minister's office—already have enhanced centralized decision-making. But to address performance deficits, India's leaders would need to strengthen oversight and to conduct independent technical audits of organizations such as the Department of Atomic Energy and the DRDO. Perhaps more critically, new linkages would need to be forged between the Strategic Forces Command and the Integrated Defence Staff in order to develop operational concepts for carrying out limited counter-force in a crowded theatre of war.[87] This would include working through command and control procedures to maintain positive launch authority, rather than delegating launch authority to military commanders in the field. These 'software' system requirements are just as important as nuclear hardware in signalling credibility, yet tend to receive far less attention. In India and elsewhere, it is easy for participants in policy debates to focus on hardware—which in principle can simply be purchased—rather than on software that requires reforming institutions.

That being said, the hardware requirements for credible limited nuclear options are daunting. These challenges stem in part from the requirement to be able to identify, target, and strike conventional military forces and mobile nuclear assets in a short time period. It would be tempting for the Indian bureaucracy to try to circumvent these broader requirements by fitting a small warhead on an existing short-range delivery system and declaring that to be a sufficient capability. But absent a strategy that considers the implications for escalation, as well as adoption of operational concepts that make execution of limited nuclear options credible, a rudimentary capability alone will not produce escalation dominance. Adoption of anything short of the full capability the requirements described below would raise dangers to the extent that it would allow India's National Command Authority to avoid thinking through the challenges of controlling escalation and fighting nuclear war.

Fissile material requirements for counter-force targeting can be sizable, given the need to cover a very large set of military targets in addition to cities. Even minimally defined counter-force options, recognizing concerns about escalation and a desire to limit nuclear damage, could exceed 100 targets. Considering the need for some level of redundancy in targeting, India would potentially need to treble its current stockpile of nuclear weapons.[88] Growth in the arsenal is limited by relatively modest plutonium production from the Dhruva reactor, which is sufficient to add perhaps five weapons per year to the arsenal.[89] Thus, to develop limited nuclear options in the short-term, India would need additional plutonium production pathways. One option would be to utilize one of its larger, unsafeguarded nuclear power reactors. A second future option would be to separate plutonium from the blanket of the prototype fast breeder reactor under construction.[90] Finally, India has announced plans to build a Dhruva-2 reactor, which may yield greater plutonium output.[91] Any of these options could, with varying degrees of time and cost, satisfy larger plutonium requirements.

A second requirement would be short- and medium-range ballistic and cruise missiles with high accuracy. India's current fleet of Prithvi and Agni missiles can carry heavy payloads, but they are not sufficiently accurate for targeting the array of nuclear and conventional military assets needed for escalation dominance, especially mobile missiles and associated enabling platforms. Instead, these missiles are best suited for targeting cities for massive retaliation. In the last several years, India has begun to develop more accurate cruise and ballistic missiles. One of these, the 150 kilometre-range Prahaar, is advertised as a tactical, battlefield weapon and was touted by DRDO as having 'high maneuverability, very high acceleration and excellent impact accuracy'.[92] Many Pakistanis believe that Prahaar was developed as India's answer to the Nasr. However, at 42 centimetre in diameter and with a payload of just 200 kilograms the missile is exceedingly slim and light and may not be able to carry any of India's existing nuclear warheads. One promising cruise missile, the Nirbhay, can carry heavier payloads, but since it uses Russian-made engines India may not be permitted to use it to carry nuclear weapons. (The same reportedly is true of the BrahMos cruise missile, an Indian–Russian joint venture.[93]) To improve this situation, India would need to develop an indigenous propulsion system for cruise missiles. Meanwhile, the Shaurya—the land-based version of the 750 kilometre-range Sagarika sea-launched ballistic missile—is capable of carrying a 1,000 kilogram warhead and reportedly has an accuracy of 20–30 metres, which with a nuclear payload could make it suitable for counter-force targeting.[94]

The Prahaar may be India's top bet for a highly-accurate delivery system capable of executing limited nuclear options, especially on the battlefield. But a major question is whether India could miniaturize a nuclear warhead to fit on this small missile. Because India's other ballistic missiles all have diameters of a metre or more and can carry 1,000 kilogram payloads, it seems reasonable to guess that these characteristics describe India's standard nuclear fission design, purportedly a 25 kiloton warhead.[95] Shrinking a warhead of this size and weight up to 60–70 per cent would be a major engineering feat. (It is worth recalling that India claims to have tested in 1998 a lightweight, tactical nuclear weapon design with a 12 kiloton yield.) Miniaturization on this scale is not impossible, of course. The US W54 warhead, for example, weighed approximately 50 pounds and had a diameter of some 27 centimetres. However, having conducted so few full-scale nuclear tests, India could not have very high confidence in the reliability of such a small weapon, which would add considerable risk to employment of limited nuclear options.

Finally, as with the sophisticated use of airpower described in Chapter 3, mastering operation of the command, control, communications, computers, intelligence, surveillance, and reconnaissance (C4ISR) and information fusion requirements for nuclear counter-force targeting, especially against mobile assets, is exceedingly difficult. One way to understand the enormity of this challenge is to consider the steps and systems involved from targeting to detonation. Assuming India might seek to destroy Nasr missile batteries with ballistic or cruise missiles following a Pakistani nuclear strike against Indian armoured battalions, India would need continuous real-time visual coverage from drones or satellites, as well as other signals intelligence, in order to identify and discriminate Nasr missiles from other military systems. Once the missiles were identified, information would need to be communicated securely through the Nuclear Command Authority (NCA) to the Strategic Forces Command for targeting. The NCA would also want to ensure that Indian conventional forces were not in the vicinity in order to diminish chances of fratricide. This requires constant communications through the Integrated Defence Staff. The NCA would also need to consider meteorological data to ensure that prevailing winds would not blow radioactive fallout to Indian population centres or agricultural areas. In the interim, it would have placed Indian nuclear forces on alert and dispersed them to the field, making them also vulnerable to a broader Pakistani counter-force attack. If Pakistan observed or was concerned that India might be readying to use nuclear weapons, Pakistani commanders, rather than losing their nuclear weapons, might instead opt to use them. This suggests that India would need to perform the above steps in a very short time-period, with air-tight secure communications and low visibility.

Little is publicly known about the systems India has in place in order to fulfil these requirements. As Nagal observed, 'since a large part of C4ISR is confidential in nature, doubts will always be raised on the efficacy of the systems in place'.[96] Interviews with current and former senior Indian officials suggest that not all of these capabilities currently exist. For instance, a recently retired high-ranking Air Force officer indicated in an interview, 'We still have a long way to go to get to the point where we can react quickly with precision. We are not in a position to react quickly now. You need constant intelligence with high accuracy, which we don't have.'[97] India will need to double its current fleet of four intelligence, surveillance, and reconnaissance (ISR) satellites, this officer added, as noted in Chapter 3.

Two additional matters regarding the capability requirements for limited nuclear options deserve mention, but will not be discussed in greater detail. The first is cost. Until now, India's nuclear weapons programme has been relatively inexpensive, as it has not relied on a massive dedicated production complex with attendant long lifecycle costs. Instead, for fissile material and delivery vehicles, India largely has depended on multi-purpose facilities and technology research and development programmes to fulfil nuclear weapon requirements. Production of the capabilities described here, even if done at relatively small scale, would necessitate financial outlays considerably greater than what India has spent to date. The second matter is security. Protecting a relatively small nuclear complex against internal and external threats is a major challenge, and there continue to be widespread doubts about the measures and practices India has in place. That challenge becomes much harder when smaller, mobile nuclear missiles, kept at higher levels of alert, are added to an arsenal. Neither of these matters is trivial; both must be considered before a decision is made to adopt limited nuclear options.

* * *

The advent of nuclear deterrence between India and Pakistan has reinforced India's tradition of restraint in the conduct of warfare. Understandable frustration over the 2001 attack on the Indian parliament and then the 2008 attack on Mumbai has prompted many in the Indian security establishment to seek new options and capabilities to punish and compel Pakistan through robust conventional military retaliation to future terrorist attacks. To make conventional retaliation to terrorism credible, however, requires overcoming the risks that Pakistan would initiate the use of nuclear weapons to deter and/or defeat effective Indian conventional operations. A singularly experienced policymaker and adviser in New Delhi put the challenge to us this way in a 2014 interview:

Our nuclear situation is still ambiguous, 17 years after the tests. We don't have strategic doctrine of any kind. But twice we came close to wider wars with escalatory potential—in 1999 and 2001-2002. If you are going to have the bomb, it imposes upon you a duty to say how you will manage the clear and present danger of conflict escalating to when you might be faced with using it.[98]

This chapter has examined the challenges that inhere in this objective.

India's current nuclear doctrine and posture are fundamentally sufficient as long as Indian leaders believe they will not authorize the Indian Army to make major thrusts into Pakistani territory, or the Air Force to conduct major missile or bombing missions against the Pakistani heartland in response to a terrorist attack. With this premise it is reasonable to conclude that Pakistan will have no occasion to use nuclear weapons against India.

India's current posture of massive retaliation is sufficient to deter Pakistan from initiating major conventional warfare on Indian territory and from conducting large-scale nuclear attacks on the Indian homeland, as long as India's nuclear forces and command and control can survive a Pakistani nuclear first strike.

If, on the other hand, Indian leaders want to promote policies and capabilities to conduct robust conventional military operations on Pakistani territory, then India may need to increase its capabilities and plans to conduct limited nuclear operations against Pakistani conventional and military forces. As discussed in Chapter 2, Indian leaders would need to resolve the disjuncture between a limited offensive conventional military doctrine and defensive nuclear doctrine in order to prepare for the probability that conventional warfare escalates to nuclear use. India could seek to employ a limited nuclear options strategy, as a way to achieve escalation dominance, but there is no basis for confidence that it would attain this objective better than India's existing capability.

Despite this assessment, if India does decide to move towards development of nuclear counter-force options, it is imperative to avoid two mistakes that have been common in past Indian policy and practice. The first is to make premature announcements of capability. There is an unfortunate tendency in India, verging on standard operating procedure, to announce or publicly discuss operational concepts or weapons systems before they actually exist. This was arguably the case with the ill-fated Cold Start doctrine, and is true of many of the strategic capabilities tested and touted by DRDO. Whatever changes India does or does not make to its nuclear policy and capabilities in years ahead—including pursuing limited nuclear options—it should seek to avoid this strategic mistake, which only serves to feed Pakistan's worst-case analysis and result in countervailing capabilities that further disadvantage India. In the intervening period—which would necessarily be many years—the Indian government would do well to avoid doing or saying things that give the impression it has either the capability or intent to use limited nuclear options.

The second mistake is to default to half-measures. It is entirely plausible, based on history in other states with nuclear weapons, that DRDO might develop a nuclear version of the Prahaar that would be delivered to the military before there is any attendant process for working through the circumstances under which the system might be used and what it would mean for escalation control. In many ways, this situation could be more dangerous for India than a formal decision to patiently adapt force posture and capabilities in parallel.

Regarding India's debate on nuclear doctrine, a threat of 'punitive' retaliation may be more credible than 'massive' retaliation, though it doesn't obviate questions of proportionality and escalation control. The picture may be a bit clearer regarding India's NFU policy, which is very much integral to India's image as a 'responsible' nuclear state. Even with a change of view on limited nuclear options, and acquisition of more versatile weapon systems, India faces no need to use nuclear weapons first. To declare otherwise would sacrifice many of the political, moral, and strategic advantages India has gained by sustaining NFU. It is worth noting that China, despite concerns about change in its nuclear doctrine, continues to retain a NFU policy and India presumably would not want to attenuate that.

Though there may be reasons that India would adjust its nuclear policy as its capabilities evolve and the deterrence environment changes, the answers to India's strategic challenge from Pakistan are unlikely to be found at this level. As Nagal concludes, 'To prevent proxy war/sub conventional conflicts calls for different strategy, linking our nuclear policy to the balance of the war spectrum does not fit India's strategic thought, it is fraught with dangers and misadventures.'[99] Given the asymmetric stakes involved in a potential conflict and divergent beliefs about nuclear weapons, the potential for a confrontation to escalate to nuclear use cannot be ruled out. For, as Vijay Shankar observes,

Deterrence in essence is a mind game that does not brook any other logic than total escalation when confronted by a nuclear strike. Notions of counter force strikes, flexible response and limited nuclear options do not make sense in the face of total escalation. India's incentive to keep below the nuclear threshold is as pressing as it is for Pakistan. This is deterrence at play.[100]

Notes and References

1. For a collection of statements and speeches by Indian strategists, see J.K. Jain, *Nuclear India* (New Delhi: Radiant Publishers, 1974), 3–102.

2. George Perkovich, *India's Nuclear Bomb: The Impact on Global Proliferation* (Berkeley: University of California Press, 2001); Raj Chengappa, *Weapons of Peace: The Secret Story of India's Quest to Be a Nuclear Power* (New Delhi: HarperCollins, 2000); and Gaurav Kampani, 'New Delhi's Long Nuclear Journey: How Secrecy and Institutional Roadblocks Delayed India's Weaponization', *International Security* 38, no. 4 (Spring 2014).

3. Rajesh Rajagopalan, 'India's Nuclear Policy', paper for National Institute for Defense Studies, Japan, International Symposium on Security Affairs, 18 November 2009; Ashley Tellis, *India's Emerging Nuclear Posture: Between Recessed Deterrence and Ready Arsenal* (Santa Monica: RAND Corporation, 2001), 261–9.

4. Feroz Khan, *Eating Grass: The Making of the Pakistani Bomb* (Stanford: Stanford University Press, 2012).

5. See discussion in P.R. Chari, Pervaiz Iqbal Cheema, and Stephen P. Cohen, *Four Crises and a Peace Process: American Engagement in South Asia* (Washington, DC: Brookings Institution Press, 2007); and P.R. Chari, 'Nuclear Signaling in South Asia: Revisiting A.Q. Khan's 1987 Threat', Carnegie Endowment for International Peace, 14 November 2013.

6. Narang, *Nuclear Strategy in the Modern Era*, 15–17.

7. United Nations Security Council Press Release, 'Security Council Condemns Nuclear Tests by India and Pakistan', 6 June 1998. Available at: http://www.un.org/press/en/1998/sc6528.doc.htm.

8. See discussion in Narang, *Nuclear Strategy in the Modern Era*, 267–73. See also Peter Lavoy, *Asymmetric Warfare in South Asia: The Causes and Consequences of the Kargil Conflict* (Cambridge: Cambridge University Press, 2009); and Lambeth, 'Airpower at 18,000'.

9. Rakesh Sood, 'Should India Revise its Nuclear Doctrine?', Centre for Nuclear Non-Proliferation and Disarmament, Policy Brief No. 18, December 2014.

10. National Security Advisory Board, 'Draft Nuclear Doctrine', 17 August 1999.

11. Rajagopalan, 'India's Nuclear Policy', 99.

12. Prime Minister's Office, 'Cabinet Committee on Security Reviews Progress in Operationalizing India's Nuclear Doctrine', Press Release, 4 January 2003.

13. There was a third addition to the scope of the doctrine released in 2003: that India would retain the option to use nuclear weapons to respond to chemical or biological attack. This change is less germane to the discussion here, but further muddles the doctrine. See Scott D. Sagan, 'The Evolution of Pakistani and Indian Nuclear Doctrine', in Scott D. Sagan (ed.) Inside Nuclear South Asia (Stanford: Stanford University Press, 2009).

14. The test of the short-range Nasr missile in April 2011 was described as adding to deterrence 'at all levels of the threat spectrum'. See Inter-Services Public Relations, Press Release 94, 19 April 2011. Available at: https://www.ispr.gov.pk/front/main.asp?o=t-press_release&id=1721&search=1. In a 21 October 2011 discussion at the Stimson Center, Zamir Akram, Pakistan's Ambassador to the Conference on Disarmament in Geneva, used the term 'full spectrum' to describe Pakistan's deterrence posture.

15. Sood, 'Should India Revise Its Nuclear Doctrine?'

16. Quoted in Celia Dugger, 'The Kashmir Brink', New York Times, 20 June 2002.

17. Narang, Nuclear Strategy in the Modern Era, 281.

18. P.R. Chari, 'India's Nuclear Doctrine: Stirrings of Change', Carnegie Endowment for International Peace, 4 June 2014.

19. Interview, New Delhi, 26 April 2014.

20. Jaswant Singh, Remarks before the Lok Sabha, 15 March 2011. Available at: http://164.100.47.132/debatestext/15/VII/z1503-Final.pdf, 114–15.

21. The 2014 BJP election manifesto is available at: http://bjpelectionmanifesto.com/pdf/manifesto2014.pdf. It is worth noting that discussion of the nuclear program falls on page 39 of the 42-page document, which is indicative of the general lack of importance given to nuclear issues relative to domestic and economic priorities in Indian politics and, arguably, governance.

22. For good reviews of the Indian nuclear debate in 2013–14, see Chari, 'India's Nuclear Doctrine'; and Manoj Joshi, 'The Credibility of India's Nuclear Deterrent', and Shasank Joshi, 'An Evolving Indian

Nuclear Doctrine', both in Michael Krepon and Julia Thompson (eds) *Deterrence Instability and Nuclear Weapons in South Asia*, (Washington DC: Stimson Center, 2015).

23. Ajit Doval, Keynote Address at the 6th Munich Security Conference Core Group Meeting in New Delhi, 21 October 2014. Available at: https://www.securityconference.de/news/article/ democracy-is-one-of-the-most-powerful-tools-for-dealing-with-security-problems/.

24. Interview with former Indian Strategic Forces Commander, New Delhi, 14 November 2014.

25. Sood, 'Should India Revise Its Nuclear Doctrine?'

26. 'Modi says Committed to No First Use of Nuclear Weapons', *Reuters*, 16 April 2014.

27. B.S. Nagal, 'Checks and Balances', *FORCE*, June 2014.

28. Chari, 'India's Nuclear Doctrine'.

29. Rajagopalan, 'India Nuclear Policy', 100.

30. Chatham House Rule Seminar at Institute for Peace and Conflict Studies, New Delhi, 11 November 2014.

31. Shyam Saran, 'Is India's Nuclear Deterrent Credible?', speech at the India Habitat Centre, New Delhi, 24 April 2013.

32. Chatham House Rule Seminar at Institute for Peace and Conflict Studies, New Delhi, 11 November 2014.

33. Raja Menon, 'A Mismatch of Nuclear Doctrines', *Hindu*, 22 January 2014.

34. Chari, 'India's Nuclear Doctrine'.

35. Joshi, 'The Credibility of India's Nuclear Deterrent', 44.

36. Manpreet Sethi, 'Counter Pak Nuke Tactics', *New Indian Express*, 24 July 2014.

37. B.S. Nagal, 'Perception and Reality', *FORCE*, October 2014.

38. Fissile material stockpiles estimates for India and Pakistan from International Panel on Fissile Materials. Available at: http://fissilematerials.org.

39. Jaswant Singh, Remarks before the Lok Sabha, 114.

40. Kampani, 'New Delhi's Long Nuclear Journey'.

41. Pravin Sawhney and Vijay Shankar, 'Is the Navy's Newest Sub Worth the Price?', *Hindu*, 25 January 2012.

42. For a good analysis of India's nuclear submarine program, see Rehman, 'Murky Waters'.

43. K. Santhanam and Ashok Parthasarathi, 'Pokhran-II Thermonuclear Test, A Failure', *Hindu*, 17 September 2009.

44. Gaurav Kampani, 'Is the Indian Nuclear Tiger Changing Its Stripes? Data, Interpretation, and Fact', *Nonproliferation Review*, Fall 2014.

45. Santhanam and Parthasarathi, 'Pokhran II Thermonuclear Test, A Failure'.

46. See discussion in Tellis, *India's Emerging Nuclear Posture*, 519–22.

47. Cohen and Dasgupta, *Arming Without Aiming*, 32.

48. Kampani, 'Is the Indian Nuclear Tiger Changing Its Stripes?'

49. Nagal, for example, argues that 'Our programme for weapons delivery platforms has not fully delivered at the pace required by national security, and a detailed performance audit is required to address the shortcomings and deficiencies, and bring about structural changes in the way strategic programmes are organized.... Other aspects for future development are improved guidance systems, miniaturization, bigger SSNNs, anti-satellite capability, space based sensors, earth penetrating systems and host of new technology required to overcome protection/defensive systems.... The surveillance and monitoring system for 360 degree coverage is a technological challenge which requires massive infrastructure and sensors in space, land, air and sea.' Nagal, 'Checks and Balances'.

50. Narang, *Nuclear Strategy in the Modern Era*, 281–2.

51. Forrest E. Morgan, Karl P. Mueller, Evan S. Medeiros, Kevin L. Pollpeter, and Roger Cliff, *Dangerous Thresholds*, 15.

52. Lawrence Freedman, *The Evolution of Nuclear Strategy* (New York: St. Martin's Press, 1981), 218.

53. Herman Kahn, *On Escalation: Metaphors and Scenarios* (New York: Frederick A. Prager, 1965), 290.

54. Nicholas D. Wright, 'Neural Prediction Error is Central to Diplomatic and Military Signalling' in Hriar Cabayan, William Casebeer, Diane DiEuliis, James Giardano, Nicholas D. Wright (eds) *White Paper on Leveraging Neuroscientific and Neurotechnological (NeuroS&T) Developments with Focus on Influence and Deterrence in a Networked World* (US Department of Defense Joint Staff, 2014); Jack S. Levy, 'Prospect Theory and International Relations', *Political Psychology* 13, no. 2 (June 1992): 283–310.

55. Narang, *Nuclear Strategy in the Modern Era*, 257–82.

56. Ali Ahmed, 'The Interface of Strategic and War Fighting Doctrines in the India-Pakistan Context', *Strategic Analysis* 33, no. 5 (2009): 708.

57. 'Policy for Planning the Employment of Nuclear Weapons', US National Decision Memorandum 242, 17 January 1974. Available at: http://www.nixonlibrary.gov/virtuallibrary/documents/nsdm/nsdm_242.pdf.

58. See Freedman, *The Evolution of Nuclear Strategy*; and Robert Jervis, *The Illogic of American Nuclear Strategy* (Ithaca: Cornell University Press, 1984).

59. Evan Braden Montgomery and Eric S. Edelman, 'Rethinking Stability in South Asia: India, Pakistan, and the Competition for Escalation Dominance', *Journal of Strategic Studies*, 2014, 18.

60. Montgomery and Edelman, 'Rethinking Stability in South Asia', 18.

61. Wright, 'Neural Prediction Error is Central to Diplomatic and Military Signaling'.

62. Jervis, *The Illogic of American Nuclear Strategy*; and Robert Jervis, 'The Nuclear Revolution and the Common Defense', *Political Science Quarterly* 101, no. 5 (1986).

63. As Henry Kissinger succinctly argued, 'A deterrent which one is afraid to implement when it is challenged ceases to be a deterrent.' Henry Kissinger, *Nuclear Weapons and Foreign Policy* (New York: Harper and Brothers, 1957), 134.

64. Shyam Saran, 'The Dangers of Nuclear Revisionism', *Business Standard*, 22 April 2014.

65. Vergese Koithara, *Managing India's Nuclear Forces* (Washington DC: Brookings Institution Press, 2012), 245.

66. Ahmed, 'Cold Start', 462.

67. Bharat Karnad, 'South Asia: The Irrelevance of Classical Nuclear Deterrence Theory', *India Review* 4, no. 2 (2005): 190.

68. Interview with former senior Indian official, New Delhi, 27 October 2013.

69. Bernard Brodie, *Strategy and the Missile Age* (Santa Monica, CA: RAND Corporation, 1959), 334–5.

70. P.R. Chari, 'Nuclear Crisis, Escalation Control, and Deterrence in South Asia', Stimson Center Working Paper, April 2003. Available at: http://www.stimson.org/images/uploads/research-pdfs/escalation_chari.pdf.

71. Brodie, *Strategy and the Missile Age*, 310–11.

72. Chari, 'Nuclear Crisis, Escalation Control, and Deterrence in South Asia'.

73. V.R. Raghavan, 'Limited War and Nuclear Escalation in South Asia', *Nonproliferation Review*, Fall–Winter 2001, 16.

74. Neil Joeck, 'Prospects for Limited War and Nuclear Use in South Asia', in Michael Krepon and Julia Thompson (eds), *Deterrence Stability and Escalation Control in South Asia* (Washington, DC: Stimson Center, 2013), 108.

75. Interview with former Indian official, New Delhi, 25 April 2014.

76. Khan and French, 'South Asian Stability Workshop'.

77. Author email correspondence, 19 August 2015.

78. Koithara, *Managing India's Nuclear Forces*, 205.

79. See, for example, Alan Robock and Owen Brian Toon, 'South Asian Threat? Local Nuclear War = Global Suffering', *Scientific American*, January 2010.

80. Nagal, 'Perception and Reality'.

81. 'BMD in Final Stages of Development', *Hindu*, 3 August 2015. Available at: http://www.thehindu.com/news/national/andhra-pradesh/bmd-in-final-stages-of-development/article7493545.ece.

82. Sushant Singh, 'Interceptor Missile Test 7 Times, DRDO's Rajinikanth Moment Still Far', *Indian Express*, 4 May 2015.

83. Sawhney and Wahab, 'Capability First'.

84. See discussion in Kampani, 'Is the Indian Nuclear Tiger Changing Its Stripes?'

85. Interview with former Pakistani military officer, Islamabad, 18 November 2014.

86. Kampani, 'New Delhi's Long Nuclear Journey'.

87. See discussion in Kampani, 'Is the Indian Nuclear Tiger Changing Its Stripes?' and Rajagopalan, 'India's Nuclear Policy'.

88. Hans M. Kristensen and Robert S. Norris, 'Worldwide Deployments of Nuclear Weapons, 2014', *Bulletin of the Atomic Scientists*, September 2014.

89. Derived from production estimates produced by the International Panel on Fissile Material. Available at: www.fissilematerials.org.

90. Z. Mian, A.H. Nayyar, R. Rajaraman, and M.V. Ramana, 'Fissile Materials in South Asia: The Implications of the US-India Nuclear Deal', IPFM Research Report #1, September 2006, 24.

91. Mihika Basu, 'BARC Proposes Two New Research Reactors Under 12th Plan', *Indian Express*, 13 February 2012.

92. T.S. Subramanian and Y. Mallikarjun, '"Prahaar" Missile Successfully Test-Fired', *Hindu*, 21 July 2011.

93. Pravin Sawhney and Ghazala Wahab, 'Capability First', *FORCE*, May 2014.

94. 'India Unveils Shaurya – Submarine Launched Missile,' *Defense Update*. Available at: http://defense-update.com/products/s/shaurya_missile_170210.html. See also Arun S. Vishwakarma, 'India's Multifunction Missile for Credible Deterrent', *Indian Defence Review*, January–March 2009.

95. Kampani, 'Is the Indian Nuclear Tiger Changing Its Stripes?'.

96. Nagal, 'Perception and Reality'.

97. Interview with former senior Indian military officer, New Delhi, 24 April 2014.

98. Interview with former senior Indian policymaker, New Delhi, 25 April 2014.

99. Nagal, 'Perception and Reality'.

100. Author email correspondence, 19 August 2015.

6

NON-VIOLENT COMPELLENCE

The imbalance of potential risks and benefits of conventional military actions and covert operations makes it clearer why Atal Bihari Vajpayee and Manmohan Singh exercised restraint after the 2001 and 2008 terrorist attacks on the Parliament and Mumbai, respectively. Even if India did undertake covert operations, as Pakistan asserts, Indian leaders refrained from conventional military retaliation. They maintained the nation's focus on development while seeking to mobilize international opinion to harm Pakistan's reputation internally and globally. New Delhi's restraint was not merely the product of necessity due to the lack of feasible forceful options; it also reflected a judgement that the nation's strategic interest was better served by avoiding escalation of violence.[1] It is impossible to know what India would have gained and/or lost if it had responded with military force instead, but the course Indian leaders did take resulted in a Pakistani sense of loss from the Mumbai attacks and their aftermath, and the onward rise of India's international power and reputation.

Looking ahead, India is naturally determined to enhance its military and covert action capabilities. This still leaves open the possibility that non-violent compellence in some circumstances could be more cost-effective to turn the people and authorities of Pakistan and the international community against actors who would conduct terrorism in India. As the great Chinese philosopher Sun Tzu reportedly said, 'The perfection of strategy would be...to produce a decision without any serious fighting.'[2]

UN Security Council Resolution 1373, adopted in 2001 after the Al-Qaeda attacks on New York and Washington, obligates all states to take actions to prevent and suppress terrorists' efforts to recruit, organize, train, fundraise, and carry out attacks. This is a Chapter VII resolution, deeming major acts of terrorism a threat to international peace and potentially subject to forceful response by the UN and/or member states. Months after Resolution 1373 was passed, and again in 2008, India suffered high-profile terrorist attacks. The US and China protected Pakistan from being exposed to UN debate over sanctions for its failures in the counter terrorism domain. Indeed, the UN Security Council issued no resolution after the Mumbai attack, unlike in the aftermath of the 9/11 attacks on the US, and the 2005 bombings of trains in London. The Council's limp response only intensified India's frustration over the veto-wielding states' tendencies to shape the Council's actions to their own narrow interests. Yet, this does not negate the potential value of improving India's capacity to mobilize international political, economic, and moral power to counter terrorism against India.

Recognizing that the Security Council is not the most plausible vector for mobilizing and channelling power, India could still use the obligations set out by UN Resolutions such as 1373 as the basis for pressing states bilaterally and regionally to hold Pakistan to account. India's power to influence other key states will increase as its economy grows. Military modernization, as reforms are implemented, will enable India to project greater power in its region and beyond, adding to its international leverage. In addition, India's political leaders, diplomats, and globally-renowned civil society figures—including authors, musicians, economists, Bollywood stars, cricket players, etc.—have untapped potential to mobilize their counterparts and audiences in other countries to ostracize Pakistan for failures to combat terrorism emanating from its territory. Many of the most globally influential states— the United Kingdom, France, Germany, the US, and China, for example—increasingly feel threatened by Islamist terrorists. These states can be put on the defensive for refusing to hold Pakistan to account.[3]

India's aim, and that of states that would join it, would not be to interfere in the internal affairs of Pakistan. Rather, the aim would be to mobilize non-violent pressure to hold Pakistan's government accountable for failing to do its utmost to prevent violent threats to international security that originate on its territory.

Non-violent compellence can take several forms. One of the most common—economic sanctions—can be imposed by states bilaterally, through regional blocs such as the EU, and, with greater difficulty, through multilateral institutions and the UN. Sanctions can restrict imports and exports, financial transactions, and insurance. Akin to sanctions, states can reduce or eliminate various forms of economic and military aid they otherwise provide to Pakistan. Going further, contributors to the International Monetary Fund (IMF) could be induced to delay or withhold support to Pakistan, though this would be a less likely course.

Political isolation is another category of non-violent pressure. Elected governments and their security establishments are not immune to the internal discord that can be generated by pointed international rebukes and protests. Leaders of other states can cancel or postpone bilateral meetings with their counterparts and withdraw invitations to participate in international forums. This can cause humiliation and impede the targeted state's pursuit of its interests with counterparts. When continuing engagement would be more effective, bilateral and multilateral meetings can be used to convey the importance of Pakistan's doing more to uphold its sovereign obligations regarding international terrorism. Official statements issued from such meetings could record the expectations that Pakistan must do better if it is to avoid material harm to its relations with other states. Travel bans against officials and their family members can impose personal costs for a state's failure to fulfil its counterterrorism obligations. These and other actions can affect a country's 'brand,' which in turn can affect attractiveness for investment.

Twenty-first century communications techniques also can be utilized to mobilize popular campaigns within a targeted country and among the larger international community to undermine the legitimacy of government leaders and policies that allow terrorism to continue. Chinese internet activists have been mobilized in this way to protest against perceived Japanese and American bellicosity. An international social media movement to challenge the legitimacy of Israel's ongoing occupation of Palestinian territory has caused deep concern in the Israeli government. Pakistan's record of failing to prevent terrorism against India (and Afghanistan) is clear enough to warrant protests of this sort, especially if another major terrorist attack tied to actors based in Pakistan occurs.

Of course, a strategy of non-violent compellence will be more effective to the extent that India (or any other state) is not acting from a position of weakness. Withholding the exercise of real options to act forcefully and effectively endows a policy of self-restraint with moral–political power and creates leverage over the opponent and the international community: if non-violent pressure does not work, harsher measures are the alternative. To make such a policy most effective, India would still need to reform its management of national defence. It would still need to acquire intelligence, reconnaissance, and strike capabilities that would enable its army, navy, and air force to prevail if Pakistan chose to respond militarily to non-violent pressure. And, because the nuclear shadow would hover over the competition, India still would need a reliable, survivable nuclear force postured to deter conflict escalation. Building up this military strength will take time; meanwhile, honing non-violent strategies and capabilities can occur in parallel, with little cost.

Finally, for non-violent pressure to have a decisive impact on Pakistan, India would need to persuade other influential states and populations to join it. India alone does not have sufficient economic, political, and social connectivity with Pakistan to make Pakistani leaders and society feel threatened by severance of these bilateral connections. Some combination of governments and civil society organizations in the US, Europe, Australia, Japan, and, ideally, Muslim-majority states, including the UAE and Iran, would need to be motivated to cooperate with India. To develop the capacity to build such cooperation, Indian leaders would need to move beyond their traditional focus on demonstrating and preserving Indian autonomy and instead create coalitions for the purpose of countering Pakistan's perceived state-enabled terrorism. This would distinguish India as a twenty-first century global power that can motivate others to help it pursue common values and purposes, rather than a national power that only can resist demands from others.

Strategic Risks and Benefits

Within India and abroad, experts and pundits in recent decades have not analysed New Delhi's traditional practice of non-violent compellence in strategic terms. This is natural: international security experts tend to focus on military capabilities and doctrine much more than on non-military means of motivating adversaries to change policies. Moreover, political leaders in India generally do not frame their actions in strategic terms, including the exercise of military restraint. Though Gandhi and the Indian independence movement employed non-violence with great strategic effect, Indian leaders and security professionals in recent years have preferred not to invoke this model of strategy and instead have compared India's policies with those of the United States, Israel, and to a lesser extent China.

Yet, as we have suggested earlier, the strategic results that the US and Israel have obtained by using military power have been mixed at best. In twenty-first century conditions, the use of military force along lines developed in the nineteenth and twentieth century yields diminishing returns. As events in the Middle East, Western Europe, Ukraine, Afghanistan, and East Asia suggest, conflict is becoming more diffuse and the utility of conventional military force more uncertain.[4] This chapter offers a cursory assessment of the potential risks and benefits of non-violent compellence as a general category compared with those of conventional military and covert options.

One category of risk involves mistaken intelligence and the targeting of kinetic forces and covert on-the-ground agents against terrorists and related infrastructure. Attacks that hit empty sites or innocent civilians, or that miss their targets, can cause embarrassment and various forms of backlash within the region or the broader international system. The consequences can vary. Pressure can mount to conduct further attacks to rebuild credibility following mistakes. Or if no follow-up action occurs, the leadership may lose credibility for failing to redeem a mistake.

The more forceful a kinetic or covert operation is, the higher the risk that Pakistani leaders and/or terrorists will feel the need to retaliate. Their retaliation, in turn, will press Indian leaders to react or else risk losing face. The shadow of nuclear war would loom over this escalatory process. Non-violent compellence could conceivably prompt Pakistani authorities and/or terrorist groups to respond violently, but the relative risks of escalation are slight compared with the most ambitious kinetic options.

The costs of mobilizing for and conducting major military operations can be significant, and must be envisioned even if the initial Indian action is modest in intensity and cost. Non-coercive policies can impose some costs on India, but given the low levels of Indo-Pak economic interdependence, the risk here is slight.

If the risks of non-violent compellence are low relative to conventional military and some covert operations, their potential benefits may be comparatively limited too. A non-violent strategy will not satisfy near-term popular and partisan demands for retribution which will be highest immediately after a terrorist attack. Sanctions and some forms of political isolation would take time to implement and the pain they would impose on Pakistan would not be apparent for even longer. Leaders pursuing this strategy could be accused of softness. In the case of Narendra Modi, who came to office in New Delhi with a reputation for toughness, eschewal of force could be especially disappointing to his followers. (However, the opposition political parties, who are all to his left, would not be very credible if they tried to make a big issue out of his restraint.) While Manmohan Singh and the Congress party did not suffer for the government's measured response following the Mumbai attack in 2008—they were returned to government in the 2009 elections—the political dynamics affecting the Modi government could be different.

Non-violent compellence would not bring the benefit of harming terrorists directly, which could be achieved by well-targeted air strikes and on-the-ground operations. Yet, if the strategic aim is to motivate Pakistani authorities and society to turn against anti-India terrorists, then the absence of attacks on individuals or terrorist infrastructure would not dramatically lessen the potential benefit of non-violence. Moreover, the data on the effectiveness of targeted killings of terrorists in the Middle East, Afghanistan, and Pakistan do not indicate clear strategic benefits from such operations.[5]

Experienced, thoughtful Indians who have served at the highest levels in the prime minister's office, the RAW, and the MoD seem to share this broad analysis. As a former senior RAW officer put it in an interview:

Suppose we were to do something big to Pakistan, then where would we be? What would the international fallout be? Migration? Can we handle that? What would be a humiliating defeat for the ISI? How do you define that? Loss of territory? India would not want to hold any Pakistani territory. It would be a liability. Weakening their industry? Not really. So then it's a question of punishment. You pulverize them, push them deeper into poverty, which creates more social discontent. Then the US comes in and bails them out so it doesn't get worse. And the Pakistanis divert that to weapons to use on us.[6]

Today and in the foreseeable future, the choice Indian leaders are likely to make will be between doing nothing and doing too much. Not reacting may be politically and strategically infeasible. Overreacting would be strategically unwise. As a former prime ministerial advisor put it: 'In hindsight, how the US responded to 9/11 was a disaster, whereas Indian restraint in 2008 made Pakistan lose.'[7] Or, as the former RAW official quoted just above put it: 'if your adversary is committing suicide, it doesn't make sense to murder him.'[8] These strategic insights point to the potential value of non-violent compellence.

Non-Violent Compellence Options and Capabilities

In considering possible modes of non-violent compellence against Pakistan, Indian strategists must weigh not only desired near-term effects but also longer-term ones. Inflicting economic pain and political isolation may satisfy interests to punish Pakistan and to create policy pressures on the state to demobilize terrorist groups. But if economic weakness and political isolation undermine the positions of progressive Pakistani political–economic forces and/or spur recruitment to militant organizations, India's long-term interest could be harmed. Here the question becomes: Are the destabilizing effects of non-violent compellence worse than those that would follow army-centric operations in Pakistan and/or airstrikes and/or covert operations? The answer depends in large part on the risks of escalation to major warfare that possible kinetic operations would entail. Relatedly, Indian strategists must calculate which options are more likely to motivate Pakistani authorities and influential circles to change the state's policies toward anti-India terrorist groups. As suggested in Chapter 3, for example, limited airstrikes on terrorists and their infrastructure could be less likely to motivate major policy changes in Pakistan than might more lasting economic sanctions and political isolation. These are questions Indian decision makers would need to address, seeking insights from Pakistani sources.

Economic Sanctions

States and international bodies weigh many factors in determining whether, when, and how to impose economic sanctions. We discuss below the interests that key states and international bodies likely would factor into decisions regarding whether to support Indian requests to sanction Pakistan. But first it is useful to consider strategic questions. Whom would those imposing sanctions seek to punish and to what ends? If the aim is to motivate a state's decision makers to change policies and behaviours, can sanctions be targeted precisely to affect them? If sanctions cannot be targeted so precisely, and/or it is judged that decision makers will only respond to pressures mounted by wider society, then should sanctions with wide socio-economic effects be pursued? Beyond the moral issues of collective punishment, would the economic losses inflicted through sanctions improve or vitiate prospects for the long-term peaceful development of the sanctioned country? Entities considering imposition of sanctions also should be clear about what the targeted state must do in order to have sanctions reduced or removed and how satisfaction of such requirements would be measured and sanctions relieved.

The results of economic sanctions historically are mixed. A classic study by Hufbauer, Schott, and Elliott in 1990 concluded that economic sanctions were effective approximately one-third of the time.[9] A recent comprehensive study suggests that the target state's membership in international institutions and the imposition of harsh economic costs are the factors most positively correlated with sanctions effectiveness.[10] The most effective, and rarest, sanctions are those imposed on a global basis under authorization by the UN. The succeeding waves of economic sanctions imposed by the UN Security Council on Iran over its threatening nuclear activities are the most potent example. Iran was unable to collect revenue from oil sales, was cut off from the international financial and insurance systems, and was ultimately compelled to acknowledge that it needed relief by agreeing to negotiate deep constraints on its nuclear activities. Sanctions that are not joined by a targeted state's key export, import, and finance partners have relatively weak effects. Similarly, if a targeted state can find substitute sources of imports and finance and destinations for exports, sanctions will not be materially decisive.

Pakistan is paradoxically less vulnerable to economic sanctions than it might seem.[11] The country's GDP in dollars at the official exchange rate was estimated in 2014 to be $246.9 billion.[12] The GDP per capita ranks 174th in the world.[13] Economic growth for years has remained below the 5–7 per cent per year rate that the IMF reports is 'needed to absorb new entrants into the labor market and achieve improvements in living standards for wide segments of society'.[14] Indeed, over the past decade, Pakistan's annual GDP growth has lagged behind that of Bangladesh, formerly the poorer half of Pakistan. While the Bangladeshi economy has grown at an average of 6.2 per cent, Pakistan's growth has remained around 4 per cent, after reaching a low of 1.7 per cent in 2008.[15] Meanwhile, the Pakistani Rupee has depreciated at an alarming rate, from 62 rupees per US dollar in January 2008 to 104 rupees per US dollar in August 2015, with a low of 108 rupees per dollar in December 2013.[16]

The Pakistani economy depends significantly on remittances from workers abroad, IMF support, aid from the United States, and project funding from China.[17] Public debt is high and the tax-to-GDP ratio 'remains among the lowest in the world', according to the IMF. 'Private investment, including FDI and exports are still much below desired outcomes'.[18] In the first half of 2015, the Pakistani Board of Investment reported that FDI into the country declined by 58 per cent compared to the previous year and amounted to only $825 million.[19] Since 1984, Pakistan has received over $10 billion in loan payments from the IMF. Between 2008 and 2010 alone, Pakistan was provided credits worth $5.2 billion.[20] Though Pakistan sought to end the IMF programme in 2011, the two sides entered into an agreement for a loan worth $6.6 billion after Nawaz Sharif's election in May 2013.[21] Pakistan's Finance Ministry cited its 2014–15 budget outlay as Rs 4,302 billion, or approximately $42.2 billion.[22] Thus, the $1.721 billion in economic and security aid provided in 2014 by the US comprised over 4 per cent of the budget.[23]

Pakistan's political economy is so troubled, so fails to create conditions for giving young people confidence in their secular future, and is so dependent on international assistance that the states that provide this assistance are highly reluctant to cut it off. This is the paradox. Responsible states that otherwise would condemn governments that allow transnational terrorists to operate are disinclined to sanction Pakistan for fear that doing so will make the environment more conducive for terrorism. Diminished economic dynamism would undermine non-madrassa educational and employment prospects for the young. Punishment by outsiders could reinforce the narratives proffered by militant leaders. Reduced budgetary resources could diminish the government's capacity to combat militants and impose the writ of the state. These propositions are all debatable, of course, but Indian officials and their supporters would need to refute them if they are to muster support for sanctions.

A particularly challenging and interesting tactic would be to persuade the IMF to assess how risks of major terrorism emanating from Pakistan against India would affect Pakistan's capacity to make future required payments to the IMF. The IMF rules require the staff to assess that a recipient of funds will be able to repay them with a 'high probability'.[24] On this basis, for example, the IMF refused to contribute to the July 2015 European bailout of Greece.[25] It is reasonable to ask whether Pakistan would be able to make its repayments to the IMF in the event of another major terrorist attack attributed to Pakistan that precipitates a military conflict with India. Such analysis should include the possibility that an ensuing conflict could escalate to the use of nuclear weapons. Under such conditions, would the IMF conclude that Pakistan would be able to make its scheduled payments? If not, then should not the IMF factor Pakistan's anti-terrorism policies into its decisions when extending finance to Pakistan? Whatever the outcome of such deliberations within the IMF would be, Indian officials in New Delhi and representatives in the IMF could increase the salience of the counterterrorism agenda by raising these questions. Discussing such issues could add uncertainty to the calculations of potential investors in Pakistan, strengthening incentives for the government to demonstrate its commitment to prevent terrorism.

The US, China, and Security Assistance to Pakistan

While India would be the presumed initiator of efforts to impose sanctions on Pakistan, China and the US would be keys to determining whether meaningful sanctions could be implemented.

China is vital in several ways. Beijing can and most likely would veto any effort to adopt UN sanctions on Pakistan. India could still urge others to raise the issue in the UN, if only to shine an international spotlight on China's unwillingness to penalize a state that was once again associated with a major terrorist attack on India, notwithstanding China's own concerns about terrorism. Also, China is Pakistan's leading source of imports and its second-largest export market (behind the US). China has the strategic motivation and resources to provide substitute aid and financing to Pakistan in the event that other sources cut them off.

The US is Pakistan's biggest export market and, with one interruption, has long been its greatest source of economic and military aid. It is also Pakistan's greatest single source of FDI and has been surpassed only by the combined resources of European donors.[26] According to data provided by Pakistan's Board of Investment, US assistance accounts for 22 per cent of all foreign investment into Pakistan between 2007 and 2015.[27] Between fiscal years 2002–15, the US provided over $31 billion in aid to Pakistan.[28] Of this, a little more than $20 billion was dedicated to security-related issues and reimbursements for Pakistani support of US-led military operations in the region. Almost $10.5 billion was economic assistance. In 2010, of the $5.1 billion in development aid Pakistan received, the US accounted for 56.3 per cent.[29] In 2014 alone, the $1.2 billion in security assistance provided by the US comprised approximately 17 per cent of Pakistan's annual defence budget.[30]

From these data it is safe to say that there is no prospect of effective economic sanctions on Pakistan if the US does not participate. If the US were willing to sanction some combination of aid, trade, and investment into Pakistan, China could backfill some of the Pakistani losses, perhaps joined by Persian Gulf states. In terms of development aid, in 2011, the US provided 30 per cent of Pakistan's total and Japan (14), Germany (4), the United Kingdom (8), Australia (2), Canada (2), and other EU institutions (6) provided another 36 per cent of the $4.15 billion received that year.[31] These likeminded states conceivably could be persuaded to withhold some amount in an effort to hold Pakistan accountable for failing to fulfil its counterterrorism obligations yet again. There is little historical basis to think China would make up much of this type of lost aid. China exports to and invests in Pakistan but generally does not offer significant budgetary assistance.

It is not self-evident that Indian leaders would be able to persuade US executive branch and legislative leaders to support sanctions on Pakistan. Much would depend on the circumstances of the triggering terrorist attack in India, and on the overall status of US relations with Pakistan at the time. The US sanctioned Pakistan heavily over its nuclear weapon programme between 1991 and 2001, after Washington no longer needed Pakistan's help to drive Soviet forces from Afghanistan. These sanctions saved US taxpayers some money, but while they were in place, the Pakistani intelligence services helped create the Taliban in Afghanistan, Pakistan's nuclear weapon programme raced ahead, and the A.Q. Khan network proliferated sensitive nuclear equipment and know how to Iran, Libya, North Korea and perhaps others.[32] It is impossible to prove that any of these developments would not have occurred if the US had not sanctioned Pakistan. In any case, the 11 September 2001 attacks made Pakistan strategically important to the US again. Sanctions were duly lifted and large amounts of aid began flowing.

Between the 9/11 attacks and the time of this writing, a number of disturbing terror-related events and trends have been associated with Pakistan, prompting some experts and congressional members to question the ongoing provision of aid to the country.[33] It is impossible to know whether Pakistani authorities would have cracked down on anti-Indian and anti-American groups if the US had significantly cut assistance. But American officials worry that cutting support could motivate Pakistanis to become more indulgent of such groups.

In these American debates, distinctions are made between economic and security assistance to Pakistan. Few argue that the former should be cut. Rather, criticism of economic assistance tends to focus on lack of consensus on objectives, cumbersome bureaucratic and accounting procedures, inadequate staffing of bodies that deliver aid, and security challenges for aid providers.[34] Most observers support the continuance of efforts to cultivate human capability in Pakistan, which is a primary objective of aid. Reluctance to significantly curtail economic assistance and development aid also obtains among other leading donors to Pakistan.

Security assistance is a different story. The main beneficiaries of security assistance are the Pakistani military, either directly or through intelligence and constabulary bodies. The military, including the ISI, are the most powerful and capable agencies in Pakistan. It is the Army and the ISI who earlier cultivated groups such as the Afghan Taliban, the Haqqani network, the LeT, Jaish-e-Muhammad, and others that have targeted American and Indian interests. And it is the ISI—directly and through enabling police bodies—that would be necessary to pacify these actors. Thus, to the extent that the Pakistani security establishment has benefited from American financial assistance, the argument goes that it should be denied these benefits in the future if it does not demonstrably act to prevent further violence against Indian and American interests in Afghanistan and India.[35]

Few officials and analysts dare to predict that significantly reducing security assistance *will* cause the Pakistani security establishment to change its behaviour. Rather, the argument is that cutting (sanctioning) assistance *might* have this effect, and if it does not, at least the US would not be funding actors who work against its interests. The main counterargument is that continuing assistance provides the US more influence over its recipients than would obtain if assistance were removed, and that the partial cooperation this assistance brings is better than the reduced cooperation that arguably would follow if the aid were cut. The American argument here resembles one that Pakistani officials make in explaining why they are reluctant to act against groups such as the LeT and its affiliates. (That is, the Pakistani state can more effectively curtail violence by seeking to reconcile such groups to the rules of the state than by forcefully trying to eradicate them.) Some also worry that if the US reduced its security assistance to Pakistan, China would become more influential there, which would be contrary to Washington's interest in balancing China's growing power.

Indian officials and analysts generally are much less conflicted than their American counterparts. New Delhi has long urged the US to take a harder line against the Pakistani military and curtail provisions of funds and equipment to it. The Indian argument is less that actual reduction of support to Pakistan will change the security establishment's behaviour, and more that curtailing assistance will weaken that establishment. Once weakened, it will be more interested in preventing Pakistan-affiliated actors from attacking Indian interests. Pakistani leaders then would want to avoid inviting Indian reprisals which Pakistan would then be less able to rebuff.

These arguments, too, cannot be proved or disproved except through future experience. This is an inherently risky proposition. As previous chapters discussed, it will take considerable time and effort for India to acquire conventional military and intelligence capabilities that would enable it to prevail in a contest for escalation dominance with Pakistan. No doubt India's prospects would be better if Pakistan were deprived of the assistance it has been receiving from the US. But would these prospects be so much better that Pakistan would perceive its own disadvantages and therefore do more to ensure that actors operating in Pakistan do not attack India again? Whether or not the most plausible answer to this question is 'yes', it is natural for Indians to want the US to reduce assistance to Pakistan.

For purposes of motivating Pakistani authorities *now* to demobilize violent anti-India groups, it would be better if the US committed in advance to sanction the Pakistani security establishment in the event of another major attack on India. Yet, for sound reasons, Washington would insist on reviewing the specifics of any act and the evidence of Pakistani complicity before deciding on the appropriate response. Still, by using confidential, high-level diplomatic channels to seek advance commitments by the US to sanction Pakistan if evidence ties it to a future major attack, India would drive US officials, including in Congress, to the likely fallback position of saying privately that if and when an attack occurred they would be inclined to pursue sanctions. Word of such communications would eventually reach Pakistan.

If India could muster support in the US for cutting security assistance, and support in the EU, Japan, and Australia for curtailing economic assistance, this could raise the costs of the Pakistani security establishment's unwillingness to demobilize anti-India groups. The strategy would be to make Pakistan appeal to China for greater assistance to make up for any amount and type of aid that was being withdrawn by the US and others. If Beijing assented, then China would feel more acutely the burden of carrying Pakistan. This could strengthen China's interests in urging Pakistani leaders to take actions in the counterterrorism domain that would limit China's exposure to Pakistani risk. However, China generally does not provide the type of economic and development assistance that Pakistan receives from its current donors. More likely would be increases of Chinese security assistance, though this too generally does not take the form of cash transfers.[36] If China were unwilling or unable to substitute fully for the hypothetical losses, Pakistani leaders could conclude they need to change policies in order to regain the lost assistance from the US (and others).

The US historically has spared China the burden of providing more to Pakistan.[37] Washington has done this for multiple reasons, including its reflexive desire to prevent China from gaining influence outside its borders, including in Pakistan. India, too, reflexively opposes greater Chinese influence in South Asia. Chinese cooperation with the Pakistani nuclear and missile programmes, and more recently in providing platforms to the Pakistani Air Force and Navy, poses direct threats to India. Yet, Pakistan is so burdened by economic, social, political, and security challenges that it may be a 'prize' that the US and India should hope China wins. To date, the Pakistani military has been exceptionally responsive when China has (usually privately) demanded action to protect Beijing's interests.[38] Beijing is wary of terrorist threats to its Western provinces, threats which have been incubated in and/or transited through Pakistan. While Chinese leaders clearly welcome competition between India and Pakistan that keeps India beleaguered, they also display clear aversion to war between the two countries. Thus, if China were to take a larger position in Pakistan, the effect could be more positive than typically assumed in Washington and New Delhi. And, if Beijing were to demur in filling the assistance role previously played by the United States, this message would shake the Pakistani security establishment.

This analysis illustrates the priority that Indian leaders would need to place on persuading the US to make Pakistani leaders perceive that another major Pakistan-sourced terrorist attack on India would jeopardize Washington's security assistance to Pakistan. It would not be easy to convince policymakers who have invested heavily in working with Pakistan. However, if, in the event of a major terrorist attack, this request were framed as part of a well-considered strategy that has weighed sanctions against more potentially escalatory alternatives such as airstrikes on Pakistani Army and ISI targets or armoured incursions, American counterparts would be compelled to take it seriously. In a sense, the power to persuade US officials to withhold assistance to the Pakistani security establishment is a capability that India would need to buttress, much like it also needs to strengthen its army, air force, and intelligence capabilities.

Specific Counterterrorism Sanctions

Economic sanctions can affect the broad interests of targeted states and thereby, it is hoped, motivate them to change policies. The UN Security Council also has adopted sanctions that specifically target individuals alleged to be involved in terrorism. Security Council Resolution 1267 was adopted in 1999 after the Al-Qaeda attacks on the US embassies in Nairobi and Dar es Salaam. This resolution ordered states to freeze the assets of the Taliban for harbouring Osama bin Laden and his associates. These sanctions were expanded by Resolution 1333 in December 2000, directly targeting bin Laden and other Al-Qaeda leaders. Thereafter a mechanism for listing individuals and entities to be sanctioned under these resolutions was created. On this basis, in 2006 and 2008 the US, encouraged by India, sought to place Hafiz Muhammed Saeed and JuD, the parent organization of LeT, on the list of individuals and entities to be sanctioned for having been involved in terrorist activities. However, China imposed a 'technical hold' on this move citing a lack of evidence. Following the Mumbai attacks, under international pressure, China lifted its hold and Hafiz Saeed and the JuD were sanctioned. The Pakistani government then duly sealed many offices of JuD, detained dozens of the group's leaders, including Saeed who was placed under house arrest. The names of eleven JuD leaders were put on the state's Exit Control List.[39]

The 'case' of Saeed and JuD has bounced fitfully in and out of the Pakistani legal system since 2009. The details are beyond the scope of this book, and include Pakistani courts' judgements that insufficient legal evidence has been provided by India and others to adjudicate trials against Saeed and the JuD. Saeed remains free and visibly active in Pakistan and the JuD continues to operate. The US government in 2012 issued a $10 million reward for information that would lead to the arrest and conviction of Saeed. Apparently no one has been able or willing to collect it.

Several broader points are relevant to the challenge of using non-violent means to target individual terrorists and organizations that may be involved directly or indirectly in anti-India terrorism.

First, implementing sanctions on individuals and organizations suspected of terrorism requires the cooperation of states in which they live and operate. The intentions and capabilities of law enforcement and judicial bodies in Pakistan tend to be unamenable to effective cooperation, especially with India. For example, a Pakistani Foreign Office spokesman explained that the international sanctions on individuals such as Hafiz Saeed do not require Pakistan to bar him from 'moving within the country. There is no bar on speaking, and there is no requirement of keeping people behind bars'.[40]

Second, even if these bodies are able and willing to prosecute suspected individuals and entities, legally admissible and persuasive evidence is difficult to acquire and provide. States that may have such evidence may be reluctant to provide it for fear of revealing secret sources and methods by which it was acquired. This reluctance can then be interpreted by officials and some citizens in the state where the sanctioned individual resides as 'proof' that the charges are unfounded.

Third, a number of states and civil society organizations, particularly in Europe, argue that the process of listing individuals and entities pursuant to Resolution 1267 is legally and morally dubious. In a report commissioned by the UN Office of Legal Affairs in 2005, a Yale University-trained German professor of law, Bardo Fassbender, concluded that the absence of due process, including the opportunity for individuals and entities to have their entry onto the list evaluated by an impartial institution, and the absence of impartial processes for removing individuals and entities from the sanction list, make the implementation of this resolution 'untenable under principles of international human rights law'.[41]

This brief assessment does not undervalue the satisfaction that the people and the Government of India and other states would enjoy from seeing individuals and groups evidently involved in terrorism brought to justice by Pakistan and the international community. Quite the contrary, such outcomes would augment broader campaigns against transnational terrorism. But as the US and others whose practices are less controversial have found, it is difficult to apprehend and legally prosecute and judge terrorism suspects. This is one reason why the US (and occasionally Pakistan) resorts to targeted killings.[42] But, as discussed in the chapter on covert operations, targeted killings may be beyond India's intelligence and operational capabilities and may not be a practice India wants to 'normalize' in the competition with Pakistan.

Beyond the difficulty of legally targeting and convicting individual terrorism suspects, the challenge for India is to persuade other key states, especially China, to support further UN-based initiatives to hold individuals, organizations, and the state of Pakistan to account if future acts of terrorism are attributed to actors affiliated with Pakistan. The fact that the UN Security Council did not adopt a Chapter VII resolution following the Mumbai attacks indicates the height of the challenge. The more persuasive the shareable evidence that India can provide regarding the identity and affiliations of attackers, the stronger the political–diplomatic argument will be for cooperation with India. And, in a reflection of realpolitik, India's leverage to press other states to support sanctions on Pakistan will be greater as India's capacity to use force or covert coercion to retaliate grows.

Political Isolation

Pakistan is fundamentally open to the international community. It has a relatively free and independent media, access to the internet, freedom of travel, and eagerness to trade. Pakistani officials participate in all manner of international institutions and conferences. Therefore, Pakistani citizens, business people, and officials gain personal and professional benefits when their country is well regarded. Conversely, they may suffer, in varying degrees, when Pakistan is seen as a pariah.

The effects of national reputation may be conceptualized as a facet of 'soft power'. Putting the matter in terms of power conveys how statecraft can be mobilized to compete in the soft power domain as well as in the more traditional fields of 'hard power' or military contestation. Herein lies an opportunity for India. By persuading other states to clarify that they would politically and socially condemn and, where appropriate, isolate Pakistan in the event of another major attack on India, Indian officials and civil society leaders could buttress those in Pakistan who do not want their state to be associated with terrorism.

The motivating idea would be that terrorism—within Pakistan and projected from it—is self-destructive. The internal destructiveness of terrorism has now registered in the society and in the security establishment, as reflected in the Army's Operation Zarb-e-Azb to crush insurgents in the Federally Administered Tribal Areas. It is less clear that the state's resolve extends to groups that primarily target India, including Afghan-based groups. But, when former military leaders in private suggest that Pakistan deserves credit for the absence of a major terrorist attack in India since 2008, they implicitly acknowledge that some national interest made the high command take steps to prevent such attacks. Other private conversations with military officers and political elites also register that groups Pakistan cultivated years ago to conduct jihad against India in Kashmir have morphed and become threats to Pakistan, too. Further, the popular feeling that the RAW was behind the Mumbai attack, upon analysis, reveals the sense that Pakistan lost from this attack and India gained. In the words of a high-ranking general responding to a question in November 2015 about LeT and other groups that have perpetrated violence against India, 'this extremism brings a bad name to our country. So we are not going to allow these groups to act'.[43]

Pakistan is used to India suspending high-level diplomatic interactions, sporting competitions, and other forms of exchange after major episodes of violence. Reasonable arguments are adduced both for and against such interruptions of intercourse. Some say it is a direct and less destructive way to register protest and inflict punishment. Anurag Thakur, secretary of the Board of Control for Cricket in India (BCCI), has bluntly linked sporting and politics, stating 'if you do not have good relations, you can't have good cricket'.[44] Others say that breaking ties merely rewards the terrorists and their patrons—who prefer conflict to peace—and has become ritualized to the point of losing potency. Thus, the authors of *Non-Alignment 2.0* recommend that 'Instead of breaking off talks in the event of a major provocation, we should declare that we favour a continuation of the dialogue.... We also need to adopt policies that will work towards the creation of constituencies in Pakistan that have a stake in peaceful and friendly relations with India.'[45]

A more ambitious and perhaps more powerful approach for India would be to mobilize other states and international bodies to express in some way that Pakistan's continued unwillingness or inability to control the projection of violence into other states is intolerable. Representatives of other states and international bodies could convey this as they find most appropriate in any given circumstance. The Indian request simply would be to demonstrate fidelity to international counterterrorism norms by speaking and acting towards Pakistani counterparts in ways that observably convey protest. Mounting a campaign of this sort would require dedicated, painstaking effort by Indian leaders, diplomats, and where relevant civil society leaders. It would also require well-formulated and privately tested messages that would articulate the basis for requesting international support in ways that would be difficult for others to resist.

The August 2015 Joint Statement by the Governments of India and the UAE is a model that India could seek to induce other states to emulate. This statement denounced 'terrorism in all forms and manifestations, wherever committed and by whomever, calling on all states to reject and abandon the use of terrorism against other countries, dismantle terrorism infrastructures where they exist, and bring perpetrators of terrorism to justice'. Many in Pakistan correctly perceived that this language was directed at their country, and saw it as an example of Indian soft power eroding Pakistan's standing in a country—the UAE—that is important to Pakistan.[46]

Beyond the UAE, success in creating international pressure on Pakistan would require cooperation from the US, the EU, Japan, and, ideally, other Persian Gulf states. It can be assumed that China would block UN action. Other states within the South Asian Association for Regional Cooperation (SAARC) would also be reluctant to act against fellow member Pakistan. Nevertheless, Indian officials and consultants could offer other states a menu of ways to shame Pakistan and demonstrate support for India. The wider the range of options, the more difficult it would be to refuse Indian requests to act.

In addition to pointed statements like those issued by the US and the UAE, specific measures could include expressions of solidarity with the victims of terrorism, whenever political leaders and officials meet Pakistani counterparts. Bilateral official meetings could be postponed in the aftermath of a terrorist attack, to be reconvened when Pakistan has demonstrated determination to bring perpetrators to account. Visa-processing for travel of Pakistani officials and their families could be delayed. The strategic point is that Indian officials could draw on their own insights, experiences of other countries, and advice from consultants to prepare a catalogue of measures that key states could consider applying to Pakistan in the event of another major terrorist attack, and India could seek commitments from these states to act in some way.

In the past, India (like other states in other contexts) has cut off sporting competitions with Pakistani teams as a form of political sanction. The impulse to react this way is natural. Yet, it would be worthwhile to consider alternative forms of social protest. Denying average Pakistanis the pleasure of seeing their athletes compete against India and in international events may inflict some punishment, but it could just as easily reinforce a sense of victimhood. Instead, Indians might consider letting competitions proceed and using them to convey psychologically effective messages that sow antipathy for the perpetrators and facilitators of terrorism. For example, India could stipulate that events go forward only if both teams agree to observe jointly a symbolic act, such as a moment of silence, or to read a statement condemning terrorism, similar to the anti-racism campaign in global sport. Civil society organizations or paid consultants could be enlisted to organize expressions of peaceful protest that could be directed at Pakistani athletic teams and thereby be broadcast via radio, television, and social media reporting. Indian teams (and perhaps those from other sympathetic countries) could at a planned time collectively make gestures to commemorate victims of terrorism: they could wear commemorative symbols on their uniforms, or audiences at events could be given commemorative t-shirts or scarves which would be highly visible on television and in social media images. The aim would be to confront Pakistani participants and audiences with the effects of actions their state has failed to prevent.

One object lesson of how *not* to convey such messages was offered by the Shiv Sena in October 2015. On 12 October, thuggish activists poured ink over the head of the Observer Research Foundation's Sudheendra Kulkarni, a former BJP leader, as he was en route to host the launch of former Pakistan Foreign Minister Khurshid Kasuri's memoir at an event in Mumbai.[47] A week later, Shiv Sena militants attacked the headquarters of the BCCI shortly before former Pakistan Foreign Secretary Shaharyar Khan was to meet with the Board's head, Shashank Manohar.[48] These events coincided with harsh anti-Muslim rhetoric and episodes of violence elsewhere in India that produced growing concern over 'intolerance' in India. When the Indian government and civil society do not differentiate themselves from Pakistan in delegitimizing and striving to prevent extremist violence and rhetoric, the country's soft power declines.

Fortunately, Shiv Sena and other hateful groups do not represent the whole of India's potential to mobilize soft power. The Indian government could explore ways to mobilize positive soft power with little risk or cost. The point would not be to create a new state bureaucracy to conduct social mobilization, but rather to work with civil society, including businesses, to explore how Indian financial and human resources could be mobilized against international terrorism that threatens India. India now has a corporate social responsibility (CSR) requirement that businesses with net profits of at least $800,000 donate 2 per cent of their net profits to organizations serving the public good.[49] If initiatives to promote public education about the costs and consequences of terrorism qualified to receive such funds, the social capital market could respond in potentially interesting ways. It is difficult to see major risks of conducting an experiment to this end.

While non-violent action may seem like a 'softer' option than a BJP-led government would be likely to pursue, the importance of reputation is recognized by one of its leading officials. In an interview shortly before taking office with Modi, this man remarked:

Pakistan lost a lot of its international reputation and standing after Mumbai. They know it. They talk about it. Many other countries communicated that this was beyond the pale. Gulf states sent Pakistani workers home, or hired fewer of them, and started hiring more Indian Muslims. China and others expressed their dismay. Reputation is very important for a country.[50]

Similarly, a former high-level defence official and advisor to the Vajpayee government emphasized that 'the Mumbai attack didn't work for the Pakistanis or the LeT in many ways, including mobilizing the disaffected Muslims in India. The Mumbai attack was too appalling. It lacked resonance'.[51]

Building on the importance of reputation in international affairs, the Indian government—or at least advisors close to Narendra Modi—has proved quite adept at using social media and campaign-style events to generate enthusiasm for the prime minister and his vision for India, especially during his foreign travels.[52] These techniques could be matched with messaging that is well tested to resonate with international audiences that India seeks to mobilize to hold Pakistani officials to account for terrorism. Such messaging would need to be more subtle and constructive than the often hate-filled, bellicose rhetoric that the online world evinces in the aftermath of an attack. Effectiveness depends on maintaining the moral high ground.

Naval Blockade

Perhaps the most robust form of non-violent compellence would be a naval blockade. Indeed, a naval blockade would verge on war. We discuss this possibility in order to be analytically thorough. The discussion is brief because it is readily apparent that India (like all other states except perhaps the US) lacks the capabilities to impose a naval blockade that would be strategically effective.

The goals of a naval blockade would be to impede Pakistani imports and exports enough to cause significant economic pain that would weaken the country and in turn prompt political backlash against the government, including the ISI. To relieve the pressure, Pakistani authorities would, according to the strategy behind a blockade, be willing to take demonstrable counterterrorism measures demanded by India.

As the scholar Walter Ladwig has recently noted, India would not be able to impose a blockade in waters near to Pakistan's three major ports of Karachi, Qasim, and Gwadar because Pakistan's land-based aircraft would hold Indian surface ships at risk, and India's attack submarine fleet is inadequate to perform all the functions required to control this space.[53] Implementing a blockade further away from ports and Pakistani defences would require a much larger Indian fleet and a sophisticated capability to distinguish ships travelling to and from Pakistan from those that are conducting trade with other states. Ideally intelligence services would analyse shipping and port data to discriminate ships that should be interdicted from those that should not be, and aerial platforms would monitor traffic and cue Indian vessels to suspect ships. For the foreseeable future India will lack this suite of capabilities.

Even if India did have the means to discriminate ships for interdiction and a large enough surface and submarine fleet to create an effective blockade, it would face political and strategic risks that would outweigh the putative benefits. Presumably India would resort to a naval blockade only if it had failed to persuade at least some of Pakistan's key trading partners to impose sanctions on such trade. (A blockade to enforce sanctions that had been agreed upon could insult states that had demonstrated political solidarity with India by adopting sanctions.) States that were unwilling to sanction export/import trade with Pakistan would likely see Indian attempts to stop, search, and potentially interdict their ships as an act of aggression. A fairly large percentage of shipping into Pakistan emanates from China and Gulf states. Would Indian leaders order naval commanders to interdict Chinese vessels? If so, is it reasonable to expect Chinese ships to cooperate? And if Chinese ships would not cooperate, how would Indian naval personnel be instructed to respond? Conversely, if Indian forces were instructed not to risk confrontation with Chinese vessels, would India not look strategically weak at precisely a time when it was seeking to demonstrate potency? Similar calculations, albeit less challenging, would need to be made regarding shipments of oil and other goods from Gulf States. India nurtures positive relations with the UAE, Saudi Arabia, Qatar, and other Pakistani trade partners. Indeed, in 2012, India imported nearly $43 billion worth of crude petroleum from Qatar, Yemen, Saudi Arabia, and the UAE alone.[54] If Indian leaders could not persuade these states to voluntarily curtail trade with Pakistan in protest to another major terrorist attack, they should expect these states to resist a potential blockade in ways that would undermine India's overall strategic position.

In any case, it is difficult to see what sea-borne trade other than oil India could interdict that would coerce the Pakistani security establishment to meet Indian demands. Compared with worker remittances, IMF support, and US and Chinese aid and investment—which could only be impeded by political agreement—seaborne trade is less vital. Moreover, blockades historically have taken months and years to affect the target state's strategic calculations.[55] Correspondingly, the state contemplating a blockade must then be prepared to sustain the economic, diplomatic, and military burden of maintaining it a long time.

This simple, largely heuristic discussion has omitted the possibility that a naval blockade would lead to armed conflict. Our aim has been to identify an option on the boundary between non-violent compellence and kinetic military action. India could impose a naval blockade intending to put the burden on Pakistan to initiate actual firing between forces. But Pakistan's navy could challenge a blockade, and/or the army could open a counter-operation along the International Boundary. Pakistani officials in the past have suggested that an Indian attempt to economically strangulate Pakistan, perhaps by a naval blockade, could prompt Pakistan to use nuclear weapons.[56] Indian planners would prepare for such escalation, both out of defensive necessity and to deter

Pakistan from forcibly resisting the blockade. This preparation initially would involve Indian land and air forces, which in turn would be matched by the Pakistan Army and Air Force. Competing mobilizations would set the stage for the risks of escalation and the competition in risk-taking that we have addressed in other chapters.

Mobilizing Non-Violent Campaigns

Indian foreign policy has long focused on preserving national autonomy. This is essentially a negative objective—to prevent others from dictating to India. It made eminent sense when India was 'post-colonial'; that is, newly independent and relatively weak in the international system. But now India is much stronger and aspires to be a global power. Global powers seek not only to block the moves of others—which India readily can do now—but also to persuade others to join them in pursuing shared objectives.[57]

During the Cold War, the US mobilized states in the non-communist world to join it in developing and promoting norms of human rights and democratic capitalism and in building institutions such as the World Bank, the IMF, NATO, and the General Agreement on Tariffs and Trade. In the 1990s, when the Soviet Union collapsed and the US briefly enjoyed a unipolar moment, it managed to expand free trade with others in the World Trade Organization and, not always consistently, to promote liberal norms. Since the invasion of Iraq in 2003, which much of the world did not support, and the relative decline of US economic preponderance, exacerbated by the financial crisis of 2008 and the rise of China, the US has found it more difficult to rally others. Global problems such as terrorism, climate change, cyber security, public health, and human rights cannot be redressed without international cooperation. But, neither the US nor any other single state has been able to persuade or coerce the most pertinent states in the international system to cooperate sufficiently.

This is to say that it is difficult for one state to mobilize others to join it on issues such as countering terrorism, our focus here. Yet, India has potential to lead more in this regard than it has thus far. Cooperating with India to motivate Pakistan to fulfil its sovereign obligations to prevent interstate terrorism does not require other states to sacrifice much.

India has strengths to draw upon. The growing size of the Indian market for foreign goods and services—especially as reforms are implemented—provides leverage. India's soft power resources continue to grow: India's campaign to promote regional infrastructure connectivity, the appeal of Bollywood, the state's capacity to manage free and fair elections on a tremendous scale. These are just some assets that build India's credibility as a positive actor. Social media techniques amplify their potency and reach.[58]

Yet, for the Indian government to take full advantage of this potential, leaders, political parties, and civil society will need to engage in a more forthcoming way with international counterparts. The habits of autonomy-seeking will have to evolve into tactics of coalition-building.

The story of India's effort to gain international cooperation in the development of peaceful nuclear energy demonstrates both the opportunities and pitfalls for such coalition-building. Indian leaders, beginning in the early 2000s, persuaded the US government to lead an international effort to change the rules that restricted India's access to nuclear commerce. Indian leaders marshalled a strategic argument that nuclear energy and a relatively unconstrained military nuclear programme could enable India to balance China's rising power. This was especially appealing to the US. India touted the commercial gains that US, French, and Russian technology suppliers could obtain if rules were changed to open the Indian market to them. Other states whose support was needed, including in the EU, were motivated to support the prospective deal in order to earn goodwill in the Indian market. India also argued effectively that issues of equity were involved, and that if India was to continue practicing solid non-proliferation policies it should not be denied nuclear cooperation that other states enjoy. Finally, the Indian diaspora, particularly in the US, was mobilized to tie its electoral and financial support of political candidates to their support for a nuclear deal.

Each of these types of arguments and tactics could be used to mobilize support among leading international states for peaceful pressure on Pakistan to counter terrorism. In principle, most states would be more amenable to this agenda than they were to removing non-proliferation restrictions on India.

However, the nuclear exemption that was cleared by the Nuclear Suppliers Group in 2008 also offers cautionary lessons. Discord within Indian politics made nuclear cooperation controversial. Seven years later, issues of legal liability have not been fully resolved to the satisfaction of international vendors and Indian contractors. No additional foreign-supplied nuclear power plants are yet under construction. Indian officials and some political factions continue to resist transparency and other safeguard procedures that most other countries think are necessary and reasonable.[59] India continues to frustrate requests by non-nuclear-weapon states to ratify the Comprehensive Test Ban Treaty and adopt a moratorium on producing fissile materials for nuclear weapons. Thus, while Indian commentators complain about the unfulfilled expectations of the nuclear deal, so too do the states that accommodated India's (and the United States) pressures to make the deal.[60] In short, if the nuclear deal demonstrated India's potential to play a leading role in the give and take of coalition-building to change the international system, it also reinforced doubts about this leadership.

A campaign to mobilize international support to hold Pakistan accountable in the counterterrorism domain would be based on widely shared values and clear UN norms. It would not be favouritism for India. Yet, it is in the nature of psychology and international affairs that other states asked to join such a campaign would expect something from India in return. States that seek to maintain good relations with Pakistan will be mindful that there are disputes between it and India. In particular, such states will feel that pressure on Pakistan would be more effective if there were also benefits that Pakistan could receive for acting more diligently to demobilize terrorist groups that threaten India. For example, many states would feel that they would have a stronger basis for demanding more from Pakistan if India demonstrated a more forthcoming approach to negotiating a resolution of the Kashmir issue. If instead, an Indian campaign appeared one-sided and strictly focused on demands of Pakistan, other states' leaders could feel it was both inequitable and unworkable, and therefore not worthy of their commitment.

No doubt this view would rankle in India. On the merits, states' obligations to prevent their territory from being used for terrorism are not conditional. (The same could have been said, and was, about India's argument that it needed a nuclear deal in order to continue to be a responsible upholder of nuclear non-proliferation norms.) The Kashmir issue is complicated historically and otherwise, and India will not be pressed by others to shape its approach to it. Nor is it clear that if a settlement were reached on Kashmir, militant elements in Pakistan, including in the security establishment, would change their behaviour towards India. These and other arguments could and would be made against efforts by other states to broaden a prospective Indian campaign to pressure Pakistan.

In some ways, Israel's experience with the Palestinians and the broader international community is instructive here. Much as Israel's use of intelligence and coercion to fight terrorism offers useful comparisons for Indians to consider, Israel's inability to resolve its issues with the Palestinian Authority and, more problematically, Hamas, has diminished international support for it and exacerbated tensions within Israel.[61] Israelis are increasingly troubled by international campaigns to boycott their products and question the legitimacy of their state's positions. Palestinian leaders and others carry great responsibility for failures to achieve reconciliation, too, of course. But the fact remains that international actors become reluctant to apply pressure on one set of parties to a dispute if they do not believe that the other party is demonstrably committed to reach equitable outcomes too.

* * *

Non-violent compellence is less risky and can be more cost-effective than conventional military operations and the more robust forms of covert operations. But this does not mean that the effects will be potent enough to change the Pakistani security establishment's behaviour. Still, one advantage of non-violent action compared with violence is that its effects can be tested at little risk and cost. India can try to mobilize an international campaign with a narrow focus on Pakistan's counterterrorism obligations, and test its effectiveness.

The essence of a non-violent strategy is to leverage India's growing economic, political, cultural, and military power to persuade other amenable, influential states to cooperate with it. However, potential capabilities mean little if they are not mobilized and guided by strategies and plans. As well-informed journalist Manoj Joshi has suggested, 'The true measure of a country's capabilities does not lie in its military or clandestine services' clout, but its ability to effect a favourable transformation in the behavior of its adversaries through a mix of strategies. While military strength is an important ingredient, it is not the key one. Soft power plays as much of a role here, as does hard power, but most of all it requires skilled operators to use the two together.'[62]

The need for enhanced capabilities in this domain is similar to the needs of the Indian military. Yet, in the case of non-violent compellence, India has untapped societal resources that could be cultivated at significantly less cost compared to military modernization. Within India and its diaspora, thousands of entrepreneurs, economic analysts, cultural leaders, and social media practitioners have skills that could be deployed to identify ways to mobilize non-violent pressure on the Pakistani security establishment. Leading Indian and international consulting firms could be contracted to develop strategies and tactics that Indian government agencies would be less likely to contemplate due to manpower shortages, the skill sets of their personnel, and their traditional predilections.

Whomever Indian leaders choose to task with developing non-violent means of compellence, the US would have to be a primary object of their effort. India alone lacks the necessary coercive leverage. The role of US as provider of economic and security assistance and international finance to Pakistan makes it a necessary partner in any move to peacefully compel Pakistani security leaders to change. Without American cooperation, India is unlikely to be able to persuade other key states such as Japan, the EU, Australia, and the UAE to follow suit. For such cooperation to be possible, both Washington and New Delhi's approaches to Pakistan would have to change. Washington would have to be more willing to withhold cooperation from Pakistan, and New Delhi more willing to negotiate with it.

In other words, Indian officials would need to display the temperament and resources for coalition-building. This is a capability that India needs to muster in any case if it is to achieve its aspirations in the twenty-first century. As China's military strategy has recognized, it is advantageous in certain cases to eschew large-scale violent conflict and 'to bring political, public opinion, physiological and spiritual pressure to the enemy'.[63]

Finally, we recognize that compared to threats of military action the exertions described in this chapter may seem 'soft'. But India's overriding strategic interest is to act in ways that maintain the global political–moral high ground while imposing greater costs on Pakistan than on India. It is to India's advantage to exploit Pakistan's self-made vulnerabilities and avoid playing to its relative strengths—military capabilities, including nuclear. Actions that stimulate escalation of military conflict invite risks and costs that may be greater than those imposed on India by terrorism. In this sense, as the US ought to have learned in the aftermath of the second Iraq War, overreaction is more dangerous than tempered reaction. Indian leaders and the Indian polity have recognized this in the past, from the non-cooperation movement that brought independence through the crises of 2001–2 and 2008. India can and should augment its hard power, but there is no reason it cannot at the same time tap the potential of its superior soft power.

Notes and References

1. For an insightful analysis of India's tradition of strategic restraint, see Sunil Dasgupta and Stephen P. Cohen, 'Is India Ending its Strategic Restraint?' *The Washington Quarterly*, Spring 2011: 163–77.

2. Quoted in Lawrence Freedman, *Strategy: A History* (Oxford: Oxford University Press, 2013), 137.

3. A recent judgement by the little known Asia Pacific Group on Money Laundering (APG), an autonomous, 41-state-member international organization committed to the enforcement of standards against money laundering and terrorist financing, may be a positive step in this direction. In late June 2015, India successfully brought Pakistan (a member of the APG) under monitoring to ensure its compliance with UN sanctions against Pakistani citizens, including Zakiur Rehman Lakhvi, Dawood Ibrahim, and Hafiz Saeed. Though China attempted to protect Pakistan from the oversight of the Financial Action Task Force, another inter-governmental body of which Pakistan is not a member, over 40 state members and organizations (including the US) joined India in referring the matter to the APG (which is an Associate Member of the Task Force). As a result, the Group will now 'closely monitor' Pakistan's implementation of UN sanctions against terrorists. See 'UN Sanctions on Dawood, Lakhvi: India Ensures Asia Pacific Group will Monitor Pakistan', *Times of India*, 29 June 2015. Available at: http://timesofindia.indiatimes. com/india/Asia-Pacific-Group-to-monitor-Pak-compliance-of-UN-sanctions-on-Dawood-Lakhvi/articleshow/47869665.cms.

4. Rupert Smith, *The Utility of Force: The Art of War in the Modern World* (New York: Random House, 2007).

5. As noted in Chapter 3, the scholarly literature on the strategic effects of targeted killing of leadership suggests that the results are mixed at best. A recent paper concluded that there is little basis 'for making general pronouncements on whether targeted killing is or is not an effective counter-terrorism tactic'. See Carvin, 'The Trouble With Targeted Killing', 1. See also: David, 'Fatal Choices'; Price, 'Targeting Top Terrorists', 9–46; and Cronin, *How Terrorism Ends*.

6. Interview with former RAW official, New Delhi, 26 April 2014.

7. Interview with former senior official, 27 April 2014.

8. Interview with former RAW official, New Delhi, 26 April 2014.

9. Gary Clyde Hufbauer, Jeffrey J. Schott, Kimberly Ann Elliott, and Barbara Oegg, *Economic Sanctions Reconsidered*, 3rd Edition (2007). Available at: http://www.iie.com/publications/briefs/sanctions4075.pdf. For a nuanced assessment of the impact of different types of sanctions, see also Meghan O'Sullivan, *Shrewd Sanctions: Statecraft and State Sponsors of Terrorism* (Washington, DC: Brookings University Press, 2003).

10. Navin A. Bapat, Tobias Heinrich, Yoshiharu Kobayashi, and T. Clifton Morgan, 'Determinants of Sanctions Effectiveness: Sensitivity Analysis Using New Data', *International Interactions* 39, no.1 (2013): 89–90. Additionally, they find that even the threat of sanctions is likely to be more effective if it is authorized by international institutions, would impose severe costs, and pertain to highly salient issues. Authors' results were based on analysis of the 'Threat and Imposition of Economic Sanctions' dataset.

11. It is important to note that Pakistan's military is a major shareholder in Pakistan's economy, which has multiple ramifications for the impact of sanctions, which were briefly discussed in Chapter 4. On the one hand, this could open up avenues of direct financial pressure on the military if sanctions could be targeted to military industries. On the other hand, the military could insulate the economy from external shocks because military industry crowds out normal business that would increase Pakistan's economic interdependence. See Ayesha Siddiqa, *Military Inc.: Inside Pakistan's Military Economy* (London and Ann Arbor: Pluto Press, 2007).

12. By comparison, the World Bank places India's 2014 GDP at $2 trillion. By further comparison, the US Department of Defense's budget for 2014 was $526.6 billion. See World Bank, 'India', accessed 15 August 2015. Available at: http://data.worldbank.org/country/india; The White House, 'Department of Defense', accessed 26 August 2015. Available at: https://www.whitehouse.gov/sites/default/files/omb/budget/fy2014/assets/defense.pdf.

13. Central Intelligence Agency, 'The World Factbook', last modified on 11 August 2015. Available at: https://www.cia/gov/library/publications/the-world-factbook/geos/pk.html.

14. International Monetary Fund, *Pakistan: Seventh Review Under the Extended Arrangement and Modification of Performance Criteria*, Country Report no. 15/162, 2 July 2015, 17.

15. World Bank, 'GDP growth (annual %)', World Bank, accessed 26 August 2015. Available at: http://data.worldbank.org/indicator/

NY.GDP.MKTP.KD.ZG?order=wbapi_data_value_2010%20 wbapi_data_value%20wbapi_data_value-first&sort=asc.

16. 'XE Currency Charts (USD/PKR)', XE, accessed 3 September 2015. Available at: http://www.xe.com/currencycharts/?from=USD&to= PKR&view=10Y.

17. Remittances to Pakistan amounted to 6.9 per cent of GDP from 2010–14, the 15th highest ratio of any country in the world. 'Personal Remittances, Received (% of GDP)', World Bank, accessed 3 September 2015. Available at: http://data.worldbank.org/indicator/ BX.TRF.PWKR.DT.GD.ZS.

18. International Monetary Fund, *Pakistan*, 17.

19. Pakistan Board of Investment, 'Country Wise FDI Inflows,' July 2015, accessed 26 August 2015. Available at: http://boi.gov.pk/ ForeignInvestmentinPakistan.aspx.

20. Center for Global Development, 'Aid to Pakistan by the Numbers', accessed 26 August 2015. Available at: http://www.cgdev.org/page/ aid-pakistan-numbers.

21. Center for Global Development, 'Aid to Pakistan by the Numbers'. This 'bailout package' will be disbursed over three years in order to ensure that Pakistan maintains adequate cash reserves.

22. Government of Pakistan, Finance Division, 'Federal Budget 2014–15: Budget in Brief', 3 June 2014. Available at: http://www.finance.gov. pk/budget/Budget_in_Brief_2014_15.pdf.

23. Congressional Research Service, 'Direct Overt U.S. Aid Appropriations for and Military Reimbursements to Pakistan, FY2002-FY2016', 10 February 2015.

24. Paul Blustein, 'Laid Low: The IMF, the Euro Zone and the First Rescue of Greece' (Centre for International Governance Innovation, CIGI Paper No. 61, 7 April 2015), 2.

25. Landon Thomas Jr., 'The Greek Debt Deal's Missing Piece', *New York Times*, 15 August 2015. Available at: http://www/nytimes. com/2015/08/16/business/international/the-greek-debt-deals- missing-piece.html?_r=0.

26. United Nations Conference on Trade and Development, 'Pakistan', accessed 26 August 2015. Available at: http://unctad.org/Sections/ dite_fdistat/docs/webdiaeia2014d3_PAK.pdf.

27. Board of Investment, 'Foreign Investment,' Prime Minister's Office, Government of Pakistan, accessed 26 August 2015. Available at: http://boi.gov.pk/ForeignInvestmentinPakistan.aspx.

28. Congressional Research Service, 'Direct Overt U.S. Aid Appropriations for and Military Reimbursements to Pakistan, FY2002-FY2016'. 30 September 2015. Available at: http://www.fas. org/sgp/crs/row/pakaid.pdf.

29. Susan B. Epstein and K. Alan Kronstadt, 'Pakistan: US Foreign Assistance' (Congressional Research Service Report, 1 July 2013).

30. Comparison of CRS 'Direct Overt U.S. Aid' report and Pakistan's 'Federal Budget 2014–15' (Rs 700.1 billion, or USD 7 billion) using 2014 currency conversion rate.

31. Center for Global Development, 'Aid to Pakistan by the Numbers'.

32. A.Q. Khan began selling nuclear technology and know-how in 1987 and continued into 2003.

33. In December 2001, militants believed to be from the Jaish-e-Muhammad attacked the Indian Parliament. In July 2008, the Indian embassy in Kabul was attacked, killing 58, and the US attributed the attack to agents of Pakistan's ISI. In November 2008, Mumbai was attacked. In 2011, Osama bin Laden was located and killed in Pakistan. Washington and other powers perceive that the Pakistani security establishment played a double game with and against the United States. It has cooperated against some terrorist/militant targets and, on the other side, has at least tolerated violence against US, NATO, Afghan, and Indian personnel and interests.

34. Nancy Birdsall, Milan Vaishnav, and Daniel Cutherell, 'More Money, More Problems: A 2012 Assessment of the US Approach to Development in Pakistan' (Washington, DC: Center for Global Development, July 2012).

35. Charles R. Kaye, Joseph S. Nye Jr., and Alyssa Ayres, *Working With a Rising India*, Independent Task Force Report No. 73 (New York: Council on Foreign Relations, 2015), 7.

36. Most sources detailing military assistance from China to Pakistan emphasize arms sales, while there is almost no discussion of cash transfers from China, which are not a hallmark of its foreign direct investment. For instance, the touted China-Pakistan Economic Corridor will involve considerable Chinese investment in Pakistan, but little if any of this will be accomplished by cash aid, rather through infrastructure construction contracts with Chinese industry.

37. China did not offset the assistance that the US curtailed during the 1990s.

38. President Musharraf's decision to attack the Lal Masjid ('Red Mosque') in 2007 is widely seen as a response to pressure from China. In an unusually strongly worded statement, Chinese ambassador Luo Zhaohui 'required' that Pakistan investigate the attack, 'round up the culprits, properly handle the follow-up issues and take effective measures to protect all the Chinese in Pakistan'. See 'Press Release of the Chinese Embassy', 10 July 2007. Available at: http://pk.chineseembassy.org/eng/zbgx/t338801.htm.

39. Atiq Durrani, 'UN Security Council Resolution 1267 and Hafiz Saeed', *Pakistan Kakhuda Hafiz*, 27 September 2014. Available at: http://www.pakistankakhudahafiz.com/news/national/un-security-council-resolution-1267-hafiz-saeed/.

40. Asad Hashim, 'Despite Sanctions, Pakistan's "Terrorists" Thrive', *Al Jazeera*, 20 May 2015. Available at: http://www.aljazeera.com/indepth/features/2015/05/sanctions-pakistan-terrorists-thrive-150518065848142.html.

41. Bardo Fassbender, 'Targeted Sanctions and Due Process', (Study Commissioned by the United Nations Office of Legal Affairs, 20 March 2006, final text), 5.

42. In a 2012 speech, the then-US Attorney Gen. Eric Holder justified targeted killings of US citizens abroad 'if the individual poses an imminent threat, capture is not feasible, and the operation were executed in observance of the applicable laws of war.' Jonathan Masters, 'Targeted Killings', Council on Foreign Relations, last updated 23 May 2015. Available at: http://www.cfr.org/counterterrorism/targeted-killings/p9627.

43. Chatham House Rule Seminar, 18 November 2015.

44. 'Attack Puts India-Pak Cricket Series in Jeopardy', *Al Jazeera*, 27 July 2015. Available at: http://www.aljazeera.com/news/2015/07/attack-puts-india-pak-cricket-series-jeopardy-150727140204607.html.

45. Sunil Khilnani, Rajiv Kumar, Pratap Bhanu Mehta, Lt. Gen. (ret.) Prakash Menon, NandanNilekani, Srinath Raghavan, Shyam Saran, and Siddharth Varadarajan, *NonAlignment 2.0: A Foreign and Strategic Policy for India in the 21st Century* (New Delhi: Centre for Policy Research, 2012): 40–1.

46. Jawed Naqvi, 'Modi Steps into Pakistan-UAE Breach', *Dawn*, 18 August 2015. Available at: http://www.dawn.com/news/1201143/modi-steps-into-pakistan-uae-breach; 'Modi in the UAE,' *Dawn*, 20 August 2015. Available at: http://www.dawn.com/news/

1201503; Raja Riaz, 'Pakistan's Poor Handling Brings UAE, India Closer', *Daily Times*, 20 August 2015. Available at: http://www.dailytimes.com.pk/national/20-Aug-2015/pakistan-s-poor-handling-brings-uae-india-closer.

47. Manasi Phadke and Zeeshan Shaikh, 'Shiv Sena Attacks Sudheendra Kulkarni over Kasuri Book, Then Brags about It', *Indian Express*, 13 October 2015. Available at: http://indianexpress.com/article/india/india-news-india/shiv-sena-attacks-sudheendra-kulkarni-over-kasuri-book-then-brags-about-it/99/print/.

48. Agence France-Presse, 'Shiv Sena Activists Storm BCCI HQ Over Shaharyar-Manohar Meeting', *Dawn*, 19 October 2015. Available at: http://www.dawn.com/news/1214126.

49. For a clear legal description of the CSR requirement enacted by the Indian parliament in August 2013, see Jones Day Publications, 'India's New Corporate Social Responsibility Requirements – Beware of the Pitfalls', April 2014. Available at: http://www.jonesday.com/Indias-New-Corporate-Social-Responsibility-Requirements--Beware-of-the-Pitfalls-04-15-2014.

50. Interview, New Delhi, 25 April 2014.

51. Interview with former defence official, New Delhi, 23 April 2014.

52. Modi's September 2014 visit to the US and August 2015 visit to the UAE are pertinent examples.

53. Ladwig, 'Indian Military Modernization and Conventional Deterrence in South Asia', 22–3.

54. $6.16 billion, $697 million, $24.4 billion, $11.5 billion, respectively. See Observatory of Economic Complexity, 'Products That India Imports from Saudi Arabia (2012)', accessed 26 August 2015. Available at: https://atlas.media.mit.edu/en/explore/tree_map/hs/import/ind/sau/show/2012/ (repeated search for each dyad).

55. Robert A. Doughty and Harold E. Raugh, 'Embargoes in Historical Perspective', *Parameters* 21 (Spring 1991): 29.

56. Interview with then-head of Pakistan's Strategic Plans Division, Gen. Khalid Kidwai, quoted in *Nuclear Safety, Nuclear Stability, and Nuclear Strategy in Pakistan*, A Concise Report of a Visit by Landau Network Centro Volto, January 2002; as cited in Narang, *Nuclear Strategy in the Modern Era*, 80.

57. For a more systematic discussion on Indian power, see George Perkovich, 'Is India a Major Power?' *Washington Quarterly* 27, no. 1 (Winter 2003–4): 129–44.

58. For an insightful discussion of India's soft power, see Itty Abraham, 'The Future of Indian Foreign Policy', *Economic and Political Weekly* 42, no. 42 (20 October 2007). See also, Huma Yusuf, 'The India Brand', *Dawn*, 26 October 2015. Available at: http://www.dawn.com/news/1215355.

59. John Carlson, 'Nuclear Cooperation with India—Non-Proliferation Success or Failure?' Carnegie Endowment for International Peace, 15 February 2015. Available at: http://carnegieendowment.org/files/India_-_nuclear_cooperation_15_Feb_15_2.pdf.

60. Pravin Sawhney and Ghazala Wahab, 'Not a Big Deal', *FORCE*, August 2015, 12–18.

61. For an insightful discussion of the consequences of the stalled Israeli-Palestinian diplomatic process, see Hilal Baraug, 'Israel's Other Existential Threat Comes from Within', *New York Times*, 20 August 2015. Available at: http://www.nytimes.com/2015/08/21/opinion/israels-other-existential-threat-comes-from-within.html?ref=opinion&_r=0.

62. Manoj Joshi, 'The Modi Government is Missing the Big Picture on Pakistan', *The Wire*, 25 August 2015. Available at: http://thewire.in/2015/08/25/the-modi-government-is-missing-the-big-picture-on-pakistan-9138/.

63. Peng Guangqian and Yao Youzhi (eds), *The Science of Military Strategy* (Beijing: Military Strategy Publishing House, 2005), 465.

CONCLUSION

We began this book by stating the exceptionally difficult national security problem India confronts in Pakistan: to motivate Pakistani leaders to act decisively to prevent future attacks on India, and if an attack occurs, to desist from escalating in reaction to India's response.

India cannot reasonably expect that Pakistani authorities will be willing and able to destroy groups such as LeT while at the same time seeking to eradicate the numerous militant groups that now more directly threaten the internal security of Pakistan. Rather, the reasonable objective is for Pakistan to make demonstrable, persistent efforts to delegitimize and prevent future terrorist attacks on India; that is, to pacify the tactics Pakistani-based actors use to pursue their political demands on India regarding Kashmir and other issues.

In the title and throughout this volume we have used the verb 'motivate' to convey the purpose of India's potential policies and actions. Chapters 2–5 focused on coercive forms of motivation—compellence and deterrence via army-centric, air force-centric, covert, and nuclear means. In Chapter 6, we explored the potential of non-violent compellence to motivate changes of behaviour in Pakistan. We have analysed these possible options in terms of criteria that follow the sequential logic of decisions Indian leaders could make in a crisis and/or conflict with Pakistan. In particular, Indian decision makers must calculate how, with highest probability of success and most acceptable costs, to:

- satisfy the domestic political–psychological need for punishment, and thereby prevent loss of support for the government;
- motivate Pakistani authorities to act decisively against terrorists and thereby build Indian confidence, to the extent possible, that such terrorist acts will not be repeated;
- deter Pakistani authorities from escalating conflict in reaction to punitive moves India would make; and
- bring the conflict to a close in ways that do not leave India worse off in terms of casualties, costs, and overall power than it would have been if it had not responded militarily, or had responded with less destructive means than it chose.

Now we summarize how each of the considered options fares against these criteria.

A proactive, army-centric policy like the one discussed in Chapter 2 would, if effective, satisfy a natural Indian desire to inflict serious punishment on the Pakistani state for failing to uphold its international obligations to prevent terrorism from its territory. Quick, effective, limited army incursions into Pakistan-administered Kashmir and/or the Pakistani heartland could, theoretically, cause enough damage to the Pakistani military's interests to motivate it to accommodate India's counter-terrorism demands in order to end the conflict. However, prudent analysis suggests that India for the foreseeable future will lack the requisite capabilities to prevail in a quick, limited military conflict on Pakistan-held territory. If Pakistani forces could prevent a quick Indian victory, countervailing actions by the Pakistani military and mobilized militants would probably confront India with a choice of escalating beyond the original plan, and/or facing either a protracted war of attrition against Indian forces in Pakistan, or withdrawing. If India chose to escalate, and succeeded, Pakistan could be inclined to use nuclear weapons against Indian forces, raising the prospect of mutually devastating nuclear war. This would portend damage to India that would greatly exceed the injury incurred through the initial terrorist attack. In such scenarios, including those wherein Indian forces cause great damage to the Pakistani military, it is difficult to see how the result would leave Pakistani authorities with the motivation and capability to eradicate anti-India terror groups.

As Chapter 3 explored, limited, primarily airborne strikes on targets in Pakistan could carry lower risks of escalation, depending on the targets. Focusing destruction on terrorist infrastructure in Kashmir would minimize the probability of major military responses by Pakistan. However, the less vital the targets are to Pakistani authorities, the less likely their destruction would be to motivate these authorities to take decisive measures against anti-India groups. For this reason, and also due to the potential that targets could be missed or misidentified causing embarrassment to India, precision strikes in Pakistani Kashmir could offer relatively limited domestic political benefits to Indian leaders and no significant prospect of compelling a change in Pakistani policy.

Conversely, more ambitious targeting of assets in the Pakistani heartland would invite Pakistan to mobilize its air force, army and proxies to contest India. Indian and Pakistani military leaders acknowledge that India would need to mobilize its army to prepare for such Pakistani responses. Thus, it could be difficult to contain the escalatory potential of air strikes against targets in the Pakistani heartland. Depending on the platforms and delivery systems that India used, it would risk losses of its own forces, also with political and escalatory implications. While it is tempting to see Israeli and American uses of air power against Hamas, Hezbollah, Iraq, and Afghanistan as examples of effective air power, nuclear-armed Pakistan is much more able to defend itself than those targets. India lacks the utter advantages in intelligence, surveillance, reconnaissance, and delivery systems that Israel and the US enjoy over their adversaries. As Israel and the US have learned, too, even technically effective air strikes do not cause motivated terror groups to cease and desist.

A RAND Corporation report produced soon after the 11/26 Mumbai attack aptly summarizes the gist of our analysis in Chapters 2 and 3: 'Despite some Indian interest in military options, there do not appear to be at present any military operations that can have strategic-level effects without significant risk of military response from Pakistan.'[1] The more potent the Indian military actions in terms of damaging the Pakistani military, the higher the risk of escalation to the use of nuclear weapons, as Indian officials and experts have noted.

Chapter 4 explored the potential deterrence and compellence value of covert operations that India conceivably could conduct directly against terrorists and their infrastructure, or more broadly, against the interests of the Pakistani state. Acquiring the human and technical resources to identify and constantly monitor targets, as well as agents able to attack them and escape without being identified, would require considerable time, money, and leadership. Although the targeted killing of anti-India terrorists could yield political dividends in India, even if the state were to deny responsibility, success in such operations would invite retaliation by Pakistan and its agents, including those it could recruit in India. The escalatory risks of covert operations can be minimized to the extent that violence is eschewed or tightly focused on belligerent targets. However, as Pakistan's use of terrorism by proxies has demonstrated, the more dramatic the violence of a covert operation, the greater the pressure on the targeted state to retaliate. In the past, concerns about blowback and harm to India's international reputation (in comparison with Pakistan's) have dissuaded Indian leaders from waging covert violence against Pakistan.

India has been more inclined to pursue less violent forms of covert action to threaten the interests of the Pakistani security establishment. While it has done less of this than Pakistan alleges, an implicit Indian threat to foment political unrest in Pakistan—for example, in Balochistan and Karachi—could establish a more symmetrical dynamic between the two states at the level of sub-conventional conflict. This could create a negotiating logic whereby Indian restraint could be 'traded' for demonstrable Pakistani action to prevent terror attacks on India. However, New Delhi's reluctance to concede the moral high ground and negotiate on issues related to proxy competition may reinforce the status quo. If India were perceived to be more actively fomenting political and economic disorder in Pakistan—let alone violence—other states that are highly concerned about Pakistan's stability and governance would be expected, again, to urge both to desist from competition and invest greater energy and creativity in conflict resolution.

Chapter 5 considered possible Indian interests in modifying its nuclear doctrine and capabilities. We recounted ongoing Indian debates over retaining or changing the declared policies of NFU and massive retaliation as well as related questions about the adequacy of India's nuclear capabilities. Our focus was on whether and how India could most effectively utilize nuclear doctrine and capabilities to manage the risks of escalation that could ensue from conventional military and covert operations in retaliation to further terrorism emanating from Pakistan. NFU is not a major impediment in this regard. India would lose more than it would gain by changing this policy. Massive retaliation, on the other hand, may not be a credible, hence effective, threat to deter Pakistan from conducting limited nuclear strikes on invading Indian conventional forces. By revising this policy and adding rungs on the escalation ladder between conventional war and massive nuclear retaliation—to seek escalation dominance—India conceivably could pose a more symmetrical deterrent balance to Pakistan. This could in turn strengthen the credibility of potential Indian conventional military responses to terrorism.

Yet, notwithstanding the theoretical attractiveness of controlling nuclear escalation, there is no historical experience to indicate that nuclear war can be kept limited. While proponents of this form of nuclear deterrence argue that the non-occurrence of limited nuclear war validates their assumptions, analysis suggests that the rational limiting of nuclear conflict in the fog of war cannot be relied upon. Recent research in neuroscience and experimental psychology highlights the risk of 'prediction errors' that could lead opponents to miscalculate each other's signalling in such a conflict. This problem could be exacerbated when one of the actors may not be as unitary as deterrence theory assumes. For example, if Pakistani authorities did not feel they were responsible for a terrorist attack that prompted India to initiate military conflict, they would view India as the aggressor. Pakistanis, then, could be more inclined to see their use of nuclear weapons against India as a defensive measure, displaying the relatively greater resolve associated with defenders compared with aggressors.

During the Cold War, the US and USSR played the escalation dominance game for decades. Then, after some daunting experience, they concluded that it was unwinnable and excessively costly. In the 1970s, they turned to détente and arms control to manage their competition. (Of course, Moscow and Washington continued to contest each other in the 'Third World', at great cost to the inhabitants of the states where they fought.) India and Pakistan have not yet drawn similar conclusions. While signs appear that leaders in India and Pakistan recognize that they cannot achieve their fundamental aims by initiating conventional war, the role of militants as instigators makes cooperative management of their competition more difficult. India does not perceive that the Pakistani security establishment has decided fundamentally to do all it can to demobilize anti-Indian terror groups. Thus, a three-part argument bedevils efforts to apply arms control between India and Pakistan: when Indian or external diplomats urge negotiation of nuclear restraint measures, Pakistanis counter that India must also be willing to limit its conventional military capabilities. Indians then respond that Pakistan must eradicate terrorist groups that threaten India. If approximate symmetries are achieved within and between the two states' nuclear, conventional, and sub-conventional capabilities, the way could be opened for negotiations to stabilize and manage the overall competition. (To be sure, the role of third parties—particularly China and the US—in India's and Pakistan's security calculations would complicate bilateral negotiations to limit military forces.)

Meanwhile, speaking and acting as if India is able and willing to engage in limited nuclear conflict with Pakistan could augment deterrence, but it would do so with grave risks. At the very least, given the time, technical innovation, and expense that would be required for India to change its nuclear posture and doctrine, it would be unwise for India to declare such changes before it has the demonstrable means to implement them.

Before deciding whether and how to pursue any of the conventional, military, and nuclear policies and capabilities we have explored, Indian officials and commentators might well contemplate the observation of a recent leader of the Integrated Defence Staff. 'We can't fight a big war in a nuclearized environment,' he said. 'The international system is moving away from such wars. This is the big problem!'[2] It is this insight that would make prudent Indian officials and strategists search for less escalatory policies and capabilities.

Non-violent compellence, the focus of Chapter 6, explored the potential utility of Indian efforts to mobilize other influential states and civil societies to impose economic and political penalties on the Pakistani state if it fails to prevent terrorism against other states. Because India's direct connections with Pakistan's economy, society, and political–military establishment are relatively minor, India needs others, particularly the US, to cooperate in exerting compellent leverage on Pakistan. Pakistan's economy is sufficiently weak and internationally disconnected that it is improbable that economic sanctions could be deployed to decisive effect. Security assistance, particularly from the US, is a different matter. If Pakistani authorities fail to prevent more major terrorist attacks against India, a strong case can be made that curtailing security assistance to the military is the least the US and others could do in order to avoid the alternative of more dangerous Indian military action. Still, the most promising form of non-violent compellence could be an international campaign to ostracize Pakistani leaders, either by boycotting them or by directly confronting them for their failures. Here, there may be untapped potential for Indian civil society to utilize social media and other means of mass communication to embarrass Pakistanis over the terrorist acts that their leaders allow to continue.

Non-violent compellence would require India to engage in international coalition-building. While this is what great powers seek to do, India has not yet fully embraced this mode of influence.

To succeed, Indian leaders would need to mobilize talented actors beyond its diplomatic and intelligence services, within India and in the broader international community. Twenty-first century modes of operating and communicating would need to be developed. To be effective—both in mobilizing the international community and in imparting messages that could affect Pakistani opinion—Indian leaders would need to complement the objective of ostracizing Pakistan with demonstrations of goodwill towards it. This means conveying a recognition that challenges such as Kashmir will require durable, forthcoming negotiations with Pakistani authorities as well as disaffected Muslims in Kashmir.[3] If India insists that a dispute does not exist, or that talks will not involve adjustments of all parties' positions, international observers and Pakistanis reasonably conclude that it will be more difficult to prevent violence.

Non-violent compellence is a 'softer' means of motivating Pakistan than violent covert operations or conventional war. It may therefore be unattractive from the standpoint of Indian domestic politics. However it also carries few costs and no risk of escalation. Unlike most military options, it plays to India's strength and Pakistan's weakness. Also unlike military alternatives, non-violent compellence would not prompt the US, China, and other influential powers to intervene to stay in India's hand. Quite the contrary, an Indian effort to build international support for non-violently motivating Pakistani authorities to change their behaviour, in lieu of or prior to military alternatives, would create pressure on others to cooperate with India. If others, including the US, refused to participate in Indian-led efforts, India would be in a stronger position to withstand external pressure not to use force against Pakistan.

Taken together, the chapters summarized here present a number of paradoxes and dilemmas that stem from the condition of Pakistan today. The military, including its intelligence service, is the strongest institution in the country. Yet, it also is bedevilled by violent actors that threaten Pakistanis, the state, and others (particularly India). The military nurtured and used some of these actors to wage proxy conflict with India, Afghanistan, and the US. But now Pakistan finds itself daunted by the prospect of controlling these actors, if not disbanding them. Partly as a result of these developments, Pakistan finds itself falling further behind India in all measures of well-being, security, and international reputation. The country is struggling to reverse self-destructive trends even as it still threatens Indian interests. India could push Pakistan closer to *self*-destruction, but does not have a clear interest in doing so. India itself is vulnerable to retaliatory forms of violent subversion that Pakistan could still mobilize. India could seek to impose lesser damage on Pakistan in order to motivate its leaders to curtail potential threats of terrorism, but Pakistan is too poor and economically disconnected from India and others to make economic sanctions a reliable tool. This leaves politics in its various forms, including international mobilization of political pressure paired with negotiation, as the least risky potentially effective alternative. Clausewitz famously wrote that war is merely the continuation of politics by other means. In Indo-Pak relations, which have involved plenty of warfare, politics may be the continuation of warfare by other means.

The analysis conducted in these pages leads us to risk the occupational hazard of predicting the following developments. India will sluggishly reform the institutions required to develop and implement national security strategy and policies toward Pakistan. India will continue to pursue capabilities to implement strategy in ways that reflect bureaucratic and political predilections more than clear, efficient strategic purpose. Military and intelligence capabilities will be acquired slowly and less coherently than a clear strategy would indicate, and the results will be suboptimal. (This of course is not unique to India.) However, elements in the technical establishment will remain tempted to tout capabilities prematurely, feeding Pakistan's worst-case assessments of Indian intentions and capabilities. Government leaders with the most power and creativity to develop new approaches and capabilities for mobilizing 'soft power' to affect hard problems will not have the time and interest to do so. Traditionally understaffed departments will be left to design and implement policies.

If these predictions prove somewhat accurate, limited capabilities combined with the precedence of other national priorities and the historically beneficial results of relative restraint in the use of force make it most probable that in the event of another high-profile attack Indian leaders would opt for the following actions: largely symbolic airborne attacks on terrorist-related targets in Pakistan-administered Kashmir; more aggressive covert operations to kill at least one major terrorist target; increased covert financial support for groups that challenge the Pakistani establishment in Balochistan, Karachi, and perhaps elsewhere; and exertion by Indian diplomats to move other states to protest against Pakistan in the event of additional terrorist attacks on India.

These predictions are not recommendations. India's strategic community is too talented and independent to need or heed any recommendations we might offer. If the analysis contained in these pages is persuasive—in varying degrees—Indian colleagues will draw their own appropriate conclusions from them.

We close, instead, with an observation. We did not devote a chapter, let alone the bulk of this book, to options of conflict resolution. Even if India's ultimate intent is to make peace with Pakistan, India would need to enhance its coercive strategy, capabilities, and doctrines. 'To make peace, prepare for war' is an incomplete guide to statecraft, but it is an important element of it. India needs to prepare for the most probable contingencies. Given the circumstances in Pakistan, it is prudent to consider that these contingencies include the risk of more terror, with the nuclear shadow creating imperatives to limit escalation. 'Not war, not peace' is the most likely condition in which Indians and Pakistanis will operate for the foreseeable future.

In this condition, when Indians reform institutions, develop strategy, and acquire capabilities, they will have the opportunity to consider more than coercive options. The chapter on non-violent compellence lays the foundation for a less traditional direction of security analysis (although it echoes the strategy of Gandhi and the Indian independence movement). Even with a focus on military and covert operations, the need for greater attention to diplomacy and conflict resolution arises unavoidably in the analysis of how to motivate Pakistan to change its behaviour.

India and Pakistan are approaching rough symmetry at three levels of competition: sub-conventional, conventional, and nuclear. One of the countries may be more capable in one or more of these domains, but each has now demonstrated enough capability in all three domains to deny the other confidence that it can prevail at any level of this violent competition without suffering more costs than gains. This condition of rough balance and deterrence across the spectrum of conflict amounts to an unstable equilibrium. Any number of actions by leaders and/or non-officials, taken by mistake or on purpose, could destabilize it. But, at the same time, the existence of a basic balance creates an opportunity for leaders to take steps to stabilize and pacify the Indo-Pak competition. Diplomacy and deal-making cannot shift balances of power and deterrence, but they can solidify them through explicit agreements that clarify expectations and standards of behaviour. Such agreements—essentially, negotiated accommodations—raise the stakes for any authorities that would subsequently violate them. This is all the more relevant when major outside powers have a stake in the stabilization that has been achieved. In this case, a coalition of stakeholders has an interest in motivating the parties to meet their obligations, including by punishing them for failing to do so.[4]

Some Indian leaders and some national security experts have perceived the need to complement coercive capabilities and policies with magnanimous diplomacy. Atal Bihari Vajpayee manifested this approach by beginning the so-called Lahore Process in February 1999, shortly after the nuclear tests. He demonstrated even more resolve by supporting back-channel diplomacy with Pakistan *after* the Kargil conflict and the 2001 parliament attacks. Indeed, any Pakistani and Indian leader who would offer positive inducements to the other in order to pacify the two states' relationship must expect opponents to undertake violent actions to destroy their initiative.

For nearly 70 years—before they acquired nuclear weapons and after—Indian and Pakistani leaders have tried various means to achieve their objectives toward each other. Sometimes this involved direct and proxy conflict; other times diplomacy. But 70 years on, the situation remains one of neither peace nor war.[5] Pakistan has fallen further behind India and its own aspirations in the process. There are signs that much of its population and some of its leaders recognize, as Pervez Musharraf did between 2003 and 2007, a need to focus on more constructive ambitions. A long-time Indian defence official and analyst assessed this possibility with insight that deserves quoting at length:

The problem is not the entirety of the ISI. But, given how long they have worked with various mujahidin groups, and how much they have done together, there must be some elements still in the ISI, or network of alumni, who will want to continue the jihad, especially against India over Kashmir. Even if and as the army leadership shifts its focus, and really does believe the greatest threat is internal, and that they have got to get control over violence within Pakistan, and they have an interest in normalizing with India, there must be elements who will resist this and keep trying to fight India.

The smarter ones realize that India as a state cannot be made to fall apart. Whatever these guys can do, whatever kinds of attacks, or support for disaffected young guys here, India will withstand it. It just won't fall apart and proxy war won't make it fall apart. At the same time, India and Pakistan can't fight a big war. There will be a level of conflict of some kind that will continue, but it won't lead to a major conflagration.

So, between those two realities, at some point the Pak leadership and even the army will realize it makes more sense to stop, especially when the proxies are now threatening Pakistan itself.[6]

This experienced official and observer was describing a sense of stalemate and rough deterrent balance that, in part, had made it possible for Nawaz Sharif to win election in Pakistan while campaigning for improved relations with India. The subsequent months after that interview in April of 2014 featured the cancellation of foreign secretary-level talks on security issues and a sharp escalation in violence along the LoC. This also demonstrated the way in which recalcitrant forces in both countries could impede this agenda. But our interviewee nonetheless continued by turning to the Indian political scene, where the election that would bring Narendra Modi to power was weeks away.

I can't understand our guys' attitude toward Pakistan. The larger state in every relationship ultimately has to recognize that the smaller states can't negotiate one for one and tit for tat. The bigger state has to be willing to give more. It's counter-intuitive: if we're bigger, we can force them to give in and do what we want. But, the psychology of it is the opposite.

The only way forward with Pakistan is that we have to be seen conceding more than we are getting. The reality is that we would be getting enormously more by normalizing relations and ending their story of conflict, etc. We would gain greatly overall.

It's going to take a very big man to do that. He would have to accept not getting another term, and the people who depend on him would have to accept that too, which is very hard. The dividend for normalizing relations won't be felt in three to four years, before the next election would happen.[7]

It is much more politically risky, hence rarer, for leaders to compromise with adversaries in negotiations than it is to authorize potentially costly uses of force. No leader benefits at home by seeming to give something to an adversary, which essentially is what negotiation and compromise require. A former Indian foreign secretary reflected this reality in an October 2013 interview: 'Nawaz says "you must give me something so I can get the Army to sign up to making peace and restraining jihadi groups." We can't do that. Either you want to change policy and rein these groups in, or you don't. And if you want to do it and you can do it, then do it.'[8]

The perspectives of these former senior Indian officials obviously diverge. The more recalcitrant view seems to be more prevalent, including within the Modi government. The veteran journalist R. Jagannathan summed up this mindset and approach:

Any concession on J&K [Jammu and Kashmir] will only convince the Pakistani generals that they were right all along in pursuing a path of mindless antagonism to India. The ISI will keep sending terrorists over to do damage. Let's not fool ourselves that talks will solve this problem.

For India, this means four or five things: we have to keep strengthening our resolve to fight terror and roll with the punches when we can't prevent it; we have to give it back to Pakistan without raising the stakes where it becomes an open war with the nuclear threat hanging over us; we have to develop covert capabilities inside Pakistan so that they know two can play the dangerous game; we have to diplomatically explain to the world what we are doing and why Kashmir *isn't* the issue, but Pakistan's ideology-driven terrorism is; and, lastly, we have to keep talking to Pakistan to convince them they cannot win and to tell the world dialogue isn't a problem for us. Underlying it all we have to give a consistent message: enmity with India has costs. If you try to harm us we will harm you. We have to prepare ourselves for a 100-year war of attrition with Pakistan till the latter accepts reality or falls victim to its own follies and disintegrates.[9]

Jagannathan's October 2014 description of the way the Indian government would approach Pakistan was clearly well-informed. Events during the subsequent year largely bore it out, with one glaring exception: as of October 2015 India did not keep talking to Pakistan. If the Indian government persists in the belief that it can manage Kashmir as an internal matter without Pakistan's negotiated cooperation, New Delhi will be unable to build an international coalition that would significantly raise the cost to Pakistan of future major attacks on India. Indeed, by acting as if there is nothing to negotiate with Pakistan, Indian leaders will encourage proponents of violence in Pakistan and discourage international players who would like to fully embrace India, but are reluctant to do so if India insists that they reject Pakistan at the same time.[10] India has the power and the habits of mind and institutions to win on its own a 100-year war of attrition with Pakistan. But India cannot achieve its ambitions to be a global power if it remains bogged down in such a war.

History teaches that not all problems have solutions, or that people often will not pursue solutions because it seems easier to live with familiar problems. The analysis presented in this book shows that there are no clear solutions that India can unilaterally pursue to end the threat of violence from Pakistan. Some are more or less likely to be effective at greater or lesser risk and cost to India. But only a combination of Indian coercive and non-violent policies and capabilities, paired with a willingness to bargain, can motivate Pakistan to remove the threat of violence. It is up to Indian and Pakistani leaders and societies, with encouragement from the international community, to find a combination that will work for them. If the analysis of this book helps inform the search for this combination, it will have achieved its purpose.

Notes and References

1. Rabasa et al., 'The Lessons of Mumbai', 14.
2. Interview with former Indian military officer, New Delhi, 24 April 2014.
3. In the aftermath of cancelled talks between the national security advisors of India and Pakistan in August 2015, the knowledgeable Indian journalist Manoj Joshi reminded Indian leaders that 'It was through patient diplomacy which ignored the provocations of Kargil and terrorist attacks that Atal Bihari Vajpayee's government persuaded Pakistan to order a ceasefire along the Line of Control, resulting in a sharp drop in infiltration, violence and casualties. Again, it was through diplomacy that Vajpayee and his successor, Manmohan Singh, brought Pakistan's military dictator within hailing distance of a comprehensive settlement on the Kashmir issue by 2007.' See Joshi, 'The Modi Government Is Missing the Big Picture on Pakistan', 2015.
4. One of the strongest arguments on behalf of the US' willingness to undertake compromises and negotiate a nuclear agreement with Iran was that the willingness to do so would make it easier to generate international support for sanctions on Iran if Iran refused to negotiate in good faith. Once a nuclear deal had been reached, perceptive analysts in the US, Iran, and elsewhere concluded that if Iran violated its terms, the probability of US military action against Iran would be much greater than would have been the case if no deal had been reached. As two leading American hardliners wrote in the Wall Street Journal, 'Hawks who believe that airstrikes are the only possible option for stopping an Iranian nuke should welcome a deal

perhaps more than anyone. No American president would destroy Iranian nuclear sites without first exhausting diplomacy. The efforts by Mr. Obama and Secretary of State John Kerry to compromise with Tehran—on uranium enrichment, verification and sanctions relief, among other concerns—are comprehensive, if nothing else. If the next president chose to strike after the Iranians stonewalled or repeatedly violated Mr Obama's agreement, however, the newcomer would be on much firmer political ground, at home and abroad, than if he tried without this failed accord.' See Reuel Marc Gerecht and Mark Dubowitz, 'The Iranian Nuclear Paradox', *The Wall Street Journal*, 8 July 2015. Available at: http://www.defenddemocracy. org/media-hit/senior-fellow-the-iranian-nuclear-paradox/#sthash. HFK5wcWI.dpuf.

5. Stephen P. Cohen, *Shooting for a Century: The India-Pakistan Conundrum* (Washington, DC: Brookings University Press, 2013).

6. Interview with Indian defence official, New Delhi, 23 April 2014.

7. Interview with Indian defence official, New Delhi, 23 April 2014.

8. Interview with former Indian foreign secretary, New Delhi, October 2013.

9. R. Jagannathan, 'The New Modi-Doval Doctrine on Pakistan is More Robust than Manmohan's', *Firstpost*, 22 October 2014. Available at: http://m.firstpost.com/india/the-new-modie-doval-doctrine-on-pakistan-is-more-robust-than-manmohans-1768509.html.

10. This situation is not very dissimilar from that of Israel vis-à-vis the Palestinians and the broader international community in 2015.

INDEX

ABOUT THE AUTHORS

George Perkovich is Vice President for studies at the Carnegie Endowment for International Peace. He has worked for three decades on nuclear strategy and security issues in South Asia. Perkovich is the author of *India's Nuclear Bomb*.

Toby Dalton is Co-Director of the Nuclear Policy Program at the Carnegie Endowment for International Peace, where his research focuses on cooperative nuclear security initiatives and the management of nuclear challenges in South Asia and East Asia. From 2002 to 2010, Dalton served in a variety of positions at the US Department of Energy.